# CAREERS

## THE ULTIMATE GUIDE TO PLANNING YOUR FUTURE

**THIRD EDITION**
**DK Delhi**
**Senior Editor** Shatarupa Chaudhuri
**Editor** Upamanyu Das   **Art Editor** Noopur Dalal
**Managing Editor** Kingshuk Ghoshal   **Managing Art Editor** Govind Mittal
**DTP Designers** Anita Yadav, Rakesh Kumar

**DK London**
**Senior Editor** Ashwin Khurana   **Art Editor** Chrissy Barnard
**US Editor** Kayla Dugger   **US Executive Editor** Lori Cates Hand
**US Consultant** Nicholas Schaefer
**Managing Editor** Francesca Baines   **Managing Art Editor** Philip Letsu
**Production Editor** George Nimmo   **Production Controller** Samantha Cross
**Jacket Designer** Surabhi Wadhwa-Gandhi
**Jacket Design Development Manager** Sophia MTT
**Publisher** Andrew Macintyre   **Associate Publishing Director** Liz Wheeler
**Art Director** Karen Self   **Publishing Director** Jonathan Metcalf

**FIRST EDITION**
**DK Delhi**
**Project Editor** Rupa Rao
**Senior Art Editor** Anis Sayyed   **Project Art Editor** Mahipal Singh
**Editorial team** Priyanka Kharbanda, Deeksha Saikia,
Neha Pande, Antara Moitra, Anita Kakar
**Art Editor** Pooja Pipil   **Assistant Art Editors** Tanvi Sahu, Deepankar Chauhan
**DTP Designer** Shanker Prasad   **Senior DTP Designer** Harish Aggarwal
**Jackets Designer** Suhita Dharamjit   **Managing Jackets Editor** Saloni Talwar
**Pre-production Manager** Balwant Singh
**Managing Editor** Kingshuk Ghoshal   **Managing Art Editor** Govind Mittal

**DK London and US**
**Project Editor** Ashwin Khurana
**Art Editor** Jemma Westing
**Editorial team** Suhel Ahmed, Chris Hawkes, Andrea Mills
**Associate Managing Editor** Allie Singer
**Consultant** Kavita Sharma
**Editor** Jenny Siklos   **Editorial Director** Nancy Ellwood
**Jacket Editor** Maud Whatley   **Jacket Designers** Mark Cavanagh, Jemma Westing
**Jacket Design Development Manager** Sophia MTT
**Producer, pre-production** Lucy Sims   **Senior Producer** Mandy Inness
**Managing Editor** Gareth Jones   **Managing Art Editor** Philip Letsu
**Publisher** Andrew Macintyre
**Associate Publishing Director** Liz Wheeler   **Art Director** Karen Self
**Design Director** Phil Ormerod   **Publishing Director** Jonathan Metcalf

**Cobalt ID**
**Editor** Richard Gilbert
**Editorial Director** Marek Walisiewicz
**Art Director** Paul Reid

This American Edition, 2022
First American Edition, 2015
Published in the United States by DK Publishing,
a division of Penguin Random House LLC
1745 Broadway, 20th Floor, New York, NY 10019

A catalog record for this book is available from the Library of Congress.
ISBN 978-0-7440-5172-8

DK books are available at special discounts when purchased in bulk for sales
promotions, premiums, fund-raising, or educational use.
For details, contact: DK Publishing Special Markets,
1745 Broadway, 20th Floor, New York, NY 10019
SpecialSales@dk.com

Printed and bound in China

**www.dk.com**

MIX
Paper | Supporting
responsible forestry
FSC™ C018179

This book was made with Forest
Stewardship Council™ certified
paper—one small step in DK's
commitment to a sustainable future.
Learn more at **www.dk.com/uk/
information/sustainability**

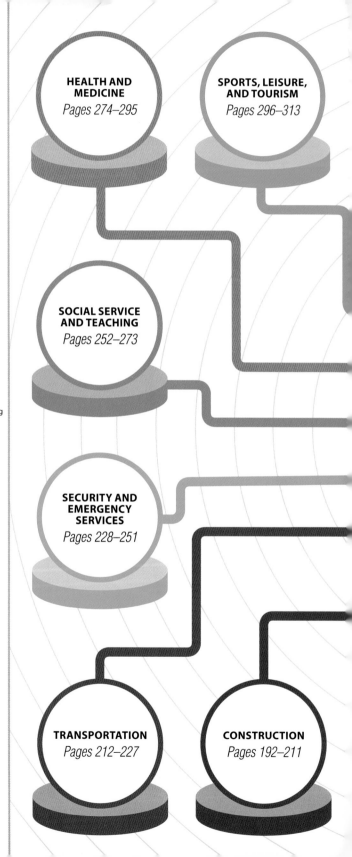

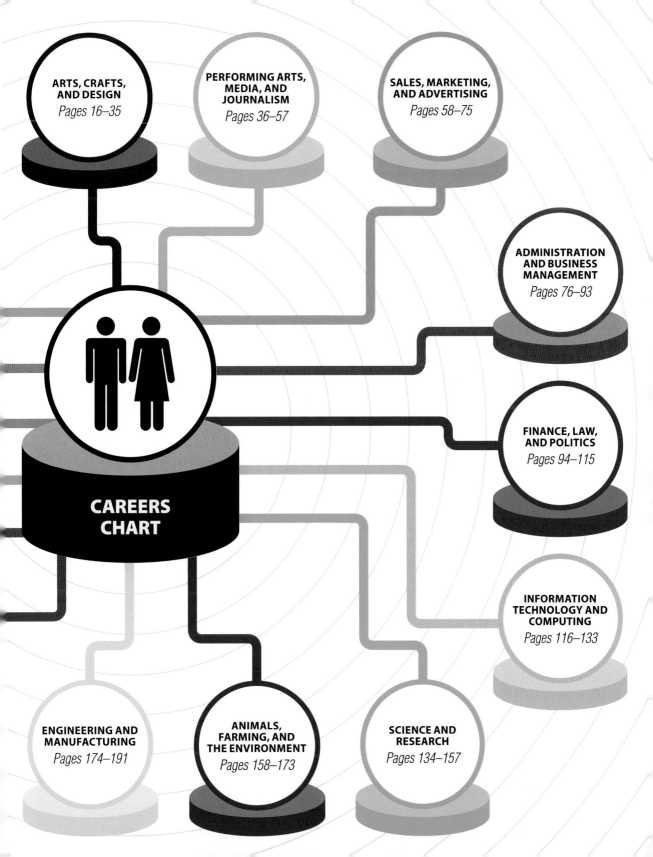

ARTS, CRAFTS, AND DESIGN
*Pages 16–35*

PERFORMING ARTS, MEDIA, AND JOURNALISM
*Pages 36–57*

SALES, MARKETING, AND ADVERTISING
*Pages 58–75*

ADMINISTRATION AND BUSINESS MANAGEMENT
*Pages 76–93*

FINANCE, LAW, AND POLITICS
*Pages 94–115*

INFORMATION TECHNOLOGY AND COMPUTING
*Pages 116–133*

CAREERS CHART

ENGINEERING AND MANUFACTURING
*Pages 174–191*

ANIMALS, FARMING, AND THE ENVIRONMENT
*Pages 158–173*

SCIENCE AND RESEARCH
*Pages 134–157*

## SALES, MARKETING, AND ADVERTISING

**58** SALES, MARKETING, AND ADVERTISING

- **60** Sales executive
- **62** Store manager
- **64** Buyer
- **66** Real estate agent
- **68** Marketing executive
- **70** Market researcher
- **72** Advertising account executive
- **74** Public relations officer

## ADMINISTRATION AND BUSINESS MANAGEMENT

**76** ADMINISTRATION AND BUSINESS MANAGEMENT

- **78** Customer service manager
- **80** Human resources manager
- **82** Project manager
- **84** Management consultant
- **86** Personal assistant
- **88** Events manager
- **90** Charity fundraiser
- **92** Translator

## INFORMATION TECHNOLOGY AND COMPUTING

**116** INFORMATION TECHNOLOGY AND COMPUTING

- **118** Software engineer
- **120** Systems analyst
- **122** Database administrator
- **124** Network engineer
- **126** IT support executive
- **128** Web developer
- **130** Game developer
- **132** Cybersecurity analyst

## FINANCE, LAW, AND POLITICS

**94** FINANCE, LAW, AND POLITICS

- **96** Bank manager
- **98** Trader
- **100** Investment analyst
- **102** Accountant
- **104** Actuary
- **106** Financial advisor
- **108** Economist
- **110** Lawyer
- **112** Judge
- **114** Politician

**174** ENGINEERING AND MANUFACTURING

176 Civil engineer
178 Drilling engineer
180 Chemical engineer
182 Mechanical engineer
184 Motor vehicle technician
186 Electrical engineer
188 Telecom engineer
190 Aerospace engineer

**192** CONSTRUCTION

194 Architect
196 Structural engineer
198 Cost engineer
200 Town planner
202 Builder
204 Construction manager
206 Carpenter
208 Electrician
210 Plumber

**296** SPORTS, LEISURE, AND TOURISM

298 Professional athlete
300 Personal trainer
302 Cosmetologist
304 Hotel manager
306 Travel agent
308 Airline cabin crew
310 Chef
312 Museum curator

**274** HEALTH AND MEDICINE

276 Medical doctor
278 Nurse
280 Midwife
282 Dentist
284 Pharmacist
286 Radiographer
288 Physical therapist
290 Speech pathologist
292 Occupational therapist
294 Optometrist

# THINKING ABOUT YOUR CAREER

Thinking about your future career can be both exciting and daunting. You need to choose which subjects to focus on in high school; make choices about further or higher education; and think about your interests, values, and skills. It is best to approach choosing a career as a process rather than a single decision. Think of it as a journey, during which you will be exposed to many influencing factors.

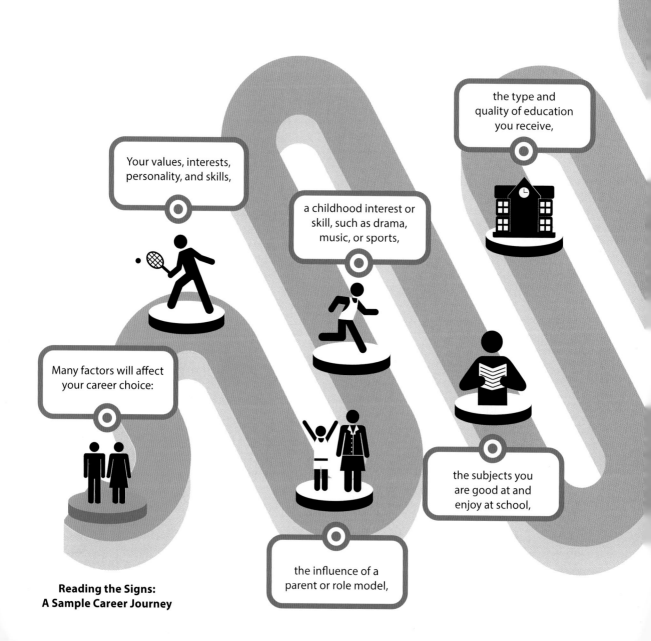

the type and quality of education you receive,

Your values, interests, personality, and skills,

a childhood interest or skill, such as drama, music, or sports,

Many factors will affect your career choice:

the subjects you are good at and enjoy at school,

the influence of a parent or role model,

**Reading the Signs:
A Sample Career Journey**

internships and apprenticeships,

the work–life balance you would like in your life,

you will find the job that is right for you!

deciding whether to attend college, and what your GPA is,

and where you live now (and where you would like to live).

and lots of hard work and dedication,

your grades in high school,

your future financial goals,

But with a desire to challenge yourself,

your after-school jobs,

# UNDERSTANDING YOURSELF

We are all individuals with our own values, interests, personality, and skills. To find a good career match, you first need to think about yourself—not only about what interests you, but your skills, personal qualities, motivators, and character. This reflection will help you plan future training and work experience, strengthen your résumé, and make informed career decisions.

### WHAT SUBJECTS DO YOU LIKE?
Which subjects do you enjoy at school? Which are you best at? How can you improve your performance in the subjects you like the most?

**Understanding yourself**

### WHAT OTHER INTERESTS DO YOU HAVE?
Do you play sports? Employers look for a range of interests beyond schoolwork. Taking part, and succeeding in, activities such as sports or the arts demonstrates you can work well with others—an important part of many jobs.

Lots of people have hobbies that develop into careers. If you enjoy drama, for example, you might go on to forge a career as an actor, but you also have skills that could be used when giving presentations or working as a teacher. If so, you could develop a portfolio career. This is where you use a specialist skill set that can be applied across a variety of industries or different employers.

Think about your hobbies and interests and how they could be put to use in the workplace.

### WHAT MOTIVATES YOU?
What is most important in your life? Do you like to build things and see how they work, or do you get satisfaction from helping others in the community? Is a high income important above all else? Do you seek excitement and challenge in your life, or are stability, freedom, and comfort more valuable?

## WHAT SKILLS DO YOU HAVE?

Think about the skills you are developing in school and during your after-school activities or jobs. You may be highly creative, be a great communicator, or have advanced IT skills; you may be good at problem-solving, or excel at working with your hands.

## WHAT ARE YOUR PERSONAL QUALITIES?

Choosing a job that fits with your personality will make you happier in your career and far more likely to be an effective employee. While you might be able to learn new skills to pursue a career, it is far more difficult to change your personality. Think about what kind of person you are, and ask others to describe how they see you.

## WHAT ARE YOUR CIRCUMSTANCES?

Do you want to work in a particular place—close to family and friends, for example, or in a big city—or are you prepared to relocate?

What are the costs of education and training in your chosen area? Can you realistically afford them?

Do you want a job that offers a flexible working arrangement? In some careers, new technology has made it possible for people to work effectively remotely, making video calls, sharing files, and holding meetings online. This allows employees to split their time between going into a workplace and working remotely, often from home, a practice known as hybrid working.

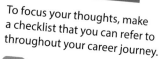

To focus your thoughts, make a checklist that you can refer to throughout your career journey.

 **FAVORITE SUBJECTS**

 **INTERESTS**

 **MOTIVATORS**

 **PERSONAL QUALITIES**

 **SKILLS**

 **OTHERS**

# TAKING ACTION

Once you have a greater understanding of who you are, what you are good at, and what type of job you would like to do, you can start to explore the world of education, training, and work. Start by looking at the job profiles in this book; they will give you a flavor of the types of careers available, and help you broaden your current ideas and learn about new opportunities.

**SEEK ADVICE**
Read up about your career or industry of interest. Talk to friends, family, teachers, or guidance counselors about your options.

**SET SOME GOALS**
Ask yourself what you want to achieve in your life and what you need to do in the short term to get to where you want to be.

**TAKE ACTION**
Once you have decided on the career you would like to pursue, you can do several things to make you stand out to potential employers.

### GET EXPERIENCE
Try to land an internship or apprenticeship in your chosen field. This will give you an excellent opportunity to talk to employees.

### START NETWORKING
Contact employers to see if they run open houses. Use social networks to connect with companies online.

**JOB**

### TRAINING AND LEARNING
Do as much research as you can to find out what qualifications you will need to enter a particular career.

### BECOME A VOLUNTEER
Offer your time to a company, nonprofit, or other organization. By doing so, you will make valuable contacts.

### RESEARCH EMPLOYERS
Find out everything there is to know about the biggest employers in your chosen sector.

### BUILD AN ONLINE PRESENCE
Use the Internet to set up and manage profiles on sites such as LinkedIn, Facebook, Instagram, and YouTube.

# GETTING THE JOB

Presenting your skills, talents, and experience to potential employers, whether in writing or in person, is a key part of getting any job. Research and good preparation are the keys to success when applying for open positions and attending interviews.

## CHOOSE YOUR WORDS
Think carefully about the words you use to describe your skills and achievements. Try to mirror the language used in the job description or on the company's website.

## RESEARCH
Use the Internet to do some online research into your potential employer. What do they do? What makes them distinctive? What is happening in their sector of the market?

## APPLYING FOR A JOB
Whether responding to an advertised job or approaching an employer, take time to think about your job application.

## READ THE JOB DESCRIPTION
Make sure you read the job description very carefully. Employers usually specify skills, knowledge, and qualifications that are essential to the job, so make sure your application indicates that you meet the specific job requirements.

## FINE-TUNE YOUR RÉSUMÉ
Don't send out the same, standard résumé or CV to all potential employers. Think about what each employer is looking for, and try to include evidence of success in these specific areas.

## PREPARE AND RELAX

Make sure you prepare thoroughly for the interview. Remember that it is natural to feel nervous beforehand, so try to find ways to relax: You could play music or do some breathing exercises.

## DRESS FOR SUCCESS

You should always be well dressed for an interview. This does not always mean wearing a suit; try to match the style of dress within the organization.

**INVITATION TO INTERVIEW**

**GETTING THROUGH THE INTERVIEW**
If an employer is impressed by your application, you may be invited to attend an interview.

**GET THE JOB**

## HAVE ANSWERS TO STANDARD QUESTIONS

Prepare answers for some of the most common interview questions, such as: "Tell me about yourself"; "Why are you interested in this role?"; "Why do you think you are the right person for this job?"

## KNOW YOURSELF

Make sure you review your résumé or CV before you attend the interview. Be clear about the skills and qualifications you have to offer the employer. Think of examples of your past achievements in advance.

# ARTS, CRAFTS, AND DESIGN

If you have artistic talent and an eye for what looks stylish, you could consider a career in arts, crafts, and design. In this sector you may be involved in creating new products, making illustrations for magazines, styling home interiors, or dreaming up the latest fashion trends.

## PRODUCT DESIGNER
*Page 18*

The everyday items we use without thinking—like cell phones, washing machines, and cars—are designed, modeled, and tested by product designers.

## TEXTILE DESIGNER
*Page 20*

Using different fabrics, including cotton, wool, and synthetic fibers, textile designers create new designs for clothing, fashion accessories, and home interiors.

## GRAPHIC DESIGNER
*Page 22*

Working on different media, from magazines to websites, graphic designers use lettering, imagery, and layout to create a visual design that conveys a clear message.

## PHOTOGRAPHER
*Page 24*

Using their technical and artistic abilities, professional photographers capture the sights of the world around us, such as weddings, landscapes, and sports events.

## ILLUSTRATOR
*Page 26*

Displaying their skills in fine arts and technical illustration, illustrators produce drawings for a variety of books, greetings cards, and product manuals.

## JEWELRY DESIGNER
*Page 28*

Working with silver, gold, precious stones, and other materials, jewelry designers keep up with the latest fashions to create jewelry, such as rings and necklaces.

## FASHION DESIGNER
*Page 30*

From *haute couture* and high-end fashion to functional footwear and everyday clothing, fashion designers set the trends and styles for the clothes we wear.

## MAKEUP ARTIST
*Page 32*

Using creative and effective makeup techniques to bring characters to life, makeup artists enhance the look of actors, models, television hosts, and private clients.

## INTERIOR DESIGNER
*Page 34*

Creating a look and feel for the places where we live, work, and relax, interior designers use furniture, paint effects, and furnishings to set the tone of interior spaces.

# PRODUCT DESIGNER

## JOB DESCRIPTION

Almost every object or device we use, from a chair to a computer, has been shaped by a product designer. In addition to creating new items, product designers may also improve existing ones or make them more user-friendly or cost-effective. Collaboration is essential—product designers develop ideas with clients, use 3-D printers to create prototypes with engineers, and assist marketing staff with promoting the product to buyers.

### SALARY

Product designer ★★★★★
Design engineer ★★★★★

### INDUSTRY PROFILE

Highly competitive • Huge demand for innovative product designers • Jobs available with manufacturers or specialized product design agencies

## ▼ RELATED CAREERS

▶ **JEWELRY DESIGNER** *see pp. 28–29*

▶ **INTERIOR DESIGNER** *see pp. 34–35*

▶ **ARCHITECTURAL TECHNICIAN** Supports an architect on the practical aspects of a construction project. An architectural technician prepares drawings and blueprints, sources suitable materials, and oversees legal and planning issues.

▶ **CREATIVE TECHNOLOGIST** Combines the skills of digital product design, art, and an understanding of people to create a link between people and brands.

▶ **DESIGN ENGINEER** Conceptualizes and develops new products as well as their manufacturing processes. Testing prototypes to ensure products function correctly and are reliable is also part of this job.

## AT A GLANCE

**YOUR INTERESTS** Art and design • Engineering • Craft technology • Graphic design • Physics • Mathematics • History

**ENTRY QUALIFICATIONS** An undergraduate degree in product design, industrial design, or engineering is required to enter this profession.

**LIFESTYLE** Product designers work regular office hours but need to be flexible to meet deadlines. Most of the design work is done on computers.

**LOCATION** Most product designers are based in offices or studios, but they may need to travel to meet clients or conduct research with the product's users.

**THE REALITIES** This is a competitive field where designers need to keep up with new technologies and design trends. Networking is key to career progression.

## CAREER PATHS

A qualified product designer needs to build a portfolio of successful work to get established. There are many fields in which you can specialize, but you may need a graduate degree for some of the more technical fields, such as biomedical engineering.

**INTERN** While getting a degree, you can gain work experience as a product design intern with an engineering company or design consultancy to build your portfolio.

**GRADUATE** This job requires a bachelor's degree. Some employers also value postgraduate degrees. Professional firms may offer you practical training.

# SKILLS GUIDE

 A high level of creativity in devising fresh ideas and new product features that will appeal to buyers.

 Self-discipline to plan and organize all stages of a project to ensure delivery on time and to budget.

 Excellent numerical skills for calculating the dimensions and proportions of a product.

 The ability to explain complex ideas to clients clearly, both verbally and in writing.

 Good computer skills for working on specialized Computer-aided Design (CAD) programs.

 Close attention to detail when working to technical specifications or client briefs.

**PRODUCT DESIGNER** The work requires you to consult with clients, research the needs of users, and then sketch ideas and develop them into plans using specialized software.

**ERGONOMIST** Focuses on the functionality of the products people use at home and in office spaces. They design new products, such as desks, kitchen equipment, or industrial tools, and try to make them safe, comfortable, and easy to operate.

**VEHICLE DESIGNER** Works in the transportation industry, creating new concepts for car bodies, lighter seats for aircraft, or clearer instrument panels for trains.

**HEALTH CARE ENGINEER** Applies engineering and design principles in the field of health care to create medical products, such as prosthetics and robotic surgical instruments.

**CONSUMER PRODUCT DESIGNER** Specializes in developing better consumer products, such as glassware, vacuum cleaners, computers, and handheld electronics.

# TEXTILE DESIGNER

## JOB DESCRIPTION

A textile designer designs woven, knitted, and printed textiles that are used to make clothes, fabrics, and furnishings. With an understanding of materials, dyes, patterns, and manufacturing processes, they produce designs for a range of decorative, durable, or protective fabrics. The work involves producing sketches and samples, and liaising with marketing and buying staff to make products that will sell.

### SALARY

Newly qualified textile designer ★★★★★
Experienced textile designer ★★★★★

### INDUSTRY PROFILE

Increasingly competitive sector, with more applicants than vacancies • Growing demand for textile designers in specialized markets, such as sports fashion and seating for car interiors

## AT A GLANCE

 **YOUR INTERESTS** Art • Craft • Fashion • Sewing • Knitting • Design technology • Mathematics • Chemistry • Information Technology (IT)

 **ENTRY QUALIFICATIONS** A degree in textile or fashion design is desirable, but it is possible to learn on the job while working in the industry.

 **LIFESTYLE** Regular office hours are the norm, but designers may have to work overtime to meet deadlines. Freelance designers can work from home.

 **LOCATION** Work is primarily based in an office or studio; designers may need to visit factories during production, or attend client briefings and trade shows.

 **THE REALITIES** The work is creatively rewarding. Most textile businesses are based in large cities, so relocation may be necessary to find a good position.

## ▼ RELATED CAREERS

▶ **JEWELRY DESIGNER** *see pp. 28–29*

▶ **CLOTHING AND TEXTILE TECHNOLOGIST** Manages the design, manufacture, and quality control of fabrics, yarns, and textiles. An expert in this field may work on fabrics for clothing, furnishings, medical supplies, or textiles for the car industry.

▶ **FURNITURE DESIGNER** Designs furniture and accessories, such as upholstered chairs and sofas. Some furniture designers work for manufacturers, creating designs for mass production; others produce items of furniture for individual clients.

Winter Olympians rely on textile designers to create "smart" textiles, such as self-warming jackets.

## CAREER PATHS

Without a relevant degree, it may be possible to enter the textile industry as a pattern cutter, creating fabric templates from drawings, or as a machinist, making garment samples. On-the-job training could lead to higher qualifications.

### INTERN OR ASSISTANT
You can gain valuable experience in the textile industry doing tasks such as creating design boards or helping prepare 3-D simulations for clients.

### GRADUATE
Earning a degree in textile design, fashion, or a related subject can help you develop the skills, creative confidence, and industry contacts to progress as a designer.

### SKILLS GUIDE

 Strong communication skills for liaising with customers, colleagues, and technical and marketing staff.

 The ability to evaluate the properties of materials used in specialty and industrial textiles.

 Creative flair for experimenting with different designs, materials, colors, textures, and weights.

 Good computer skills and knowledge of Computer-aided Design (CAD) software.

 Commercial awareness and good business sense, especially if working as a freelance designer.

### TEXTILE DESIGNER
Once qualified, you may work with fashion houses, architects, interior designers, or fabric manufacturers and retailers. You can specialize in areas such as interiors—upholstery, furnishings, and carpets—or technical fabrics, such as those used in fireproof clothing.

### TEXTILE CONSERVATOR
Works with museums, heritage organizations, and in the antiques trade to restore valuable textiles, such as tapestries, clothing, and wall and floor coverings. This job requires a thorough knowledge of design history, textile structure, and traditional manufacturing methods.

### WALLPAPER DESIGNER
Creates patterns and textures for wallpapers and other wall coverings. Most opportunities in this specialty field are freelance, or in working for textile or wall-covering manufacturers.

### FASHION DESIGNER
Designs accessories, shoes, or clothes—for mass-production or limited editions for niche markets—that mimic current trends in fabric, color, and shape, or create a new style.

### INTERIOR DESIGNER
Uses a knowledge of pattern, color, texture, and design techniques to design interior textiles and home furnishings, such as sofas, curtains, bedding, pillows, rugs, and carpeting.

# GRAPHIC DESIGNER

## JOB DESCRIPTION

Using images, colors, and text, graphic designers create compositions on screen to convey information and messages for print or electronic media. Designers must assess their clients' requirements to produce advertisements, promotional material, or logos that appeal to their target audience. Most of the work is computer-based, but the job may also involve working with suppliers, such as illustrators and photographers.

### SALARY

Junior graphic designer ★★★★★
Experienced graphic designer ★★★★★

### INDUSTRY PROFILE

Industry continually evolving due to technological developments • Wide range of employers • Self-employment common • Worldwide demand

## AT A GLANCE

 **YOUR INTERESTS** Art and design • Computers • Photography • Illustration • Project management • Advertising

 **ENTRY QUALIFICATIONS** Most designers have a degree, but some train on the job. Qualifications in art or design-related fields are useful.

 **LIFESTYLE** Designers tend to work normal office hours. However, overtime may be required to meet pressing deadlines and tight schedules.

 **LOCATION** Hybrid working is becoming common. Designers work in studios and home offices. They sometimes travel to meet clients, or can present ideas online.

 **THE REALITIES** Nearly one-third of all graphic designers are freelance. Others may expect to work for a number of different companies during their career.

## SKILLS GUIDE

 Strong written and verbal communication skills to articulate designs and ideas clearly.

 Expertise in using the latest design software, and the ability to adapt to new technology.

 Excellent design flair, artistic abilities, and creative ideas to produce innovative designs.

 The ability to listen to clients and fully understand and interpret their specific requirements and ideas.

 Good organizational skills, as multiple projects are often being handled at the same time.

 An eye for detail to ensure designs are accurate and are conveying the message required by the client.

## ▼ RELATED CAREERS

▶ **ILLUSTRATOR** *see pp. 26–27*

▶ **INTERIOR DESIGNER** *see pp. 34–35*

▶ **ADVERTISING ACCOUNT EXECUTIVE**
*see pp. 72–73*

▶ **WEB DEVELOPER** *see pp. 128–129*

▶ **ADVERTISING ART DIRECTOR** Creates visual ideas to
convey each particular message for advertising campaigns.
Works closely with a copywriter, who writes persuasive text,
or copy, for a specific target audience.

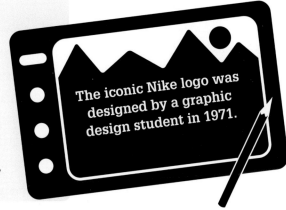

The iconic Nike logo was designed by a graphic design student in 1971.

## CAREER PATHS

Most graphic designers have a degree in graphics or
art and find work in companies involved in marketing,
communications, advertising, or publishing. They usually
specialize in one area, such as designing children's books,
magazines, websites, or user interfaces for applications.

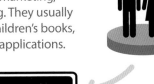

**ASSISTANT** Without a
degree, you may be able
to find work as a design
assistant, then train on the
job and progress into more
creative roles.

**GRAPHIC DESIGNER** As a graphic
designer, you will continue learning
throughout your career, keeping in touch
with new directions in commercial design
and changes in technology. You may
choose to freelance or to develop your
career in an individual company.

**GRADUATE** You
can enter the career
with a bachelor's
degree in graphic
design or a related
arts subject.

**ART DIRECTOR**
Steers the design
of a brand, campaign,
or publication, usually
heading a team of
designers or other
creative staff.

**WEB DESIGNER**
Specializes in website
design, from creating logos
to providing visual content
for their clients' brands.

**EXHIBITION DESIGNER**
Designs displays for
exhibitions, conferences,
or museums. A strong
interest in 3-D design
definitely helps in this role.

**MARKETING
CONSULTANT**
Uses design expertise
to create marketing
materials and advise on
strategy and branding.

# PHOTOGRAPHER

## JOB DESCRIPTION

Photographers combine artistic flair with technical knowledge of cameras and digital imaging to produce photographs. They work across a range of industries, from fashion and magazines to architecture and advertising. Some are self-employed, selling their images to picture libraries and media agencies. Others are hired for special events, such as school portraits and weddings.

### SALARY

Assistant photographer ★★★★★
Experienced photographer ★★★★★

### INDUSTRY PROFILE

Many different specializations • Growing opportunities in drone photography • Freelance work common • Very competitive area

## AT A GLANCE

**YOUR INTERESTS** Photography • Art and design • Travel and culture • Computers • Business management • News and current affairs

**ENTRY QUALIFICATIONS** No degree is required, making this field competitive. Many people train on the job as a photographer's assistant.

**LIFESTYLE** The work schedule may be arranged at short notice. Photo shoots can include evening and weekend work, plus travel to long-haul destinations.

**LOCATION** Photographers travel for photo shoots, working either indoors or outdoors. Others work in studios and will spend time on computers.

**THE REALITIES** Many hours are spent editing photos rather than shooting. Networking and building a reputation are key to having a successful career.

## ▼ RELATED CAREERS

▶ **GRAPHIC DESIGNER** *see pp. 22–23*

▶ **JOURNALIST** *see pp. 54–55*

▶ **WEB DEVELOPER** *see pp. 128–129*

▶ **ANIMATOR** Brings characters and images to life on-screen by using animation software to create visual effects and movements. They work in the TV, film, or computer games industries.

▶ **ART DIRECTOR** Oversees the visual style and content of a printed book, magazine, or website. Responsibilities include ensuring the work meets the brief and is delivered on time and to budget.

▶ **DRONE PILOT** Uses remote aircraft to take videos and photographs for commercial, military, and domestic projects, such as film and TV aerial shots, agricultural surveys, and construction site surveys.

▶ **TV CAMERA OPERATOR** Prepares and sets up equipment ready for use. Under the instruction of a director of photography, the camera operator records images to film or digital media.

## CAREER PATHS

Most photographers are self-employed and specialize in one area. Creating an online portfolio or website of images and skills, as well as developing both client and industry contacts, helps secure regular work.

**ASSISTANT** After finishing school, you may be able to gain experience working as an assistant to an established photographer.

**GRADUATE** A degree in photography or a related arts or design subject is useful, in addition to gaining experience as an assistant.

### SKILLS GUIDE

 Good artistic and design skills, imagination, and innovative ideas combine to get the best results.

 The ability to make people feel comfortable in front of the camera and quickly put them at ease.

 Familiarity with computer software and an aptitude with digital photographic equipment.

 Self-confidence to pursue your goals, even though jobs may be irregular at times.

 A good eye for detail, shape, form, and color; high levels of patience and concentration.

**PHOTOGRAPHER** Business acumen and self-promotion is as important to your success as technical and creative skills. You will need to keep up to date with new technology and emerging markets for images.

**MEDICAL PHOTOGRAPHER** Records medical procedures, diseases, operations, and injuries. Could also assist in crime scenes as a forensic photographer.

**LIFESTYLE PHOTOGRAPHER** Photographs families, portraits, and events, including weddings, for the general public.

**FASHION PHOTOGRAPHER** Takes shots of designers' clothing and accessories to promote fashion brands, especially in magazines. Usually works in a studio or on location.

**PRESS PHOTOGRAPHER** Produces photographs of events and the people associated with them, usually for newspapers, magazines, and websites. Often works under pressure to meet deadlines.

**CORPORATE PHOTOGRAPHER** Works in the corporate world to produce images that record or promote an organization's activities or showcase its products and brands to customers.

# ILLUSTRATOR

## JOB DESCRIPTION

Illustrators are commercial artists who produce paintings and drawings to accompany text in books, magazines, brochures, and advertisements. They usually specialize in one area, such as producing drawings for children's books, cartoons for newspapers, or technical illustrations for manuals. While some illustrators still use a pen or brush, many work on computers, graphic tablets, and digital sketchbooks

### SALARY

Illustrator ★★★★★

### INDUSTRY PROFILE

Majority of illustrators work as freelancers • Volume and type of work subject to changing trends in media industries • Bulk of jobs available in print and online media

## CAREER PATHS

There is no formal career path into this creative industry. You need to assemble a collection of your best work into a portfolio and present this to prospective clients. Your success depends not only on your artistic and technical skills, but also on your ability to network and market yourself.

**ANIMATOR** Uses digital or nondigital pictures, models, or puppets to produce multiple images called frames. When sequenced in the right order, these frames together create an illusion of movement known as animation.

**ASSISTANT** You can gain useful experience and make potential industry contacts by working as a design assistant or technical artist within a media or publishing company.

**GRADUATE** An undergraduate degree in illustration, fine art, or graphic design offers employers proof of your skills. However, potential clients will judge your ability on the quality of your portfolio and its suitability for their needs.

**ILLUSTRATOR** Developing one of several artistic styles, you can find work through personal contacts or sign on with agents who promote your work and take a commission on any jobs they find for you.

## SKILLS GUIDE

 A strong proficiency in computer applications and graphic design software.

 Effective communication skills for dealing with clients, agencies, and potential employers.

 A high level of creativity and talent to produce eye-catching work and generate new ideas.

 Good commercial awareness for negotiating fees with clients and working in a competitive market.

 Flexibility to take on different kinds of work when opportunities in a particular area become scarce.

 The ability to follow a client's brief and accurately produce complex technical illustrations.

 **BOOK OR MAGAZINE ILLUSTRATOR** Draws images that accompany articles in magazines, or which illustrate and enliven text in books, comic books and graphic novels.

 **MEDICAL OR TECHNICAL ILLUSTRATOR** Produces images of medical conditions and procedures that help people understand complex information in textbooks, instruction manuals, or sales brochures.

## ▼ RELATED CAREERS

▶ **GRAPHIC DESIGNER** *see pp. 22–23*

▶ **GAME DEVELOPER** *see pp. 130–131*

▶ **ART DIRECTOR** Leads and directs a team responsible for the design of visual concepts and images in creative industries, such as advertising, publishing, film and TV, or web design.

▶ **CARTOONIST** Uses a sense of humor and observational skills to draw cartoons or devise graphic stories. A cartoonist's work may be used in newspapers, books, magazines, and digital platforms, or by advertisers to promote products.

▶ **STORYBOARD ARTIST** Draws sequences of illustrations that show the key points in a story, which are then used as a basis for filming.

## AT A GLANCE

 **YOUR INTERESTS** Art • Drawing and painting • Graphic design • Information Technology (IT) • Science • Mathematics

 **ENTRY QUALIFICATIONS** Illustrators need good artistic training and a strong portfolio of creative work, or a degree in art, illustration, or graphics.

 **LIFESTYLE** Freelance illustrators can set their own working hours; those employed by companies work regular office hours.

 **LOCATION** Although illustrators can work at home or in a studio, they may need to visit a client's office to discuss briefs and promote their work.

 **THE REALITIES** Paid commissions may be sporadic for freelance illustrators, so many have a second job to maintain a regular income.

# JEWELRY DESIGNER

## JOB DESCRIPTION

A jewelry designer needs a strong eye for detail, a flair for fashion, and a love of creating intricate objects to succeed in their profession. They design jewelry and accessories, and make the items in their workshop using materials, such as gold, silver, precious stones, and wood. Designers without access to a workshop use the services of specialized companies to manufacture their designs.

### SALARY

Newly qualified designer ★★☆☆☆
Jewelry technician ★★★★☆

### INDUSTRY PROFILE

Competitive industry • Most jewelry manufacturers concentrated in "jewelry district" of large cities • Traditional jewelry stores have declined in numbers

## AT A GLANCE

 **YOUR INTERESTS** Craft design and technology • Art • Fashion • Computer-aided Design (CAD) • Science • Mathematics

 **ENTRY QUALIFICATIONS** A degree is an advantage, but many designers are self-taught, take vocational courses, or begin work as an apprentice.

 **LIFESTYLE** Jewelry designers generally work regular hours, but they may travel to meet suppliers, retailers, clients, and manufacturers, and to attend trade fairs.

 **LOCATION** Jewelry designers usually work in a studio or workshop. They may also work at a manufacturer's office, sharing a space with other designers.

 **THE REALITIES** Building a reputation is vital for success, so jewelry designers need to work hard to promote their work in galleries, in stores, and online.

## CAREER PATHS

Aspiring jewelry designers do not require formal qualifications—skills and experience are much more important. However, a relevant degree will increase your chances of finding a job with a large jewelry company, or give you the confidence to start your own design business, selling your work online or through galleries and stores.

**TRAINEE** You can start an apprenticeship with a designer, or an internship with a large jewelry company, learning practical skills on the job.

**GRADUATE** Employers will value certain college courses, such as jewelry design, gemology (the science of natural and artificial gems), art and design, 3-D design, fashion and textile design, and trend forecasting.

## ▼ RELATED CAREERS

▶ **PRODUCT DESIGNER** *see pp. 18–19*

▶ **FASHION DESIGNER** *see pp. 30–31*

▶ **CERAMICS DESIGNER** Shapes and fires clay to produce objects, such as kitchenware, tableware, and tiles.

▶ **WATCHMAKER** Makes and repairs watches and other timepieces. Many watchmakers are self-employed, while others work in jewelry shops and department stores.

▶ **WOODWORKER** Manufactures a variety of products, such as cabinets and furniture, using wood, veneers, and laminates.

## SKILLS GUIDE

 A high level of creativity and innovation to prepare designs to commissioned briefs.

 Good communication skills for interacting with designers, manufacturers, and clients.

 Proficient computer skills, such as the ability to operate Computer-aided Design (CAD) software.

 An ability to use fine tools to create and repair intricate pieces of jewelry.

 Commercial awareness for marketing designs and products to clients and manufacturers.

 Good attention to detail for carrying out complex design work accurately.

**JEWELRY TECHNICIAN** Uses specialized equipment in order to make jewelry. A technician will usually make jewelry in a factory or large workshop.

**SILVERSMITH** Specializes in, and principally works with, silver to make jewelry, silverware, vases, and other artistic items. They may use other metals, such as gold, copper, steel, and brass.

**JEWELRY DESIGNER** You may specialize in a specific type of work, such as bracelets or wedding rings. Once established, you may move into manufacturing, or run your own business.

**GEMOLOGIST** Gives valuations of precious jewelry for insurance purposes. This role requires formal training in the identification, grading, and pricing of gems.

Demand for gems and jewelry goes up in prosperous times, and down when an economy is flat, so a designer's income can fluctuate.

# FASHION DESIGNER

## JOB DESCRIPTION

Fashion designers create clothing, shoes, and other accessories. They use their creative expertise and knowledge of textiles, sewing, and manufacturing processes to set trends in color, fabric, and style. Those designers with a high profile often specialize in creating expensive one-off items, whereas the majority of designers work on clothing for the mass market, focusing on certain lines, such as sportswear, men's suits, or knitwear.

### SALARY

Junior designer ★☆☆☆☆
Head of design ★★★★☆

### INDUSTRY PROFILE

Market dominated by small- to medium- sized fashion houses located in large cities • Jobs in high fashion (*haute couture*), ready-to-wear (*prêt-a-porter*), and mass-market retail

## CAREER PATHS

The fashion industry is highly competitive, and you need to generate new ideas frequently. A degree isn't necessarily required to earn your first break, but you do need to show evidence of your interest and talent, such as a portfolio of fashion sketches, and have lots of determination. With experience, you can reach more senior creative positions in a fashion house or clothing manufacturer, or even start your own business.

**SPECIALIZED DESIGNER** Focuses on designing clothes for a specific area of the industry, such as menswear, footwear, activewear, or swimwear.

**ASSISTANT** If you are a naturally gifted designer, work experience in a retail store or hands-on dressmaking or tailoring skills will attract employers. With talent, a good portfolio, and internship experience, you may gain an entry-level job in fashion design.

**GRADUATE** Studying for a degree in fashion design, textile design, or fashion merchandising will develop your skills and teach you about clothing design and the business side of the industry. This improves your chances of finding a job.

**FASHION DESIGNER** In the beginning, you work on specific design products to fill an identified gap in the market. Creative freedom comes with seniority, or when you start your own company or label.

# SKILLS GUIDE

 The ability to generate lots of ideas and translate them into viable sketches, designs, and products.

 Strong numerical skills for setting dimensions and scale in patterns, and calculating production costs.

 Effective communication skills for interacting with design teams and conveying ideas clearly.

 Strong market awareness and business skills, especially for self-employed designers.

 Strong computer skills for working on Computer-aided Design (CAD) software and other applications.

 **TECHNICAL DESIGNER** Bridges the gap between fashion house designers and manufacturers, focusing on producing patterns that make the most economical use of fabric, and are cost-effective and easy to manufacture.

 **FASHION STYLIST** Advises clients on how to make themselves as stylish and confident as possible. They work in the modeling, photography, film, and subscription-box industries.

 **FASHION BUYER** Works for retail stores, purchasing stock to sell to the store's customers. Because buyers usually purchase merchandise several months in advance, they must be able to anticipate trends in fashion to meet future demand.

## AT A GLANCE

 **YOUR INTERESTS** Art • Fashion • Craft and design • Sewing • Pattern-making • Information Technology (IT) • Mathematics

 **ENTRY QUALIFICATIONS** A degree-level qualification in fashion, art, or design is helpful. However, a strong portfolio of work is a must.

 **LIFESTYLE** People in the fashion industry usually work long hours. Weekends are required in the lead-up to fashion shows and other launches.

 **LOCATION** The role is based in a studio or workshop. Fashion designers may have to travel abroad to attend fashion shows and fairs in big cities.

 **THE REALITIES** A fashion designer's work is often subject to harsh criticism. Deadlines are tight, especially when they are preparing a new collection.

## ▼ RELATED CAREERS

▶ **TEXTILE DESIGNER** see pp. 20–21

▶ **COSTUME DESIGNER** Designs clothes and accessories that actors wear in plays or films. These outfits need to be appropriate for the characters in a production and suit the period or fictional world in which the play or film is set.

▶ **DRESSMAKER/TAILOR** Creates made-to-measure items of clothing for customers, and usually runs small independent businesses, specializing in a particular type of clothing, such as customized suits or bridal wear.

▶ **FASHION MODEL** Models clothes in order to promote fashion lines to customers and the media.

# MAKEUP ARTIST

## JOB DESCRIPTION

Makeup artists work in the film, TV, theater, music, and fashion industries. They apply makeup and sometimes style hair for models or performers, whether they are trying to create a dynamic look for a model, a natural look for a TV host, or a dramatic image for a rock musician. In TV or theater, they may work with production and costume designers to design prosthetics, create a desired style, or capture a historical period.

### SALARY

Makeup artist ★★★☆☆
Makeup stylist ★★★★☆

### INDUSTRY PROFILE

Opportunities for freelance work • Employers generally based in large cities • High-profile makeup artists can charge high fees • Some makeup artists are popular bloggers

## ▼ RELATED CAREERS

▶ **FASHION DESIGNER** *see pp. 30–31*

▶ **COSMETOLOGIST** *see pp. 302–303*

▶ **BEAUTY AND FASHION BLOGGER** Shows viewers online the latest tips and trends in beauty, makeup, and fashion.

▶ **COSTUME DESIGNER** Designs clothes and accessories that actors wear in their performances. Costume designers combine their own creative instincts with extensive research into the clothes and styles associated with a particular era or location.

▶ **HAIRDRESSER** Cuts, colors, or shapes a client's hair to create the style they want. Training can either be on the job or at a technical school.

▶ **WIGMAKER** Creates wigs for a film, TV, or theatrical production. Wigmakers may work with a costume designer or director to decide on a specific look. They also design and create wigs and hairpieces for patients with medical conditions.

## AT A GLANCE

**YOUR INTERESTS** Makeup and hair • Fashion • Art • Photography and videography • Design • Drama • History • Film and theater studies

**ENTRY QUALIFICATIONS** A degree or certificate in cosmetology plus a license and work experience. Posting video tutorials online may build a following.

**LIFESTYLE** This is a demanding job with no regular schedule. Working hours are long and can stretch into the night if working on a film or video shoot.

**LOCATION** A makeup artist works mainly in theaters, film and TV studios, or in the offices of commercial video companies. Overseas travel is possible.

**THE REALITIES** Competition for work is tough, and success depends on experience and the ability to build a network of contacts in the industry.

## CAREER PATHS

An aspiring makeup artist can gain valuable experience by working for amateur theater groups, or in student fashion shows or film productions. Training at college is useful and may help you get a job assisting an established makeup artist, where you can build up your knowledge and industry contacts.

**STUDENT** You can study for a certificate in makeup design, hairdressing, or fashion design, but will need specialized training to work in any aspect of the media.

**ASSISTANT** Opportunities exist to assist an experienced makeup artist, by maintaining a makeup station and freshening makeup between shots.

**MAKEUP ARTIST**
In most cases, your work is based around contracts that run for the duration of a film or other production. You can choose to specialize in a number of areas.

### SKILLS GUIDE

 Creative flair and distinctive style to stand out in this highly competitive industry.

 The ability to create intricate styles of makeup and hair for prosthetics and wigs.

 Excellent interpersonal skills to work calmly with actors and models, often under pressure.

 Able to work well within a production team, and meet the production designer's brief.

 Physical and mental stamina to cope with the long hours and heavy demands of the job.

 Attention to detail, particularly when trying to ensure continuity during filming.

**MAKEUP AND HAIR STYLIST** Oversees the look of hair and makeup in a film or theater production. The best film makeup stylists are in great demand and may win awards for their work.

**WEDDING MAKEUP ARTIST** Provides customized makeup and hairstyles for weddings, proms, galas, and other events. They often run their own businesses.

**PROSTHETICS ARTIST** Helps create special effects, such as fake wounds or fantasy characters, using sculpting and crafting techniques. Most of this work is for film or TV.

**COSMETICS DEVELOPER**
Works with a cosmetics company to develop new products. Cosmetic developers may run promotional sessions in stores, trying out new products on potential customers, or they can showcase products through photo shoots.

# INTERIOR DESIGNER

## JOB DESCRIPTION

An interior designer shapes the look and feel of living and working spaces in homes, offices, stores, hotels, and other buildings. They may work on their own or alongside other professionals, such as architects and contractors, to create interiors that are both functional and attractive. Their work may range from advising on structural alterations to helping to select and coordinate furnishings, color schemes, and lighting.

## SALARY

Junior interior designer ★★☆☆☆
Consultancy partner ★★★★★

## INDUSTRY PROFILE

Demand for interior designers rising steadily • Main employers include design consultancies and architectural practices • Self-employment common among interior designers

## AT A GLANCE

 **YOUR INTERESTS** Interior design • Architecture • Design technology • Drawing • Arts and crafts • Materials • Sciences • Mathematics

 **ENTRY QUALIFICATIONS** Relevant training is required in order to practice. Union membership may also be required to work on larger projects.

 **LIFESTYLE** The work is often demanding and may require long or irregular hours to complete a job to a set deadline.

 **LOCATION** Interior designers work in their clients' homes, in an office, or at industrial sites. They may also have to attend exhibitions and trade fairs.

 **THE REALITIES** Clients can be unreasonable if their vision differs from that of the interior designer. Competition for work is fierce.

## CAREER PATHS

A degree-level art or design qualification is often required to become an interior designer. Before you practice, you may also need to become a member of a professional design body. With experience, you can specialize in areas, from lighting to eco-friendly furniture design.

**ASSISTANT** You may start by working alongside an established designer, sourcing materials or producing mood boards—used to illustrate the style a designer is trying to achieve. To progress, you will need to study for a degree or certificate on the job.

**GRADUATE** A degree or other higher-level qualification in design, architecture, or art history is required to work in some companies.

## ▼ RELATED CAREERS

▶ **FASHION DESIGNER** *see pp. 30–31*

▶ **ARCHITECT** *see pp. 194–195*

▶ **DECORATIVE PAINTER** Applies paint and coverings, such as wallpaper, to enhance the look of surfaces in buildings or to protect them from the elements.

▶ **EXHIBITION DESIGNER** Designs exhibitions held in museums, galleries, and heritage centers, or focuses on commercial exhibitions, such as trade shows and conferences.

▶ **SET DESIGNER** Creates sets and scenery for use in theater productions, films, and TV shows, often using Computer-aided Design (CAD) programs.

# SKILLS GUIDE

 Creativity and imagination in designing new concepts in line with contemporary trends.

 Good communication skills to explain ideas, and to negotiate with clients and suppliers.

 Excellent organizational skills to ensure each project is completed on time and within budget.

 Commercial awareness for negotiating contracts with clients and attracting new business.

 Adaptability to work on different briefs simultaneously and to follow new trends.

 Excellent numerical skills for determining costs and the amount of materials needed for a job.

 **HEAD OF PRACTICE** Heads a design team or establishes their own practice to work on interior-design projects.

 **ARCHITECTURAL DESIGNER** Specializes in working with architects at the planning stage of a new building. They design interior fittings, and may help with creating floor plans.

**INTERIOR DESIGNER** Designers may work on residential or corporate projects or focus on buildings with a specialized function, such as hospitals, restaurants, or hotels.

**LIGHTING DESIGNER** Produces functional and appealing designs for lighting. These designers create lighting concepts for a project, such as a new building, and then plan how to implement the scheme liaising with engineers, electricians, and architects.

 **FURNITURE DESIGNER** Creates new designs for furniture, balancing creativity with comfort. Some make one-off items, while others may work for large manufacturers of office or home furniture.

# PERFORMING ARTS, MEDIA, AND JOURNALISM

Performing on stage, playing an instrument, writing articles, or communicating through visual media—such as TV, film, and the Internet—can all be pursued as careers. However, each field is fiercely competitive, and you will need tenacity, dedication, and perseverance to succeed.

## MUSICIAN
*Page 38*

Combining musical talent with enthusiasm, determination, and a flair for performance, musicians entertain an audience with their melodies and compositions.

## DANCER
*Page 40*

With an inherent feel for music and movement, together with years of practice, dancers bring stories, themes, and emotions to life through rhythmic steps and routines.

## ACTOR
*Page 42*

Whether working in TV, film, and theater, or commercials and training videos, actors use their dramatic skills to portray and develop the characters they play.

## TV/FILM DIRECTOR
*Page 44*

Using commercial instinct and technical expertise, the director is the creative force inspiring actors and crew to fulfill a film's overall vision.

## TV/FILM PRODUCER
*Page 46*

Successful TV and film productions are big business. The producer ensures they make it to the screen by studying scripts, securing funding, and hiring cast and crew.

## CAMERA OPERATOR
*Page 48*

Filming dramatic performances, musical pieces, news items, and nature events, camera operators use technical skill and creativity to capture the scene in front of the lens.

## SOUND ENGINEER
*Page 50*

Rigging up equipment and checking sound levels at concerts and shows, sound engineers create pitch-perfect acoustics for the listening audience.

## WRITER
*Page 52*

With a mastery of story and language, writers use their creativity and research skills to produce fiction and non-fiction pieces for publication across a range of media.

## JOURNALIST
*Page 54*

Digging up the facts behind newsworthy events, journalists are seasoned professionals who investigate every angle to get to the heart of a story.

## EDITOR
*Page 56*

Working with the written word across books and other media, editors have overall responsibility for the quality and accuracy of the text content in a publication.

# MUSICIAN

## JOB DESCRIPTION

For most musicians, music is not so much a career as a lifelong passion. To succeed, you need natural ability, dedication, and a lot of practice. Musicians may need formal training, especially in classical music or composition, but many are self-taught. Their earnings come from performing, recording, or writing music, either alone or as part of a group or an ensemble.

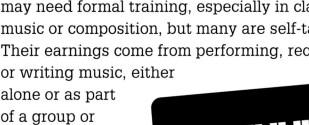

### SALARY

Orchestral player ★★☆☆☆
Successful music artist ★★★★★

### INDUSTRY PROFILE

Competitive industry • Mostly part-time and freelance work, although full-time roles in military bands and large orchestras available • Increasing demand for online soundtracks

## AT A GLANCE

**YOUR INTERESTS** Music • Entertainment • Songwriting and composition • Performance arts and culture • Creativity • IT skills

**ENTRY QUALIFICATIONS** A degree is not required, but you must be able to either sing or play an instrument, and to perform to a very high standard.

**LIFESTYLE** Rehearsals and recordings in a studio, or live performances during gigs and tours, can involve long hours. Schedules are highly irregular.

**LOCATION** Musicians may work in a recording studio, theater, school, or place of worship. If touring, international travel may be required.

**THE REALITIES** This is a hugely competitive field. Performances can be tiring and stressful, whether live or in a studio.

## CAREER PATHS

A musician's future depends partly on the genre of music chosen. If you play in an orchestra, your chances of becoming a soloist are low; if you play in a popular group, you could achieve huge, but often short-lived, commercial success.

**AMATEUR** Playing in a local band or orchestra and taking music classes will help you develop your skills, give you exposure to an audience, and may help you start a professional career in music.

**GRADUATE** If you study music at college, you will gain an understanding of theory, history, and technique. A music degree is not a guarantee of success as a performer, but it can give you access to other parts of the music business.

## ▼ RELATED CAREERS

▶ **ARTS MANAGER** Supervises activities and events that promote the arts in theaters, museums, galleries, and music festivals.

▶ **MUSICAL INSTRUMENT MAKER/REPAIRER** Uses specialized skills to create new instruments or repair ones that have been damaged.

▶ **MUSIC TEACHER** Gives music lessons to people of all ages and abilities.

▶ **MUSIC THERAPIST** Uses music creatively to help adults and children address social, emotional, or physical challenges.

▶ **VIDEO GAME COMPOSER** Composes, produces, performs, and delivers music to become integrated into a video game.

# SKILLS GUIDE

 A high level of musical ability and the confidence to perform before an audience.

 Dedication and motivation to practice and rehearse for several hours every day.

 The ability to work closely with other musicians in orchestras, and sound recordists in studios.

 Excellent social skills and the ability to self-promote in order to find paid work.

 Attention to detail and perfect timing, especially when performing with other musicians.

**POPULAR MUSICIAN**
Plays pop, jazz, or another contemporary musical genre. Only a few achieve great success, but many more make a living playing in informal settings, such as small venues, bars, restaurants, and at events such as weddings.

**CLASSICAL MUSICIAN** Performs live or in recordings as part of an orchestra, in a smaller ensemble, or as a soloist. Skill in playing more than one instrument can improve a musician's prospects.

**CONDUCTOR** Interprets musical scores, and uses a baton or hand gestures to give musical or artistic directions to performers. Some classical musicians undergo further training to become conductors in orchestras and ensembles.

**MUSICIAN** As a musician, you can work in various roles—as a performer on stage, in the theater, or as a session musician, working as a temporary member of a group in a recording studio or at a live performance. Many trained musicians become music teachers or work with record companies.

**COMPOSER** Creates original music for artists and orchestras, as well as for TV and film soundtracks, computer games, and advertising jingles.

# DANCER

## JOB DESCRIPTION

Dancers use their bodies to perform routines to music, tell stories, and express ideas for the entertainment of audiences. They can work on stage as members of a dance company or theater group, or perform in films, TV shows, and music videos. Dancers spend years training to hone their skills and build up their fitness and flexibility. They usually specialize in one genre, such as ballet, jazz, or street dance.

### SALARY

Junior in dance company ★★★★★
Experienced dancer ★★★★★

### INDUSTRY PROFILE

Opportunities exist in dance, ballet, opera, and theater companies • Highly competitive industry • Many dancers are self-employed

## CAREER PATHS

Most dancers begin their training in childhood, attending ballet classes or dance school. If you choose this career, you can continue training at vocational dance colleges or at colleges that offer undergraduate and graduate programs in dance. The physical demands and brevity of this career mean that most dancers have an additional line of work, possibly in dance teaching or therapy.

**DANCE NOTATOR** Records dance moves in a score (a plan of a dance), using figures and graphic symbols. This allows ballets and other dance pieces to be recreated at a later date or by other companies.

**ASSISTANT** In this role, you help out with classes at a dance school. You may lead students through exercises, help with choreography, or play accompanying music. Many dance students have their tuition reduced by working as part-time assistants.

**GRADUATE** An undergraduate degree in dance or in the performing arts may give your career a boost. You can also train in your chosen genre of dance at a private dance school and pass examinations by various accredited bodies.

**DANCER** Performance is an important but relatively small part of a dancer's life. You spend the bulk of your time practicing to maintain skills and fitness, preparing for auditions for new roles, or rehearsing.

## SKILLS GUIDE

 Excellent interpersonal skills to communicate with choreographers and other dancers about routines.

 The ability to work in a team with a troupe of dancers, choreographers, and others.

 An ability to master new types of dance and to meet the demands of an ongoing performance.

 A high level of physical fitness and stamina to brave the rigorous cycles of training and performance.

 Creativity to add individuality to choreography, and an innate sense of rhythm, timing, and musicality.

 Motivation and the self-discipline to train and rehearse regularly, and maintain high levels of fitness.

 **DANCE TEACHER** Trains students of all ages in different types of dance. Dance teachers work in dance and stage schools, as well as colleges, and may also teach related subjects, such as drama or performing arts.

 **CHOREOGRAPHER** Works in theater, film, and television to create routines for dancers and other performers. Planning movements to fit the music and staging, choreographers need to work closely with musical directors and costume designers.

## ▼ RELATED CAREERS

▶ **MUSICIAN** *see pp. 38–39*

▶ **ACTOR** *see pp. 42–43*

▶ **ARTS MANAGER** Plans and oversees programs of arts activities and events in theaters, museums, galleries, and music festivals.

▶ **CHILDREN'S ENTERTAINER** Provides shows and entertainment for children at parties, cruise ships, or family-centered hotels. Jobs can be sporadic or seasonal.

▶ **DANCE SCIENTIST** Works with a dance company or university, conducting research into the relationship between performance and physiology, psychology, fitness, and well-being.

## AT A GLANCE

 **YOUR INTERESTS** Dance • Music • Drama • Art • Mime • Musical theater • Self-expression • Fitness and sports

 **ENTRY QUALIFICATIONS** Training at a stage school, dance academy, or ballet school is essential. A degree in dance and choreography may help.

 **LIFESTYLE** Working hours can be long and dancers may have to rehearse and tour a lot. Keeping fit is crucial because the job is physically demanding.

 **LOCATION** Dancers work in movie and TV studios, as well as in operas, theaters, and cruise ships. More than half work as dance teachers.

 **THE REALITIES** Gigs may be irregular. Self-confidence to continue pursuing your goals is important when facing rejections at auditions.

# ACTOR

## JOB DESCRIPTION

Actors portray a character through a combination of speech, movement, and body language. They work mainly in theater, film, TV, and radio; they can also appear in corporate videos and advertisements, and record voice-overs. Usually they interpret the words of a playwright or screenwriter, working from a script under the instruction of a director, but sometimes they can improvise on a theme.

### SALARY

Actor in regional theater ★☆☆☆☆
Famous screen or TV actor ★★★★★

### INDUSTRY PROFILE

Intense competition for roles • Diverse opportunities, ranging from theater to theme parks, and from TV to teaching • An expanding industry with opportunities for online streaming roles

## AT A GLANCE

**YOUR INTERESTS** Drama • Film • Arts and literature • Languages • History • Poetry • Music • Dance • Mime • Theater • Sports and fitness

**ENTRY QUALIFICATIONS** Although a degree in drama, or training at a stage school or drama college, is not required, it may help you break into the industry.

**LIFESTYLE** Actors work irregular hours. In film and TV, days can be long and involve a lot of waiting. They may work far from home on location or on tour.

**LOCATION** Actors work in theaters, TV, film, commercial studios, and even in open-air locations, such as parks, gardens, and forests, around the world.

**THE REALITIES** Actors need to audition for roles, and rejection can be tough. There is little job security, and most actors spend a lot of time looking for work.

## ▼ RELATED CAREERS

▶ **MUSICIAN** *see pp. 38–39*

▶ **DANCER** *see pp. 40–41*

▶ **DRAMA THERAPIST** Uses theatrical techniques, such as vocal expression and role-play, to help people through traumatic experiences or emotional, physical, or behavioral challenges.

▶ **SCREENWRITER** Creates ideas and writes scripts for movies or television shows. May also adapt existing works, such as novels, for the screen.

▶ **TALENT AGENT** Promotes the skills of an actor to find them work with prospective employers, from movie studios to theater companies.

In William Shakespeare's time, in the late 16th and early 17th centuries, women were not allowed to be actors. Men played all the female roles.

## CAREER PATHS

An actor's career can be unpredictable. Training and talent may help you land good and well-paid roles, but you also need luck and perseverance to be spotted and to be selected at auditions. Finding a respected agent to represent you may help you get noticed.

**AMATEUR ACTOR** Joining an amateur drama group, or appearing in student films or stage productions, can help you get noticed as a young, aspiring actor.

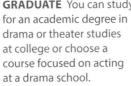

**GRADUATE** You can study for an academic degree in drama or theater studies at college or choose a course focused on acting at a drama school.

**ACTOR** You may need to join a professional body or an actor's union to be considered for some acting roles. You may need to learn new skills throughout your career, such as stage fighting and perfecting dialects, to win roles.

**VOICE ACTOR** Works on radio dramas, or provides voice-overs for commercials, animations, training materials, or audiobooks. They are hired for the quality of their voices.

**FILM ACTOR** Performs in front of cameras on movie sets, often repeating scenes several times in different "takes." Many actors start their careers in low-budget independent movies.

**TV ACTOR** Performs a role for a TV show, such as a soap opera or period drama. Some TV actors may also find work in corporate videos or in TV and online advertisements.

**STAGE ACTOR** Performs in front of audiences in a range of venues, from small, intimate studios to large open-air theaters, or even on the street.

**STUNT PERFORMER** Stands in for other actors on set when the film or TV script calls for a scene that is physically dangerous or that requires specialized skills.

# TV/FILM DIRECTOR

## JOB DESCRIPTION

Directors oversee the production of a film or TV show, and make the creative decisions that guide the rest of the crew. They link together experts in various disciplines, including actors, costume and set designers, and camera operators, and are ultimately responsible for developing a vision for the TV show or film by defining its overall shape, structure, and style.

### SALARY

Independent director ★★☆☆☆
Experienced director ★★★★★

### INDUSTRY PROFILE

A fast-evolving industry • Corporate production is booming • Rise in independent film-making due to affordable film equipment and more investors

## CAREER PATHS

There is no formal route to becoming a director, but experience, reputation, and creative energy are all important. Aspiring directors often work on low-budget independent productions early in their careers, and often come from diverse backgrounds, such as acting or screenwriting.

**GRADUATE** You can study for a degree in film or cinematography, in which you will be taught technical skills in composition, lighting, and direction and develop your creative instincts.

**CAMERA OPERATOR** If you start your career as a camera operator, you can progress to the senior position of director of photography. From there, you can go on to direct films and TV shows.

**PRODUCTION ASSISTANT** As a production assistant (or "runner") on a set, you run errands for the production team. Hard work and dedication may earn you promotion to production-based or creative roles, which may lead to an assistant director position.

Kathryn Bigelow was the first woman to be awarded the Oscar for Best Director, which she won in 2010 for *The Hurt Locker*.

**ASSISTANT DIRECTOR** As the director's second-in-command, you are responsible for all practical tasks, such as managing schedules, allowing the director to fully concentrate on the creative process.

## SKILLS GUIDE

 Strong leadership skills to take charge of a cast, technical crew, and production teams.

 Excellent communication skills to ensure the cast and crew understand what to do.

 Creative flair in interpreting a script, framing shots, and giving clear direction to actors.

 Endurance and stamina to maintain the fast pace of filming under potentially difficult conditions.

 The ability to complete the project, working within the budgets set by the producer.

**PRODUCER** Steers a TV show or film from its earliest stages—securing funds, rights, and scripts—through production, all the way to release, promotion, and distribution. Not all producers have experience as a director.

**TV/FILM DIRECTOR** Oversees the entire production of a film or TV show. With experience and success, may take on progressively larger and more ambitious projects. Some choose to move into production—the business end of the industry.

## AT A GLANCE

 **YOUR INTERESTS** Film • Theater • Drama • Art • Music • Writing • Reading • Mathematics • Languages • Information Technology (IT)

 **ENTRY QUALIFICATIONS** A bachelor's degree or higher in film production or cinematography is helpful but not required.

 **LIFESTYLE** Directors keep regular hours when planning and rehearsing. However, they often work long and irregular hours during shoots.

 **LOCATION** Film directors work in production studios, film-editing suites, on film sets, or at outdoor locations, some of which are far from home.

 **THE REALITIES** This is a highly competitive field. Working on set can be both physically and emotionally demanding.

## ▼ RELATED CAREERS

▶ **CASTING DIRECTOR** Finds suitable actors and celebrities for film or video and TV roles. They assess who will be right for the role. They also organize auditions and negotiate fees and contracts.

▶ **FILM OR VIDEO EDITOR** Works with the director after the filming has finished to select shot sequences, and arranges them in an order and style that creates a convincing and coherent story.

▶ **SCREENWRITER** Creates ideas and writes scripts for films or television shows. Screenwriters may also adapt existing works, such as novels or plays, for the screen.

▶ **THEATER DIRECTOR** Interprets a dramatic script or musical score and directs actors and technicians.

# TV/FILM PRODUCER

## JOB DESCRIPTION

The producer is the linchpin of any TV or film production. The role involves assessing scripts, buying the rights to adapt books for the screen, and securing finance before filming. The producer hires a director and crew, organizes the shooting schedule, and is responsible for ensuring that the project is completed on time and on budget, using a blend of business acumen, creativity, and technical expertise.

### SALARY

Assistant producer ★★☆☆☆
Experienced producer ★★★★★

### INDUSTRY PROFILE

Most jobs based in large cities • Competitive industry • Permanent, salaried jobs becoming rare • Growing opportunities in cable and satellite TV • Online video production

## ▼ RELATED CAREERS

▶ **TV/FILM DIRECTOR** see pp. 44–45

▶ **CAMERA OPERATOR** see pp. 48–49

▶ **SOUND ENGINEER** see pp. 50–51

▶ **DIGITAL PRODUCER** Uses social media, podcasts, and apps to generate interest in films and TV shows. They use communication, digital, and marketing skills to reach the target audience.

▶ **PRODUCTION ASSISTANT** Acts as a general assistant on a film or TV production, carrying out basic tasks, such as carrying equipment and making deliveries.

▶ **PROGRAM RESEARCHER** Contributes ideas for programs, sourcing contacts and contributors.

The Producers Guild of America includes over 7,000 members in film, TV, and new media.

## AT A GLANCE

**YOUR INTERESTS** Film • TV • Drama • Theater • Photography • Videography • Crafts and design technology • English • History • Arts • Economics

**ENTRY QUALIFICATIONS** There are no defined entry qualifications. A degree in film production or similar is useful, and a showreel of work is essential.

**LIFESTYLE** Producers work long and irregular hours to ensure that projects finish on time. Working during weekends and holidays is common.

**LOCATION** Based in an office, producers need to travel to studios, casting sessions, and to oversee location shoots, some of which may be abroad.

**THE REALITIES** Finding work is tough in this competitive industry. Balancing the creative, practical, and financial aspects of a project can be stressful.

## CAREER PATHS

There is no set path to becoming a film or TV producer, and no defined route for progression. In this industry, dedication and excellent networking skills are key to finding work.

**ASSISTANT** You can gain experience in production work in the role of an assistant. You will perform administrative tasks, working either on set or in an office.

**GRADUATE** Earning a bachelor's degree in film and TV production or media studies may increase your chances of finding work in this competitive field.

### SKILLS GUIDE

 Strong organizational skills for managing creative and technical processes on time and to budget.

 Excellent communication and interpersonal skills for team work during the production process.

 Creative flair to help interpret how a script can be presented through visual images and sound.

 Endurance and stamina for dealing with a range of responsibilities, often within tight schedules.

 Commercial awareness to manage resources effectively and raise the necessary finance for projects.

**TV/FILM PRODUCER** Working as an associate producer—who performs many of the tasks of a producer, under their direct supervision—can be a stepping stone to becoming a producer yourself. You can then specialize in a particular type of production.

**EXECUTIVE PRODUCER** Oversees the work of a producer on behalf of a studio or a project's backers. Usually focuses on the financial and creative aspects of production, as opposed to technical issues.

**COMMERCIAL PRODUCER** Produces TV commercials for advertisers, working on every aspect of the project, from writing to shooting and editing.

**CORPORATE VIDEO PRODUCER** Manages the production of videos for a range of purposes, such as business training and conferences, or award ceremonies and industry conventions.

**VIDEO GAME PRODUCER** Handles different aspects of video game development to ensure that it is being produced on schedule and to budget. This role requires an undergraduate degree in game design, computer science, or digital media.

# CAMERA OPERATOR

## JOB DESCRIPTION

The role of a camera operator involves recording moving images for films, TV shows, music videos, or commercials using digital video and film cameras. As a camera operator, you use both technical and creative skills to follow a script, visualize and frame shots under instructions from a director, and work closely with performers and other members of the crew during the shoot.

### SALARY

Camera assistant ★☆☆☆☆
Experienced operator ★★★☆☆

### INDUSTRY PROFILE

Freelance work common • Full-time employment opportunities with large broadcasting companies • A number of jobs available in corporate and training video production

## AT A GLANCE

**YOUR INTERESTS** Photography and videography • Cinema, film, and video • Art • Electronics • Design technology • Media • Travel

**ENTRY QUALIFICATIONS** A degree is useful, but practical knowledge of videography and work experience in the industry can be enough to get you a job.

**LIFESTYLE** Long hours and tight deadlines are common. Operators may also have to travel to distant or extreme locations, such as deserts or war zones.

**LOCATION** Depending on the job, camera operators may work primarily in a studio or on location. They may need to spend extended periods away from home.

**THE REALITIES** Competition for jobs is intense, and many camera operators are self-employed, moving from one contract to another.

## CAREER PATHS

Many camera operators get their foothold in the industry by working as production assistants ("runners"). Your progress will depend on your talent and commitment, as well as on the way in which you develop a network of contacts in the industry.

**ASSISTANT** With some technical knowledge of film-making, you may become a camera assistant. Your job is to assemble the cameras, and keep shots in focus. With experience you can become a camera operator.

**GRADUATE** You can study for a degree in photography, film and TV production, cinematography, or media studies, but technical ability and experience count for more than academic study.

## ▼ RELATED CAREERS

▶ **SOUND ENGINEER** *see pp. 50–51*

▶ **GRIP** Works with camera operators in the film and video industries. Grips are responsible for mounting camera equipment onto fixed or moving supports, such as cranes, and setting up lighting rigs safely. They also order and prepare equipment, and transport it to a film location.

▶ **LIGHTING ENGINEER** Sets up and operates all of the lighting equipment for video, film, TV, and theater productions. Lighting engineers visit locations to assess requirements for lighting and special effects.

# SKILLS GUIDE

Good interpersonal skills to work with performers, directors, and production staff.

Innovation and creativity to get the best possible shots during filming.

Problem-solving skills to fix any technical issues at a film shoot without affecting the schedule.

Physical strength and endurance to stand for extended periods of time, or to lift or move equipment.

Manual dexterity and good hand-eye coordination to get the best results from film equipment.

More than 25,000 camera operators work in the US alone.

**DIRECTOR OF PHOTOGRAPHY** Works with the director of the film or TV show to establish its visual style. The job involves determining how a scene should be lit, deciding which lenses and equipment should be used, and instructing camera and lighting crews.

**IMAGE TECHNOLOGIST** Develops new equipment and techniques that push the boundaries of what is possible to record on film or digital media. Imaging companies may recruit camera operators with expertise in the technical side of film-making to fill this role.

**CAMERA OPERATOR** You usually specialize in one area of work. This could be covering news stories for TV, making corporate videos, or recording sports events or concerts. With experience, it is possible to advance into more creative roles.

# SOUND ENGINEER

## JOB DESCRIPTION

Sound engineers work with musicians and film or TV producers to make high-quality recordings of music, speech, and other sounds. They oversee recording sessions, usually in a studio but sometimes on location. They set up microphones and other equipment, record different instruments or voices separately, and then mix these different recordings (known as tracks) together electronically to craft the desired overall sound.

### SALARY

Junior sound engineer ★★☆☆☆
Experienced sound engineer ★★★★☆

### INDUSTRY PROFILE

Opportunities in a range of industries, including broadcasting, music, TV, and computing and advertising • A growing sector continually evolving with development of new technology

## CAREER PATHS

Formal training in sound engineering or music technology is an advantage in this competitive industry, but some studios and broadcasting companies take on talented trainees straight out of high school. You will need to learn continually to keep up to date with digital recording technologies if you are to be considered for more senior and creative roles.

**TRAINEE** You may be able to find an employer to take you on as a trainee. This route is very competitive, and you will need good grades in mathematics, physics, and computer science. Any experience you may have from working on school productions or amateur gigs will be useful.

**GRADUATE** A degree in sound or acoustic engineering gives you an excellent foundation in the technical and creative aspects of this career.

**MIXING ENGINEER** Mixes or remixes music or sound. Mixing engineers edit the sound and manipulate the volume and pitch of individual tracks to achieve a finished mix (an electronic blend of music tracks or sounds) with the desired qualities.

**SOUND ENGINEER** As a sound engineer you record and mix sounds to realize the creative vision of the artist or film or TV producer. With experience, you can go on to manage a studio, or move into specialized roles in TV, movie, or music production.

# SKILLS GUIDE

 Good team-working skills to deal with artists and producers, often under intense time pressure.

 A good knowledge of operating a mixing console and other equipment to set sound levels.

 Scrupulous attention to detail for monitoring audio signals and keeping a log of all recordings.

 Physical strength for setting up equipment in a studio or on location at concerts and events.

 Excellent computer skills to operate state-of-the art digital systems for recording music.

 Flexibility to work the long hours needed to accommodate performers and events.

**SOUND DESIGNER** Takes responsibility for the entire sound of a production, which may be a movie, video, or computer game. Sound engineers create and edit music and sound effects, using a range of digital equipment.

**MUSIC PRODUCER** Works with artists, songwriters, and audio engineers on aspects such as songwriting, recording, and mixing. Many music producers work for record companies or are hired by artists.

## ▼ RELATED CAREERS

▶ **BROADCAST ENGINEER** Sets up and operates the sophisticated electronic systems used in TV, radio, and other digital media broadcasts. Broadcast engineers work as part of a team with producers and anchors in recording studios, in control rooms, or on location in all weather conditions.

▶ **LIGHTING ENGINEER** Prepares, sets up, and operates the lighting equipment for TV, movie, or video productions, and live events, such as concerts and theater productions.

▶ **RADIO STUDIO MANAGER** Ensures the smooth running of live broadcasts in studios and on location. Also controls the mixing of prerecorded productions prior to going on air.

## AT A GLANCE

 **YOUR INTERESTS** Electronics • Music technology • Music • Physics • Mathematics • Information Technology (IT)

 **ENTRY QUALIFICATIONS** A relevant degree is desirable, but good technical skills and experience can get you started in this career.

 **LIFESTYLE** Hours can be long and irregular. Sound engineers may be expected to work at night when studio time is less expensive.

 **LOCATION** Sound engineers may work in a studio or on location at concerts, on a movie set, or at other live events. They may have to travel extensively.

 **THE REALITIES** The work can be demanding, but working as part of a creative team with talented artists can be highly rewarding.

# WRITER

## JOB DESCRIPTION

Writers work to inform, educate, or entertain their readers. They are skilled at using the written word to convey meaning or to tell stories, and work in a huge range of industries in diverse roles. Some writers achieve fame by writing novels or working as journalists or screenwriters, but many more make their living by writing press releases, articles for magazines and websites, or copy (text) for advertisements.

### SALARY

Varies enormously depending on the type of writing and experience

### INDUSTRY PROFILE

Increasing demand for writers in online media • Fierce competition for work in every sector • Work predominantly freelance based

## AT A GLANCE

**YOUR INTERESTS** Writing • Languages • Literature and reading • Performing arts • Drama • Technical and scientific subjects

**ENTRY QUALIFICATIONS** There are no specific requirements. Some have higher degrees in professional or creative writing; others have little formal training.

**LIFESTYLE** Many writers are self-employed and set their own working hours. They usually need to meet deadlines set by publishers.

**LOCATION** Many writers adopt a hybrid working model based at home, in an office, or a studio. They may travel to meet clients or conduct interviews.

**THE REALITIES** A writer's earnings can be as unpredictable as their workload. Writing is an isolating experience, and all writers need great perseverance.

## CAREER PATHS

The majority of writers work on a freelance basis, specializing in one of many areas, from children's books to technical manuals. As with many creative jobs, there is no formal career structure, and some people can become writers without undergoing any training. Reputation, networking skills, and experience count for more than any qualifications.

**BLOGGER** Writing a personal blog or contributing to a college magazine gives you a chance to develop your writing skills. Showing your work to online or print publishers may win you a paid commission.

**GRADUATE** A degree in English or creative writing is useful, but not required. You may be better off earning a degree in another area that enables you to become a writer on a specialized subject.

## ▼ RELATED CAREERS

▶ **JOURNALIST** *see pp. 54–55*

▶ **EDITOR** *see pp. 56–57*

▶ **PUBLIC RELATIONS OFFICER** *see pp. 74–75*

▶ **COPYWRITER** Writes text on brochures, billboards, websites, emails, advertisements, catalogs, and more.

▶ **PROOFREADER** Checks documents for accuracy, grammar, spelling, and consistency before their publication.

A successful writer needs determination: J.K. Rowling's first novel, *Harry Potter and the Sorcerer's Stone*, was rejected by 12 publishers.

# SKILLS GUIDE

 Excellent writing and communication skills for creating lively and readable text.

 A high degree of creativity in inventing stories, characters, themes, and dialogue.

 Perseverance in the face of criticism from clients or the rejection of work from publishers.

 Good knowledge of computers and social media to network with potential clients and self-promote.

 Strong organizational skills to manage a schedule when working on your own.

 An eye for detail to ensure that text is accurate and free from grammatical and spelling errors.

**REVIEWER** Analyzes a variety of artistic works, including books, films, and theatrical performances, and then critiques them, in newspapers, magazines and journals, or online.

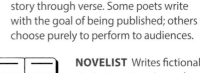

**POET** Expresses an emotion or tells a story through verse. Some poets write with the goal of being published; others choose purely to perform to audiences.

 **NOVELIST** Writes fictional stories to entertain readers. There are many genres of novels, from science fiction to romance.

 **SCREENWRITER** Writes scripts for films and TV productions, sometimes adapting existing works. Can also find work writing speeches for business leaders and politicians.

**WRITER** Some people are commissioned to write by a publisher. Others write speculatively, hoping to sell their completed work. Experienced writers can find work in many fields.

# JOURNALIST

## JOB DESCRIPTION

Journalism consists of two main related areas: researching and gathering information, and writing or presenting content. As a journalist, you will often need to be "on-the-go" to report events as they happen or to interview people on location. You will usually work on a specific subject area assigned to you. Good communications skills and strong integrity are vital.

### SALARY

Newly qualified journalist ★★☆☆☆
Experienced journalist ★★★☆☆

### INDUSTRY PROFILE

Opportunities in traditional print journalism in decline • Many journalists write for online publications • Highly competitive • Deadline-driven industry

## CAREER PATHS

Many journalists begin by writing for student publications. Once qualified, they can work in diverse media—including newspapers, magazines, TV, and online—and choose to specialize in one field, such as sports, news, features, or politics. They can progress to an editorial role, which involves managing a section of a publication or broadcast.

**BROADCAST JOURNALIST** Works for radio or TV stations broadcasting via air, cable, or the Internet. These journalists research, write, and often present stories for broadcast.

**INTERN** You can gain frontline experience from an internship and develop a portfolio of work from school publications, blogs, class assignments, or magazines and newspapers that will showcase your talent.

**GRADUATE** Some employers look for applicants with graduate-level qualifications. You can apply for entry-level positions with a media company after completing your bachelor's degree.

**JOURNALIST** With the necessary qualifications and work experience for a local newspaper, radio station, or TV station, you can choose to pursue one of a variety of specialties.

# SKILLS GUIDE

 Excellent verbal and written skills help to express ideas clearly to varied readerships or audiences.

 The ability to work with people in many teams, including editors, designers, and producers.

 Perseverance and dedication to help create and present a story for the target audience.

 The flexibility to take on stories that arise without warning and to follow them as events unfold.

 Good organizational skills to meet tight deadlines, especially when juggling multiple stories.

**NEWSPAPER JOURNALIST** Provides information to the public about events, people, and ideas. The role involves detailed research, writing, and fact-checking.

**MAGAZINE JOURNALIST** Researches and writes news articles and features for a variety of periodicals, including popular titles, business journals, and trade publications.

**ONLINE JOURNALIST** Produces content for online publication on one or many different topics. This requires good journalistic and computer skills. The ability to work in a variety of media—including video and sound—is extremely beneficial.

## AT A GLANCE

 **YOUR INTERESTS** Writing • Research • Meeting and interacting with people • Media • Social media • Computers • Current affairs

 **ENTRY QUALIFICATIONS** A degree followed by graduate training in journalism is desirable; internships are also available for on-the-job training.

 **LIFESTYLE** Work is project-based, with long and irregular hours, which can extend over weekends and holidays. Some jobs require frequent traveling.

 **LOCATION** You may be based in an office or at home, but you will need to travel to conduct interviews and research depending on your field.

 **THE REALITIES** Tight deadlines and long hours are common. Working conditions can be poor or dangerous, for example in war or disaster zones.

## ▼ RELATED CAREERS

▶ **WRITER** *see pp. 52–53*

▶ **EDITOR** *see pp. 56–57*

▶ **PUBLIC RELATIONS OFFICER** *see pp. 74–75*

▶ **ADVERTISING COPYWRITER** Produces the concise and persuasive written words, or "copy," for advertisements.

In 2017, online media sales overtook paper-based media sales for the first time ever.

# EDITOR

## JOB DESCRIPTION

Editors of books and journals are responsible for the editorial content of their publications. In this role, your duties may range from evaluating manuscripts and commissioning writers to produce text, to checking text for accuracy, spelling, and grammar. Editors may work directly with subject experts, graphic designers, and picture researchers, and liaise with sales, marketing, or production staff to promote and print the publication.

### SALARY

Editorial assistant ★★★★★
Editor ★★★★★

### INDUSTRY PROFILE

Strong competition for entry-level jobs • Low pay levels for junior roles • Book and journal publishers increasingly turning to online publication • Jobs in book publishing not always advertised

## CAREER PATHS

Most editors enter publishing as editorial assistants, helping with research, fact-checking, and basic editorial tasks. With experience they can gain promotion to manage the publication of a book or journal, and then a "list"—a themed category—of books. Some editors diversify into other roles in publishing, such as marketing or management.

**GRADUATE** Increasingly, a degree—in English or a subject related to the type of publishing you intend to specialize in—is essential to become an editor. An internship with a publishing company will give you useful experience, and you can also take industry-accredited courses in editing and proofreading.

### ▼ RELATED CAREERS

▶ **WRITER** *see pp. 52–53*

▶ **JOURNALIST** *see pp. 54–55*

▶ **ADVERTISING ACCOUNT EXECUTIVE** *see pp. 72–73*

▶ **FILM/VIDEO EDITOR** Assembles pictures and sound for film or television. A film or video editor needs a good sense of timing, attention to detail, and the ability to meet deadlines. Due to the competitive and fast-paced nature of the industry, technical skills and experience are valued just as highly as formal qualifications.

**EDITOR** After gaining experience at editorial assistant level, you can choose to specialize in a particular type of book or journal publishing.

## AT A GLANCE

 **YOUR INTERESTS** Reading • Writing • Literature • Languages • Graphic design • Information Technology (IT) • Creative writing

 **ENTRY QUALIFICATIONS** A degree is essential for many jobs in editing. Specialized publishing companies may require focused training.

 **LIFESTYLE** Editors in full-time jobs keep regular office hours, but evening and weekend work is often required, especially if freelancing.

 **LOCATION** Editors may adopt a hybrid working model by being based at home and the office. Occasional travel to trade shows or meetings may be required.

 **THE REALITIES** Editors must put in long hours of meticulous editorial work. Schedules can be demanding, especially if working on multiple projects.

## SKILLS GUIDE

 Excellent verbal and written skills to express themes, ideas, and concepts clearly to the reader.

 Strong team-working skills for liaising with authors, designers, and other publishing departments.

 A creative flair, critiquing skills, and commercial awareness to improve and refine a publication.

 Flexibility and adaptability, as publishing schedules may be revised at short notice.

 Good organizational skills, since workloads may be heavy and involve several projects at once.

 **FICTION EDITOR** Works with the author of a novel or short story to prepare the manuscript for publication. Assesses the author's work, suggests changes to make the text more engaging, corrects errors, and may advise on marketing and production.

 **NONFICTION EDITOR** Develops, commissions, and checks content for nonfiction books, such as biographies, histories, and cookery, travel, or fitness books. Nonfiction editors may liaise with subject specialists to consult on the text.

 **REFERENCE EDITOR** Plans, commissions, and ensures the accuracy of text for a range of reference works, such as dictionaries, encyclopedias, directories, and academic or scientific works.

 **ACADEMIC JOURNAL EDITOR** Prepares scholarly or scientific articles for publication and distribution to academics and researchers. Ensures that articles are read and validated by expert consultants.

 **ONLINE EDITOR** Sources, edits, and collates text and imagery for publishing on websites. Online editors are trained in specialized web-design and editing software.

# SALES, MARKETING, AND ADVERTISING

Commercial flair, an interest in selling, and knowledge of customers are vital in this fast-paced industry. Job roles are diverse and range from creating advertisements to writing press releases and predicting the public's spending habits.

## SALES EXECUTIVE
*Page 60*

The aim of sales is to grow a firm's profits by increasing revenue from its products or services. Sales executives do this by approaching clients to win new business.

## STORE MANAGER
*Page 62*

Using their leadership skills to motivate staff to achieve sales targets, store managers oversee the shops and supermarkets in which we purchase the goods we need.

## BUYER
*Page 64*

With an eye on future trends and consumer demands, buyers make decisions about what will sell, which products to stock, and how to price them.

## REAL ESTATE AGENT
*Page 66*

Real estate agents link home buyers and sellers, negotiating property sales on behalf of clients. They are most in demand when the property market is booming.

## MARKETING EXECUTIVE
*Page 68*

Clear and creative communication is the key to successful marketing. This is how marketing executives promote products, services, and ideas to customers.

## MARKET RESEARCHER
*Page 70*

Combining numerical skills with knowledge of consumer behavior, market researchers survey consumers' preferences to improve existing products and services.

## ADVERTISING ACCOUNT EXECUTIVE
*Page 72*

Interpreting the goals of their clients, advertising account executives work alongside a creative team to develop campaigns for print, television, and online media.

## PUBLIC RELATIONS OFFICER
*Page 74*

The public perception of a product, service, or company is vital to its sales and popularity. Public relations officers promote a positive public image for their company.

# SALES EXECUTIVE

## JOB DESCRIPTION

Sales executives make contact with potential customers—either individuals or businesses—to sell their company's goods or services. They develop a thorough understanding of their company's products so that they can address a customer's queries with confidence to complete a sale. They must have a good understanding of customer psychology, data and analytics, and sales strategies to be successful.

### SALARY

Retail sales worker ★★★★★
Business sales executive ★★★★★

### INDUSTRY PROFILE

Job opportunities in all commercial sectors • Demand for sales executives varies with market conditions • Financial rewards often linked to sales targets

## AT A GLANCE

 **YOUR INTERESTS** Sales • Marketing • Customer service • Finance • Business studies • Mathematics • Advertising • Languages

 **ENTRY QUALIFICATIONS** A degree is not required for most sales jobs, but one may be required when selling technical or financial products.

 **LIFESTYLE** Sales executives may need to work long hours to meet sales targets or to deal with customers in other countries and time zones.

 **LOCATION** Depending on the sector, sales executives may be based in stores or offices; they may travel widely to visit clients at their premises.

 **THE REALITIES** Competition between colleagues and rivals can be intense. The role demands a thick skin to deal with rejection from customers.

## ▼ RELATED CAREERS

▶ **BRAND MANAGER** Promotes a company or a product by managing its profile and reputation among its customers and the wider public. Uses a variety of techniques, such as advertising and public relations, to enhance the brand's image.

▶ **ONLINE MARKETING MANAGER** Develops strategies to attract customers to an online store, and ensures that the design and usability of a retail website helps to increase sales.

▶ **RETAIL MANAGER** Manages the day-to-day operations of supermarkets and stores.

Promotions can come quickly for sales executives who consistently exceed their targets.

# CAREER PATHS

Sales executives need to be ambitious and determined because career progress depends entirely on hitting sales targets. Successful salespeople are typically promoted to handle larger and more valuable clients, and may go on to join a company's management team. Sales skills are highly transferable, and it is not unusual for sales executives to move between different industries.

## SKILLS GUIDE

 Excellent communication skills for presenting product information to potential customers.

 Good interpersonal skills to handle queries and complaints in a professional manner.

 Strong organizational skills and self-motivation in planning and making sales calls and visits.

 A sound knowledge of business practices, and an awareness of customer expectations.

 Good numerical skills for calculating percentages, discounts, and profits on sales.

## SALES ASSISTANT

You may begin your career in an administrative role, supporting senior salespeople. Your employer is likely to teach you about the company's products and sales techniques before you start to deal with customers.

## SALES EXECUTIVE

Sales executives represent an organization's products or services, and build and manage relationships with customers. With experience they can move into several other fields of work.

## SPECIALIZED SALES EXECUTIVE

Works in the financial sector, selling products such as mortgages and investments, or in other fields, selling products, such as pharmaceuticals or insurance.

## KEY ACCOUNT MANAGER

Takes on responsibility for dealing with their employer's most valuable clients or product areas.

## SALES MANAGER

Coordinates a company's sales operations in a region or country, setting targets and advising staff on ways to improve their performance.

## MARKETING EXECUTIVE

Researches customer needs and behavior and plans a company's strategy to promote its products.

# STORE MANAGER

## JOB DESCRIPTION

Store managers run the day-to-day business activities of a retail store. In this role, you lead and inspire a team of sales assistants, manage staff recruitment, organize pricing, displays, promotions, and special events, and deal with customer queries. You analyze sales data to forecast future stock requirements, and are also responsible for the health and safety of customers and staff in the store.

### SALARY

Sales assistant ★★★★★
Head office manager ★★★★★

### INDUSTRY PROFILE

Vast range of potential employers • Recent decline in business for some national chain stores • Many retailers sell online • Growing opportunities in outlet and discount retailer space

## ▼ RELATED CAREERS

▶ **SALES EXECUTIVE** *see pp. 60–61*

▶ **BUYER** *see pp. 64–65*

▶ **INTERNET MARKETING MANAGER** Develops Internet-based strategies to raise public awareness of an organization's activities.

▶ **MERCHANDISE MANAGER** Decides which goods to stock, sets prices, predicts future demand, and monitors supply levels.

▶ **SALES ASSISTANT** Works on the sales floor, replenishing stock, pricing and ticketing, using checkout facilities, and serving customers.

The number of retail establishments across the US has increased even as e-commerce has grown.

## AT A GLANCE

 **YOUR INTERESTS** Business studies • Marketing • Dealing with people • Economics • Mathematics • Psychology • Information Technology (IT) • Sales

 **ENTRY QUALIFICATIONS** A good general education is sufficient, but a degree in business or retail management will hasten promotion.

 **LIFESTYLE** Shift and weekend work is normal at most stores. Overtime is to be expected in busy periods, such as during seasonal sales.

 **LOCATION** Work is split between an office in the store and the sales floor. Some travel for training and to meetings with management is required.

 **THE REALITIES** Store management is competitive and fast-paced. Long hours on the sales floor and pressure to meet sales targets can be tiring and stressful.

## CAREER PATHS

There are two main ways to become a store manager: by joining a company as a sales assistant and gaining promotion through merit, or joining a retailer's training program, which may be open to part-time students or graduates. The prospects for progression are good, with vacancies at retailers of all sizes and specializations.

### SKILLS GUIDE

 The ability to communicate well with customers and staff while maintaining a calm disposition.

 Excellent team-working skills for motivating staff to achieve a store's sales targets.

 Creativity and innovation in sales techniques and product display to increase store revenues.

 Strong leadership skills to inspire staff to reach their potential and deliver excellent service.

 Business-management skills, commercial awareness, and the ability to spot future trends.

**TRAINEE** You can join a retailer as a sales assistant and work your way up, or enroll in the company's management training program.

**GRADUATE** A degree in any discipline will enable you to join a graduate training program, but employers favor subjects such as business studies, retail management, and marketing.

**STORE MANAGER** After gaining experience, you can seek promotion to work in a larger store, or in one of the business areas of retailing, such as buying, human resources, or marketing. You may train staff on selling techniques, product lines, and consumer trends.

**OPERATIONS MANAGER** Works with store managers and regional managers to help a business to increase its profits through methods such as marketing, more efficient stock control, or improved customer service.

**RETAIL IT MANAGER** Responsible for a store's technology systems— such as point-of-sale, stock ordering, and cash accounting—IT managers install updates and resolve computer problems as and when they occur.

**HUMAN RESOURCES (HR) MANAGER** Deals with staffing issues for a large store or for a number of stores, organizing recruitment, training, payroll, and staff rotations.

**REGIONAL MANAGER** Takes responsibility for the retail activities and profitability of a number of stores in a certain area, and liaises with senior management.

# BUYER

## JOB DESCRIPTION

Every retail business needs stock—the items it sells to its customers in store, online, or by mail order. A buyer's job is to source, select, and purchase these goods. Buyers must anticipate customer demands and predict market trends. By combining excellent people skills and deep industry knowledge, they negotiate prices with suppliers and agree delivery schedules to get the best deals for their company.

### SALARY

Junior buyer ★★☆☆☆
Senior buyer ★★★★☆

### INDUSTRY PROFILE

Demand for buyers set to grow • Plenty of job opportunities in all industry sectors • Growth in certain sectors depends on market trends

## AT A GLANCE

**YOUR INTERESTS** Business studies • Economics • Mathematics • Law • Information Technology (IT) • Marketing • Languages • Travel

**ENTRY QUALIFICATIONS** Relevant work experience may be enough, but some companies may expect you to have a degree.

**LIFESTYLE** Buyers keep regular office hours. Workload may vary considerably if working in an area such as fashion, where buying activity is seasonal.

**LOCATION** Most work is office-based, but buyers need to travel regularly to meet suppliers and attend industry events and trade fairs.

**THE REALITIES** This is a demanding job as buyers make decisions that impact the company financially. Success often leads to management-level roles.

## CAREER PATHS

Buying is a key activity in the retail industry. With experience, buyers move on to manage ever-larger contracts with suppliers, or take responsibility for numerous product lines. This opens the door to higher management roles in planning, logistics (the transportation of goods), and marketing.

**TRAINEE** You can join a retail chain's management program out of high school. You may then progress to assistant buyer, checking stock levels and placing orders while training on the job.

**GRADUATE** A degree in business or a related subject is preferred. However, the profession is open to graduates of any discipline. You may also choose to do a postgraduate course in purchasing.

## ▼ RELATED CAREERS

▶ **SALES EXECUTIVE** *see pp. 60–61*

▶ **STORE MANAGER** *see pp. 62–63*

▶ **REAL ESTATE AGENT** *see pp. 66–67*

▶ **CONTRACT MANAGER** Manages the process of selecting suppliers by providing them with detailed information about the goods required and asking them to offer their best price.

▶ **PURCHASING MANAGER** Buys the equipment, goods, and services needed by government departments or large industries.

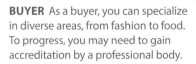

**Depending on the item or season, buyers will often buy merchandise six months before it is sold in stores.**

## SKILLS GUIDE

 Good communication skills for explaining buying choices and negotiating prices with suppliers.

 A sharp analytical approach for comparing offers from various suppliers and selecting the best.

 Good numerical skills to calculate the best deals offered by suppliers and estimate profit margins.

 An awareness of commercial needs and trends to ensure customer requirements are met.

 Good attention to detail to ensure the right goods are purchased at the right time.

**MERCHANDISING MANAGER** Controls the selling activities in a store or group of stores. This job includes tasks such as analyzing the market, planning product lines, implementing sales promotions, and pricing goods. The manager may also oversee a store's e-commerce.

**COST ESTIMATOR** Analyzes data to predict the costs of future business activities, and so determines if selling certain items will make a profit for a retail chain. The factors taken into consideration include the costs of labor, materials, storage, and transportation.

**BUYER** As a buyer, you can specialize in diverse areas, from fashion to food. To progress, you may need to gain accreditation by a professional body.

**LOGISTICS MANAGER** Oversees the transportation of products from suppliers, through distribution centers, and onto the shelves of stores.

# REAL ESTATE AGENT

## JOB DESCRIPTION

Real estate agents organize the sale, purchase, and renting of properties. They meet with sellers or landlords, value the house or apartment, and present it to potential buyers or tenants. Sales agents handle all of the negotiations between buyers and sellers, and liaise with surveyors and lawyers to ensure the sale runs smoothly. Leasing agents finalize the contractual details between landlords and tenants.

### SALARY

Trainee estate agent ★★★★★
Experienced manager ★★★★★

### INDUSTRY PROFILE

Many job opportunities, especially in big cities • Industry sensitive to economic change and housing demand • Real estate agents often move between companies

## CAREER PATHS

Realtors handle the sales and/or rentals of residential and commercial properties. An agent can work in both rentals and sales, but many focus on one or the other. To be licensed, you must take a salesperson qualifying education course and pass an exam. With experience, you may progress to handling larger property deals, conducting property auctions, or managing an agency.

**LEASING AGENT**
Specializing in the rental property market, you will oversee all aspects of leasing a property, from valuing it to finding tenants.

**TRAINEE** You can start your career as a trainee negotiator after leaving high school or college. Employers may offer a short induction course and encourage you to study for further qualifications.

RE/MAX, one of the largest real estate agencies, employs more than 100,000 agents worldwide.

**SALES AGENT** Works with buyers, sellers, lawyers, mortgage brokers and bankers, home inspectors, and others. You will oversee all aspects of the sale of a property, from valuing it and finding potential buyers, to supervising the completion of the sale.

# SKILLS GUIDE

 Excellent verbal communication skills to promote properties to potential clients.

 Flexibility to deal with a variety of challenging negotiations between a wide range of clients.

 The ability to understand the requirements of potential clients and adapt responses accordingly.

 Organizational skills to deal with many sales or rentals going through at the same time.

 Awareness of current commercial trends and escalating or declining prices in the property market.

**ASSISTANT BRANCH MANAGER** Assists the branch manager with the overall running of a real estate agency. Has a proven track record in sales, valuation, and property listing.

**BRANCH MANAGER** Handles the branch's staff and administration, and is responsible for increasing the profitability of the branch.

**AGENCY DIRECTOR** Owns or runs a real estate agency, overseeing all aspects of the business, from employing staff to attracting new clients in both the sales and rental property markets.

## ▼ RELATED CAREERS

▶ **COST ENGINEER** *see pp. 198–199*

▶ **DOMESTIC ENERGY ASSESSOR** Calculates how much energy a property uses and comes up with ways to make it more energy-efficient. They make recommendations to homeowners to save them money on their energy bills.

▶ **PROPERTY DEVELOPER** Buys, improves, then sells properties to make money. May invest in a wide range of properties, from new developments to homes requiring renovation, before selling them for a profit.

▶ **REAL ESTATE ATTORNEY** Handles all of the legal matters involved in the sale and purchase of properties. They must pass related exams before they can start practicing.

## AT A GLANCE

 **YOUR INTERESTS** Marketing • Sales • Property • Customer service • Real estate management • Economics • Business studies

 **ENTRY QUALIFICATIONS** After leaving high school or college, you begin as a trainee with a company, which may provide induction courses.

 **LIFESTYLE** Outside of regular office hours, you will likely need to attend property viewings in the evenings and on weekends.

 **LOCATION** Real estate agents usually deal with properties within a defined location. Most work in an office, while some work from home.

 **THE REALITIES** Intense pressure to meet sales targets. Basic salaries are often low (or nonexistent) and supplemented by commissions.

# MARKETING EXECUTIVE

## JOB DESCRIPTION

Marketing is the art—and science—of creating demand for a product or service. Executives in this area work to communicate positive messages about products and brands to potential customers through print, TV, and online advertising. They may also use social media, or make direct contact via email, mail, or telephone.

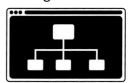

### SALARY

Marketing manager ★★☆☆☆
Marketing director ★★★★★

### INDUSTRY PROFILE

Competitive and fast-paced industry • Opportunities in company marketing departments and stand-alone agencies • Digital and social media becoming increasingly important

## AT A GLANCE

**YOUR INTERESTS** Business studies • Economics • Mathematics • Science • Information Technology (IT) • Psychology • Sociology

**ENTRY QUALIFICATIONS** A business-related degree is a great advantage, although training on the job as a marketing assistant is an option.

**LIFESTYLE** Most marketing executives keep regular office hours, but may need to work evenings and weekends when launching a new campaign.

**LOCATION** Hybrid working is increasing, with many based in an office but some working from home. Most need to travel to present work to clients.

**THE REALITIES** Job specifications—and salaries—vary widely. Pressure to deliver results can be high, and junior roles may offer limited creativity.

## CAREER PATHS

Some marketing executives work for one individual company that makes and sells products and services; others are employed by specialized marketing agencies who develop and deliver campaigns for numerous clients. It is possible to move between the two sectors to gain promotion and responsibility for larger and higher-profile campaigns.

**ASSISTANT** In this entry-level job, you assist a marketing team by preparing presentations and dealing with clients. With experience, you can progress to the role of marketing executive.

**GRADUATE** In order to enter marketing at executive level, you will need to study for a degree in a related subject, such as marketing, communications, business management, or advertising.

## ▼ RELATED CAREERS

▶ **MARKET RESEARCHER** *see pp. 70–71*

▶ **ADVERTISING ACCOUNT EXECUTIVE**
*see pp. 72–73*

▶ **ADVERTISING MEDIA BUYER** Negotiates on behalf of clients to buy advertising space in print, billboards, TV, radio, and digital media, to reach the target audience for as little cost as possible.

▶ **INTERNAL COMMUNICATIONS MANAGER** Communicates to employees through email, social media, and newsletters to inform and motivate staff about new developments.

▶ **SALES DIRECTOR** Oversees a company's sales and its position in the marketplace, directing sales strategy and managing sales staff.

## SKILLS GUIDE

 Good evaluative skills to help analyze market trends and competitors' products and services.

 Excellent numerical skills for preparing and managing budgets and accounts.

 Strong communication skills for presenting reports to senior managers and directors.

 The ability to manage, inspire, and support a team, and take the lead in client meetings.

 Creative thinking to come up with new marketing concepts and strategies.

 Good business awareness and the ability to identify target markets and analyze market-research data.

**DIRECT MARKETING MANAGER** Promotes a company's products and services by engaging directly with customers through channels such as mail shots, competitions, displays in stores, and money-off or loyalty schemes.

**DIGITAL MARKETING MANAGER** Promotes products and services through websites, social media, and email campaigns. Works to build awareness of a company or product, and to attract Internet traffic to its website.

**EVENT MARKETING MANAGER** Markets products or services by sponsoring or placing promotions, such as branded displays or handing out free samples, at public events.

**MARKETING EXECUTIVE** Most marketing executives gain experience on the job, but many employers will encourage them to study for professional qualifications. You can specialize in a particular type of marketing, or after three or more years in the job, aim for promotion to senior roles.

**FREELANCE CONSULTANT** Provides advice to companies on how best to present their products to customers. Consultants usually possess an in-depth knowledge of consumer activity and buying trends within a specific industry.

# MARKET RESEARCHER

## SALARY

Market researcher ★★☆☆☆
Market research director ★★★★★

## INDUSTRY PROFILE

Marketing agencies are largest employers • Industry in decline in Middle East and Europe, but growing in most other parts of the world

## JOB DESCRIPTION

Market researchers gather information to help organizations understand the needs and preferences of customers, and to assist with developing new products. They carry out surveys by telephone, mail, online, or in person, and analyze the results to produce reports of people's opinions about a product, brand, or a political or social issue.

## CAREER PATHS

A degree is usually required to enter the market research sector, which includes marketing agencies, businesses, government departments, or nonprofits. Early in their career, market researchers collect and analyze information. With experience, they may choose to conduct research for clients, give presentations, or manage teams on projects.

**DATA ANALYST** Specializes in using statistical and mathematical methods to analyze market research data. Data analysts interpret the results and present their findings to clients.

**HIGH SCHOOL GRADUATE** You can find work as a market research assistant if you have good writing and numerical skills; experience in customer service is also beneficial. You can combine working as an assistant with studying part-time for a degree in a related subject.

**COLLEGE GRADUATE** You need a degree, preferably in psychology, sociology, mathematics, or statistics, to enter the profession as a graduate. You may be expected to study for accreditation to improve your career prospects.

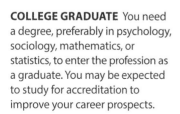

**MARKET RESEARCHER** You can stay in touch with advances in research methods by taking professional courses. You may specialize in areas such as ethnographic research—observing people at home or work to understand their needs better—or move into management or sales roles.

# SKILLS GUIDE

 Strong interpersonal skills to put people at ease while conducting market research interviews.

 Good writing skills for scripting questionnaires and preparing reports and presentations.

 Perseverance and self-motivation for completing research tasks in order to meet projected targets.

 Flexibility to work irregular hours, and to adapt to different research methods and interview styles.

 Excellent attention to detail when completing market research surveys and collating the results.

 Good numerical and analytical skills to interpret data using statistical methods.

 **RESEARCH MANAGER** Oversees the planning, execution, and analysis of market research projects, from setting goals with the client to choosing a survey method and preparing reports.

 **ACCOUNT DIRECTOR** Manages client accounts for a marketing agency, ensuring that market research is carried out in the best way and among the right customer group to suit the client's goals.

By 2029, employment of market researchers is projected to grow by 18 percent.

## AT A GLANCE

 **YOUR INTERESTS** Psychology • Sociology • Anthropology • Statistics • Mathematics • Information Technology (IT) • Business studies • Economics

 **ENTRY QUALIFICATIONS** A degree-level qualification is usually required. Prior marketing experience or working in a customer-facing job is useful.

 **LIFESTYLE** Most researchers keep regular office hours, but conducting face-to-face surveys may require working on evenings and weekends.

 **LOCATION** Although it is mainly office-based, hybrid working is increasing. Researchers may need to travel to conduct surveys or run focus groups.

 **THE REALITIES** Researchers often manage several studies at once. This is an appealing job for those who enjoy dealing with people.

## ▼ RELATED CAREERS

► **MARKETING EXECUTIVE** *see pp. 68–69*

► **INVESTMENT ANALYST** *see pp. 100–101*

► **CONSUMER SCIENTIST** Researches the tastes, needs, and preferences of existing and potential customers, and advises commercial clients on improvements to products and services.

► **DATA SCIENTIST** Acquires, manages, and utilizes electronically stored information—such as online databases—for commercial, public-sector, or charitable uses.

► **STATISTICIAN** Collects, analyzes, and interprets complex quantitative data, then presents it in a comprehensible form using graphs and charts.

# ADVERTISING ACCOUNT EXECUTIVE

## JOB DESCRIPTION

In the advertising industry, the account executive is the most important link between an agency's creative team and its clients. In this role, you work with your creative team to create an effective advertising campaign that fulfills the client's goals. Digital skills and an appreciation of online promotional tools are vital in this role.

### SALARY

Junior account executive ★☆☆☆☆
Account director ★★★★★

### INDUSTRY PROFILE

Highly competitive, fast-paced industry • Roles available in public and private sectors • Opportunities across the world

## CAREER PATHS

An advertising account executive works on the business side of the advertising industry; it is rare for individuals to move from this area into creative roles, and vice versa. Experienced account executives may, however, move into marketing roles within larger companies.

**ACCOUNT DIRECTOR** Supervises a team of account executives, and usually works on larger, complex projects with greater demands.

**INTERN** Some advertising agencies take on college interns to work in administrative roles, for example, in their media buying departments. From here, you may be able to apply for internal promotion.

**GRADUATE** A bachelor's degree in any discipline will allow you to apply for the graduate training programs run by many agencies. These programs train you to become an advertising account executive.

**ADVERTISING ACCOUNT EXECUTIVE** As you rise through the ranks, you will have the chance to work for different types of clients. Managers tend to work for clients in one specific industry, such as in food or financial services. After gaining experience, you can go on to become an account director or work on a freelance basis.

## SKILLS GUIDE

Excellent written and verbal communication skills help to tailor campaigns to meet client needs.

The ability to lead, inspire, and motivate a creative team to produce successful campaigns.

Good organizational skills to manage many complex and varied advertising projects at once.

The drive and motivation to succeed, and the ability to develop this attitude among team members.

An extensive knowledge of market trends, current media, and the client's business and competitors.

**GROUP ACCOUNT DIRECTOR** Supervises several accounts and a large staff; may even supervise advertising branches across the world.

**FREELANCE ADVERTISING ACCOUNT EXECUTIVE** Chooses either to work as an advertising consultant or to start up a new advertising company.

A 30-second advertisement for Super Bowl LV cost about $5.6 million.

## ▼ RELATED CAREERS

▶ **REAL ESTATE AGENT** *see pp. 66–67*

▶ **MARKETING EXECUTIVE** *see pp. 68–69*

▶ **PUBLIC RELATIONS OFFICER** *see pp. 74–75*

▶ **ADVERTISING ART DIRECTOR** Creates visual ideas to convey a clear message for advertising campaigns. They work with a copywriter, who writes text, or copy, for the target audience.

▶ **MEDIA BUYER** Organizes and purchases advertisement space in magazines, newspapers, TV, and online resources on behalf of clients to promote their products and services.

▶ **SALES PROMOTION EXECUTIVE** Organizes promotional marketing campaigns to encourage consumers to purchase products and services.

## AT A GLANCE

**YOUR INTERESTS** Media • Social media • Current affairs • Communications • Business management • Art • Design

**ENTRY QUALIFICATIONS** Having a bachelor's degree is generally required. Having a master's degree in business or marketing may help secure a job.

**LIFESTYLE** Official working hours are usually regular, but most account executives may need to work overtime to complete a project.

**LOCATION** You are office based, but may need to travel to meet clients and collect market research data, or go abroad for international campaigns.

**THE REALITIES** This is a high-profile job with a lot of responsibility. It can be stressful at times, but greater experience produces financial rewards.

# PUBLIC RELATIONS OFFICER

## JOB DESCRIPTION

Organizations hire Public Relations (PR) officers to manage and boost their reputations. As a PR officer, you will produce campaigns to promote awareness of a company and its products and/or services. PR officers can also work within an institution to raise awareness and visibility of the company's projects, programs, and initiatives internally.

### SALARY

Publicity assistant ★★★★★
Account director ★★★★★

### INDUSTRY PROFILE

Highly competitive job market • Majority of work in large firms • Most work located in big cities • Global opportunities • Freelance possible

## CAREER PATHS

PR officers can work within organizations, communicating with both staff and the wider public, or for agencies hired by corporate clients. They also need to develop strong relationships with media contacts.

**ASSISTANT** Right out of high school, you can take an internship or an administrative role in the PR department of a large organization, or within a PR agency.

**GRADUATE** You can study PR at college, but most employers prefer candidates with degrees in disciplines such as English, communication, journalism, or marketing.

### ▼ RELATED CAREERS

▶ **MARKETING EXECUTIVE** *see pp. 68–69*

▶ **ADVERTISING ACCOUNT EXECUTIVE** *see pp. 72–73*

▶ **EVENTS MANAGER** *see pp. 88–89*

▶ **CHARITY FUNDRAISER** *see pp. 90–91*

▶ **ADVERTISING COPYWRITER** Produces text for marketing and advertising materials. They also liaise with clients, designers, and the rest of the creative team to agree on campaign style and content.

**PUBLIC RELATIONS OFFICER** As a PR officer, you may be expected to study for higher professional degrees in order to progress to more senior roles.

## AT A GLANCE

**YOUR INTERESTS** Media • Marketing and communications • Social media • Business studies • Advertising • Current trends

**LOCATION** PR officers usually work in an office, but some may work remotely. You may have to travel to meet clients or for promotional events.

**ENTRY QUALIFICATIONS** There are no set entry requirements, but many employers expect a degree in a relevant subject, such as communications.

**THE REALITIES** Must be flexible; you will attend events scheduled at various times. Dealing with difficult people in delicate situations is a big part of the job.

**LIFESTYLE** Work hours are regular, but you will need to attend launches and events in evenings and on weekends.

PR specialists in government are known as "press secretaries."

# SKILLS GUIDE

Excellent written and verbal skills, as the job involves crafting original and memorable campaigns.

An ability to quickly grasp a client's needs and handle multiple PR campaigns at once.

A clear understanding of the interests, aims, and requirements of the client and target audience.

Exceptional planning and organizational skills for running complex and nuanced projects.

Knowledge of global events and current business trends to help create effective PR strategies.

**ACCOUNT MANAGER** Manages a small team and, within a PR agency, provides the primary point of contact for a particular client.

**ACCOUNT DIRECTOR** Liaises with senior managers to develop and deliver effective campaigns, and is often responsible for managing a large team of PR officers.

**COMMUNICATIONS MANAGER** Leads a team within a company to deliver consistent news and business messages to all staff.

**DIGITAL COMMUNICATIONS MANAGER** Deals with managing and promoting organizations through various channels, such as digital, online, and social media.

**HEAD OF COMMUNICATIONS** Develops overall creative strategy and vision for complex, innovative, and high-profile projects.

# ADMINISTRATION AND BUSINESS MANAGEMENT

Decision-making and organizational abilities are key aspects of administration and business management. There are many sectors of employment within this field, and you will need a range of skills—from problem-solving to expertise in leadership—to truly excel.

### CUSTOMER SERVICE MANAGER
*Page 78*

The public face of a business or organization, customer service managers work to ensure that clients are happy with the products and services they provide.

### HUMAN RESOURCES MANAGER
*Page 80*

People are the most valuable asset of any organization. HR managers recruit and train staff, and deal with personnel issues, such as equal-opportunity policies.

### PROJECT MANAGER
*Page 82*

Working in virtually every industry and sector, project managers ensure that projects are well-organized, run smoothly, and stay within budget.

### MANAGEMENT CONSULTANT
*Page 84*

Contracted by firms to identify problems and recommend solutions, management consultants are business experts with the skills to cut to the heart of key issues.

### PERSONAL ASSISTANT
*Page 86*

Busy executives rely on their personal assistants to organize their schedules, deal with correspondence, and supervise administrative staff.

### EVENTS MANAGER
*Page 88*

Commercial, charitable, and public events require careful planning, whatever their scale. Running them are events managers, who ensure that every aspect runs smoothly.

### CHARITY FUNDRAISER
*Page 90*

Fundraising is fundamental to the operation of every charity, and fundraisers must develop exciting and innovative approaches to bringing in donations.

### TRANSLATOR
*Page 92*

Drawing on their linguistic skills and an understanding of other cultures and traditions, translators convert written or audio material from one language to another.

# CUSTOMER SERVICE MANAGER

## JOB DESCRIPTION

The experience of buying products or using services is enhanced by impressive customer support. A customer service manager works for an organization to ensure that its clients are satisfied. Leading a dedicated team, managers handle customer queries, offer product advice, and resolve complaints. Senior managers help develop a company's policies and procedures.

### SALARY

Customer service assistant ★★★★★
Experienced manager ★★★★★

### INDUSTRY PROFILE

Many opportunities available across a wide range of organizations • More jobs resulting from the growth in online retail • Customer service skills in high demand • Target-driven work

## CAREER PATHS

Most people begin their careers as customer service assistants, learning on the job by dealing directly with clients. With experience they can progress into supervisory and then managerial roles. Customer service managers are employed in businesses such as retail, telecommunications, and financial services, as well as in government roles.

**SENIOR CUSTOMER SERVICE MANAGER** Develops policies, procedures, and staff training programs to improve customer service standards across the business.

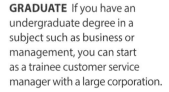

**ASSISTANT** You can begin your career as an assistant without a college degree. Employers will provide training on products and services, as well as on customer service procedures and protocols.

**GRADUATE** If you have an undergraduate degree in a subject such as business or management, you can start as a trainee customer service manager with a large corporation.

**CUSTOMER SERVICE MANAGER** Experience is crucial if you want to move up the ladder in your organization. In bigger companies, you can progress into one of several specializations or move up into a more senior role.

# SKILLS GUIDE

 Communication and motivational skills are necessary to deal with both customers and colleagues.

 Good team-working skills, to work closely with customer service agents and help their work run smoothly.

 The ability to lead and inspire staff so they can reach their potential and reflect well on the company.

 Genuine understanding and empathy to resolve a range of customer queries and problems.

 Excellent organizational skills and the ability to manage staff and high volumes of caller queries.

 Great problem-solving skills, as the job depends on effective responses to various customer complaints.

**CUSTOMER SERVICE ASSESSOR**
Trains and develops staff who are new to the customer service role. Assessors use training techniques to ensure that candidates reach the required standards of work.

**BUSINESS MANAGER**
Influences strategic business decisions based on customer satisfaction in order to increase sales. They work as part of the senior management team.

## AT A GLANCE

 **YOUR INTERESTS** Business studies • Administration • Retail • Customer care • Information Technology (IT) • Psychology • Communications

 **ENTRY QUALIFICATIONS** An undergraduate degree in business or management isn't required but can boost your chances of landing a job.

 **LIFESTYLE** Customer service managers work regular hours. Shift work is sometimes necessary to cover evenings and weekends.

 **LOCATION** You may work in an office, or remotely from home or out-of-town call centers, which is becoming more common.

 **THE REALITIES** The industry is driven by meeting quality targets. Though irate clients can be frustrating, it is satisfying to resolve their problems.

## ▼ RELATED CAREERS

▶ **HUMAN RESOURCES MANAGER** see pp. 80–81

▶ **HOTEL MANAGER** see pp. 304–305

▶ **CALL CENTER MANAGER** Oversees day-to-day running of a call center, where operators answer customer inquiries via telephone, email, or online chat. Managers organize the staff, explain their duties, and set their targets.

▶ **OFFICE MANAGER** Organizes and supervises administrative and IT tasks to ensure the smooth running of an office.

▶ **RETAIL MANAGER** Runs shops and department stores, while also managing staff. They have strong commercial skills and use displays and pricing methods to maximize revenue.

# HUMAN RESOURCES MANAGER

## JOB DESCRIPTION

Human Resources (HR) professionals deal with people in the workforce. They work for organizations and are responsible for hiring new staff, and for ensuring that employees uphold company standards and procedures. They also represent staff, negotiating their benefits and offering them new training and development opportunities.

### SALARY

HR assistant ★★★★★
HR manager ★★★★★

### INDUSTRY PROFILE

Competitive but growing industry • Jobs in companies' own HR divisions and also in external HR agencies • Industry very sensitive and responsive to movements in the economy

## AT A GLANCE

 **YOUR INTERESTS** Project management • Employment law • Marketing and communication • Psychology

 **ENTRY QUALIFICATIONS** A degree in business, psychology, management, law, or a similar subject is desirable. Some companies hire trainees at junior levels.

 **LIFESTYLE** Working hours are regular. As the "face" of an organization, HR managers have to look professional and present themselves well at all times.

 **LOCATION** Usually office-based, there are growing opportunities for hybrid working. Travel is likely, as a company may have branches in various locations.

 **THE REALITIES** Dealing with people is hard. You must be resilient yet show sensitivity when handling professional, and sometimes personal, issues.

## ▼ RELATED CAREERS

▶ **MANAGEMENT CONSULTANT** *see pp. 84–85*

▶ **EMPLOYEE RELATIONS MANAGER** Facilitates effective working relationships between management and employees. May cover all communications between the two, including employment contracts, changes to workforce planning, policy enforcement, and trade unions.

▶ **OCCUPATIONAL HEALTH PROFESSIONAL** Provides health support to employees while at work. Treating employees who become ill at work, they also maintain detailed health records for all staff.

▶ **ORGANIZATIONAL DEVELOPMENT AND DESIGN PROFESSIONAL** Works to optimize business strategy and performance by using behavioral science, systems, structures, culture, and values to guide an organization forward.

▶ **RECRUITMENT PROFESSIONAL** Finds and helps select suitable candidates for employment. They conduct necessary background checks for potential candidates.

## CAREER PATHS

Some colleges offer programs in HR management, but a business-related bachelor's degree is usually enough to apply for entry-level jobs. An HR manager's job can vary depending on the company's size; in larger companies, you can specialize in one area, such as recruitment.

**HR GENERALIST** Joining a company as a generalist, you start in a broad role, gaining an overview of relevant activities. This role can be very process-driven.

**GRADUATE** Many HR professionals start as graduate trainees. Any degree discipline is acceptable, but business, psychology, and law are very helpful.

**HR MANAGER** While HR management is a common position in most companies, with experience you may be able to progress into more senior roles or various specialties, like compensation.

### SKILLS GUIDE

 Good communication skills to interact and negotiate effectively with colleagues.

 Leadership skills and the vision to implement difficult policies and measure the impact of decisions.

 Sensitivity toward diverse viewpoints and empathy for employees' issues at work.

 Decisive problem-solving to help make employees productive and comfortable at work.

 Precision and an eye for detail in HR activities, such as recruitment drives and payroll administration.

**TALENT MANAGER** Sources, recruits, and retains key personnel for a business. They work with senior management to ensure that the needs of a business are being met by its current and future workforce.

**LEARNING AND DEVELOPMENT MANAGER** Identifies the induction and training needs of employees, and is involved in coaching and mentoring staff, from newcomers to other managers.

**HR DIRECTOR** Plays the lead role in shaping and driving an organization's HR policies, from recruitment to training.

**HR CONSULTANT** Provides HR expertise to client companies, either independently or through broader consulting firms.

# PROJECT MANAGER

## JOB DESCRIPTION

Project managers work in a range of industries to ensure that projects are completed on time and to budget. In this role, you will need to draw upon organizational and interpersonal skills to agree the project's goals with your client, draft a plan, identify risks, and assemble a team of consultants and specialists to carry out the work. You then monitor the progress of the project until its goals have been achieved.

### SALARY

Project manager ★★★★★
Senior project manager ★★★★★

### INDUSTRY PROFILE

Good pay levels • Opportunities in public and private sectors • Key role in a wide range of industries • Size and number of available projects is experiencing rapid growth

## ▼ RELATED CAREERS

▶ **HUMAN RESOURCES MANAGER** *see pp. 80–81*

▶ **MANAGEMENT CONSULTANT** *see pp. 84–85*

▶ **EVENTS MANAGER** *see pp. 88–89*

▶ **CONSTRUCTION MANAGER** *see pp. 204–205*

▶ **PROGRAM MANAGER** Manages several projects at the same time. They use a structured approach to use people and resources in the most efficient way to reach project goals.

By 2018, the number of project managers awarded Project Management Professional status reached 750,000 around the world.

## AT A GLANCE

**YOUR INTERESTS** Business Studies • Economics • Management • Accounting • Information Technology (IT) • Mathematics • Psychology

**ENTRY QUALIFICATIONS** A degree in project- or business-management, or in a subject directly relevant to the industry, is required.

**LIFESTYLE** Project managers generally work longer hours than project staff in order to ensure that the project hits targets and deadlines.

**LOCATION** Hybrid working is very common in project management roles. Local and international travel may be required.

**THE REALITIES** The job may involve changing location, colleagues, and clients for each new project. Inactivity while awaiting a new project can be frustrating.

## CAREER PATHS

Most project managers hold a degree related to the sector in which they work, or a certificate in business administration. They usually specialize in managing projects in one sector, such as Information Technology (IT) or construction.

**ASSISTANT** This role enables you to learn on the job by lending support to project managers.

**GRADUATE** A bachelor's degree followed by a graduate degree in project management offers you the best way into this career.

**PROJECT MANAGER** After gaining experience of supervising and managing projects, you can choose to specialize in one of a number of sectors. You can also seek sponsorship from your employer to study for Project Management Professional status.

**CONSTRUCTION PROJECT MANAGER** Oversees the successful delivery of construction projects, such as new housing, highways, airports, or retail parks.

**CONSERVATION PROJECT MANAGER** Plans, oversees, and delivers projects, such as breeding programs or habitat protection, for wildlife trusts, conservation bodies, or environmental agencies.

**ARTS PROJECT MANAGER** Supervises and delivers arts-related ventures, such as community arts projects, installations and exhibitions, and arts-education projects.

**IT PROJECT MANAGER** Coordinates IT projects, such as installing or upgrading computer systems, networks, hardware, and software for new or existing businesses and organizations.

**ENGINEERING PROJECT MANAGER** Manages engineering projects, such as the building of railroads, bridges, power stations, telecommunications systems, and energy networks.

# MANAGEMENT CONSULTANT

## JOB DESCRIPTION

Management consultants provide businesses with research and advice to help them grow and increase their profits. Large consultancies advise on all business areas, from supply chain management, finance, and human resources to Information Technology (IT), while smaller companies may specialize in one specific area of business.

### SALARY

Graduate consultant ★★☆☆☆
Experienced consultant ★★★★★

### INDUSTRY PROFILE

The largest consultancies employ thousands of staff and have offices all over the world • Some clients retain consultants for long-term projects

## AT A GLANCE

**YOUR INTERESTS** Management science • Business studies • Economics • Accounting • Marketing • Mathematics • Statistics • Political science

**ENTRY QUALIFICATIONS** A degree is required. Most employers will expect a graduate degree or experience that is relevant to their area of activity.

**LIFESTYLE** Long working hours and frequent travel are common. Management consultants may have to spend long periods away from home.

**LOCATION** Usually office-based, but many people have a hybrid working pattern. Visits to clients' premises locally and abroad may also be required.

**THE REALITIES** The financial rewards are high, but management consultants have to work hard and may have to deal with demanding clients.

## CAREER PATHS

Management consultancy firms offer internships and training programs for high-achieving graduates. Following a period of training, management consultants usually specialize in one area, such as helping companies rebrand, or analyzing a client's competitors or sales strategies.

**GRADUATE** You can join a consultancy as an intern after completing a degree. Competition for places is intense, but for ambitious graduates they offer the best route into the profession.

**BUSINESS PROFESSIONAL** Your chances of becoming a management consultant are highter if you have solid work experience or formal training in a profession such as law, finance, accountancy, or IT.

## ▼ RELATED CAREERS

▶ **HUMAN RESOURCES MANAGER** *see pp. 80–81*

▶ **ACCOUNTANT** *see pp. 102–103*

▶ **ECONOMIST** *see pp. 108–109*

▶ **COMPANY EXECUTIVE** Responsible for directing a company, setting its policies and targets, and ensuring that the company's managers work toward these goals. Most company executives specialize in one area, such as finance or human resources.

▶ **DATA SCIENTIST** Acquires, manages, and utilizes electronically stored information—such as online databases—for commercial, public-sector, or charitable uses.

# SKILLS GUIDE

 Good communication skills to work with senior managers and executives.

 Leadership and authority to implement change in a business or organization.

 The ability to understand and interpret complex numerical data and financial reports.

 Strong mathematical skills for collecting and processing data, and making financial projections.

 A thorough understanding of business processes, taxes, and the impact of business decisions.

 An eye for detail for analyzing data and other business-related information accurately.

## FINANCIAL CONSULTANT

Reviews a company's financial systems and evaluates its business plans in order to help it identify ways of raising money to grow. Financial consultants usually come from an accountancy background.

## STRATEGY CONSULTANT

Analyzes a business and provides advice on issues, such as how to improve the value of the company's shares, or how to diversify the company's activities. They work closely with senior management.

## MANAGEMENT CONSULTANT

In this role you examine a client company's working methods and strategies, applying your own expert knowledge to help solve a variety of business problems.

## OPERATIONS CONSULTANT

Focuses on helping a company improve its productivity by analyzing the workflow in its supply chain and looking at a company's structures and policies.

# PERSONAL ASSISTANT

## JOB DESCRIPTION

Personal assistants (PAs) support business executives and senior managers in their day-to-day work. They set up meetings for their employer, manage their correspondence, organize their travel requirements, and file documents. Experienced PAs may even represent their employers at meetings.

### SALARY

Junior PA ★★★★★
Executive PA ★★★★★

### INDUSTRY PROFILE

High demand for candidates with computing and language skills • PAs required in every sector of business

## CAREER PATHS

The role of a PA can vary enormously depending on the employer. The most senior PAs earn good salaries and have a detailed understanding of their employer's business. Ultimately, they may even move into management roles themselves.

**RECEPTIONIST** Highly experienced and skilled receptionists may be able to move into higher roles within a company's administration.

**ASSISTANT** You can begin your career as an administrative assistant after you have completed high school. You will have to carry out tasks such as keeping records, maintaining databases, and answering routine queries from colleagues, clients, or suppliers.

**GRADUATE** If you have a degree and good administrative skills, you may find a job as a PA for a senior executive. Proficiency in languages or knowledge of the employer's business sector is an advantage in most roles.

**PERSONAL ASSISTANT** With experience, you will develop knowledge of the business in which you work. You can move into more senior roles, such as human resources or office management.

## SKILLS GUIDE

 Good communication skills for negotiating with others, writing reports, and dealing with inquiries.

 Strong interpersonal skills for dealing with people at all levels in an office or organization.

 The ability to remain calm under pressure, prioritize work, and multitask when necessary.

 A thorough knowledge of standard office software and Internet research methods.

 A good understanding of business, bookkeeping, and management techniques.

 **MEDICAL PA** Works with senior doctors to manage their patient lists, arrange appointments, and ensure patients receive appropriate treatment. The job requires a thorough knowledge of medical terminology.

 **VIRTUAL PA** Operates a hybrid working model to provide administrative support to one or more business clients using email, video conferencing, and telephone.

 **EXECUTIVE PA** Combines the role of a general PA with organizing an employer's personal and social calendar. They usually work for wealthy, high-level executives.

## AT A GLANCE

 **YOUR INTERESTS** Computers • Law • Administration • Foreign languages • Business studies • Mathematics • Travel • Communications • Reading • Writing

 **ENTRY QUALIFICATIONS** PAs may be able to find work out of high school, but they may need a degree to work for some companies.

 **LIFESTYLE** Regular office hours are the norm, but tight deadlines or other demands may require overtime. A professional appearance is essential.

 **LOCATION** PAs are usually office-based, but some work remotely, as the role is suited to hybrid working. They may also need to travel with managers.

 **THE REALITIES** Some managers can be demanding. Working very closely for one individual daily can be difficult.

## ▼ RELATED CAREERS

▶ **CUSTOMER SERVICE MANAGER** *see pp. 78–79*

▶ **BOOKKEEPER** Maintains thorough records of a company's financial transactions, such as purchases, invoices, wages, and taxes paid.

▶ **LEGAL ASSISTANT** Supports lawyers in carrying out administrative or routine legal tasks to enable them to prepare for client meetings or court appearances.

▶ **OFFICE MANAGER** Oversees the efficient day-to-day operation of an office. This includes supervising administrative staff, arranging supplies of business equipment and stationery, and maintaining a healthy office environment.

# EVENTS MANAGER

## JOB DESCRIPTION

Great people skills and the ability to multitask make a successful events manager. In this job, you are responsible for organizing and running all types of events, from wedding parties to conferences. The role involves understanding a client's needs before coming up with event ideas, sourcing venues, choosing vendors, negotiating costs, hiring and managing assistants, and promoting the occasion.

## SALARY

Events administrator ★★☆☆☆
Events manager ★★★★☆

## INDUSTRY PROFILE

Multiple entry points into the field • Popular profession experiencing rapid growth • Global opportunities • Almost equal proportion of males and females in the industry

## AT A GLANCE

 **YOUR INTERESTS** Planning events • Hospitality • Marketing • Working with people • Business administration • Management • Law

 **ENTRY QUALIFICATIONS** A degree in hospitality or similar is fast becoming a requirement, but work experience in an events company may be acceptable.

 **LIFESTYLE** You will need to attend events in evenings and on weekends. Managing events is a social business and you will be surrounded by people.

 **LOCATION** Hybrid working is increasing in this field, particularly during the planning phase. Travel to events, sometimes abroad, may be required.

 **THE REALITIES** This is a fast-paced job where it is not acceptable to be late. A lot of time is spent seeing venues, meeting vendors, and networking.

## CAREER PATHS

An events manager may work on a variety of social, business, or commercial events in one particular field or industry, or specialize in one kind of event for a variety of clients. Progress in this career depends on contacts, energy, and networking abilities as much as on formal education.

**ASSISTANT** If you have a positive attitude, you may be able to find employment as an assistant or an intern in an events company after leaving school. You can progress to the level of events manager as you build up experience.

**GRADUATE** A degree in hospitality management, public relations, or marketing combined with relevant work experience such as an internship is a typical example of a route into this career.

## ▼ RELATED CAREERS

▶ **MARKETING EXECUTIVE** *see pp. 68–69*

▶ **PUBLIC RELATIONS OFFICER** *see pp. 74–75*

▶ **CHARITY FUNDRAISER** *see pp. 90–91*

▶ **HOTEL MANAGER** *see pp. 304–305*

▶ **FESTIVAL MANAGER** Organizes bands and performers, publicity, catering, logistics, and all aspects required to set up a music festival.

▶ **FOOD SERVICES MANAGER** Supervises the daily operation of restaurants and other outlets serving prepared meals.

▶ **LEISURE SERVICES MANAGER** Manages recreational venues, such as spas and gyms.

# SKILLS GUIDE

 Good communication and negotiation skills to liaise effectively with clients.

 The ability to coordinate and manage teams when working on multiple projects.

 Excellent business skills to manage the potentially large budgets involved with big events.

 Strong organizational skills to carry an events project from concept to completion.

 Good multitasking skills, as juggling a client's many needs is very important.

**WEDDING PLANNER**
Organizes and manages weddings for clients, booking venues, caterers, florists, and entertainers.

**CONFERENCE DIRECTOR**
Arranges conferences by booking speakers and venues that will attract paying delegates.

**EXHIBITION PLANNER**
Works with businesses and organizations exhibiting to the public or at trade fairs and conferences. The planner helps design and produce exhibition stands, then delivers and installs them on site.

**EVENTS MANAGER** Junior events managers are responsible for tasks such as registration of visitors and sales of exhibition space. With experience in the role, you may deal with larger clients and negotiate contracts with suppliers.

**CONCERT PROMOTER** Sets up concerts or other public events by booking artists and venues, publicizing the event, and selling tickets to the public.

# CHARITY FUNDRAISER

## JOB DESCRIPTION

Charities depend on the financial support of individuals, organizations, and governments. To increase these donations, fundraisers organize events or collections, carry out direct mail campaigns to donors, promote the charities through the media, or seek to get sponsorship and grants from companies and foundations.

### SALARY

Charity fundraiser ★★★★★
Fundraising manager ★★★★★

### INDUSTRY PROFILE

Demand for fundraisers set to grow as government funding falls • Job opportunities exist across the world • Salaries vary depending on the size and location of the charity

## CAREER PATHS

A charity will expect you to be highly committed to the cause it promotes. Some of the larger organizations provide training in fundraising and marketing skills. With experience, you may be able to move into the management of the charity, helping to set its goals and determine its fundraising strategies.

**VOLUNTEER MANAGER** Recruits, trains, and manages volunteers to carry out different tasks within a charity or other voluntary organizations.

**VOLUNTEER** If you are interested in becoming a charity fundraiser, you should seek out experience as a volunteer in your charity of interest. Some offer unpaid internships, which can be a good way for you to build contacts.

**GRADUATE** You stand a better chance of getting hired as a charity fundraiser if you have a degree in business or marketing, or one that is related to the activities of your chosen charity, such as a degree in development studies for an aid organization.

**CHARITY FUNDRAISER** You may specialize in one area of revenue, such as arranging corporate sponsorship, street collections, or legacies, if working for a larger charity. Fundraisers in smaller charities combine all these roles.

## SKILLS GUIDE

 Good communication skills across all forms of media, from social media to television.

 The ability to work in a team on a variety of tasks, from making phone calls to handling mailings.

 Great interpersonal skills and ability to manage negative responses appropriately.

 Organizational skills to train and coordinate the work of volunteers.

 Motivation and commitment to drive a fundraising project with limited funds and resources.

 Financial knowledge and commercial awareness to work with business donors.

**PLANNED GIVING PROFESSIONAL** Persuades and encourages a charity's supporters to leave part of their wealth to the charity in their wills. Legacies are an important source of income for most charities.

**LOBBYIST** Represents charities in meetings with politicians or government officials. Using their skills of persuasion, lobbyists encourage people to increase funding to the organization to help it achieve its aims.

## AT A GLANCE

 **YOUR INTERESTS** Fundraising • Planning • Psychology • Sociology • Politics • Journalism • Business studies • Economics

 **ENTRY QUALIFICATIONS** A relevant degree is useful, but hard work and commitment to the charity's causes may be sufficient to find a job.

 **LIFESTYLE** Jobs can be part- or full-time. Weekend and evening work is common in roles that involve organizing events with the public.

 **LOCATION** Much of the work is office-based, but fundraisers may need to visit potential donors, attend events, or organize street collections.

 **THE REALITIES** Competition for jobs is intense when starting out, but experienced fundraisers can command high salaries.

## ▼ RELATED CAREERS

▶ **MARKETING EXECUTIVE** *see pp. 68–69*

▶ **EVENTS MANAGER** *see pp. 88–89*

▶ **INTERNATIONAL DEVELOPMENT WORKER** Travels to countries affected by disaster, war, or poverty and helps the local people.

One-off online donations to charities increased by 26 percent in 2020 compared to the same time in 2019.

# TRANSLATOR

## JOB DESCRIPTION

A translator converts words from one language to another while making sure that the original meaning is retained. Translators are fluent in more than one language and have highly developed written and verbal skills. They also often have a good understanding of the cultures of the countries associated with the languages they are translating.

### SALARY

Newly qualified translator ★★★★★
Experienced translator ★★★★★

### INDUSTRY PROFILE

Freelance work is common • Most full-time jobs in government • There is an increasing demand for translation to and from Chinese, Russian, Arabic, and minority European languages

## SKILLS GUIDE

Excellent written and verbal communication skills to translate clearly for clients.

Fluency in multiple languages in order to translate efficiently, easily, and accurately.

A good understanding of different cultural values and how people communicate in different regions.

The perseverance to handle complex, technical, and lengthy projects, and still meet deadlines.

Attention to detail and the ability to understand and convey the correct meaning of words.

## AT A GLANCE

**YOUR INTERESTS** Languages • Literature • Science • Writing and speaking • Law • Business studies • Politics • Travel and culture

**ENTRY QUALIFICATIONS** Most employers require a bachelor's degree in languages; some require a graduate qualification. Work experience is valuable.

**LIFESTYLE** Much of the work is done on computers and driven by deadlines, which means you may need to work long hours in order to finish a project.

**LOCATION** Hybrid working is very common, with many freelancers based at home. Video conferencing is often used for meetings to minimize travel.

**THE REALITIES** Jobs may not be regular; freelance work is common in this industry. Pay rates vary according to the language and length of project.

## ▼ RELATED CAREERS

▶ **BILINGUAL SECRETARY** Uses a knowledge of one or more foreign languages to translate business communications and research materials, and to liaise with overseas clients face-to-face or by telephone. Administration skills are also essential in this job.

▶ **TECHNICAL AUTHOR** Writes user manuals, technical guides, and online blogs for a wide range of industries and products. They are highly skilled at presenting very technical information in a user-friendly way.

▶ **VACATION REPRESENTATIVE** Looks after groups of tourists on vacation in international resorts. Proficiency in the local language and the languages of clients is highly desirable.

Growth areas include creating subtitles for computer games and translating websites.

## CAREER PATHS

Translation is a degree-level profession, but graduate degrees in translation can greatly enhance your employment opportunities. Fluency in two or more languages is a key requirement, and knowledge of a specific sector, such as business, finance, or technology, is an advantage.

**GRADUATE** To find work in this field you may need a degree in modern languages and preferably a postgraduate qualification in translation. Taking language proficiency tests is another way you can increase your credibility as a translator.

**TRANSLATOR** Once qualified as a translator, you can take several routes. You could specialize in one language or more. Experienced translators may move into a number of different areas.

**GOVERNMENT TRANSLATOR**
Works for government departments, such as security and intelligence services. Governments can offer a clear and structured career path in this field.

**INTERPRETER** Converts the spoken word from one language to another between people who do not speak the same language. A clear, strong voice is essential.

**TRANSLATION AGENCY MANAGER** Sets up an independent business, and employs freelance workers to provide translation services to clients in government and the private sector.

**FREELANCE TRANSLATOR**
Registers with agencies or finds translation jobs using personal contacts. They may work in video captioning or dubbing so that TV programs or movies can reach a broader audience.

# FINANCE, LAW, AND POLITICS

Careers in this area require strong intellect, the ability to process and retain large amounts of information, numerical aptitude, and a complete understanding of legal and business issues. People skills are also vital, as these careers involve working with other professionals and the public.

**BANK MANAGER**
*Page 96*

Working in a retail banking setting, bank managers oversee the delivery of a range of financial services for personal and business customers.

**TRADER**
*Page 98*

Through buying and selling investments such as stocks and bonds, traders use their knowledge of financial markets to make profits for their clients.

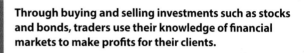

**INVESTMENT ANALYST**
*Page 100*

By researching financial data and economic and political trends, investment analysts advise banks, investors, and fund managers on the best ways to generate income.

**ACCOUNTANT**
*Page 102*

Financial accounting is fundamental to businesses of every kind. Accountants are the skilled analysts who gather and examine complex financial data.

**ACTUARY**
*Page 104*

With an advanced knowledge of statistics and economics, actuaries are skilled mathematicians who give risk advice to organizations to help them plan and make decisions.

**FINANCIAL ADVISOR**
*Page 106*

The growth of the financial services industry has led to a vast array of saving and investment products. Financial advisors help their clients make the right financial choices.

**ECONOMIST**
*Page 108*

An understanding of economic theory is vital for business strategy and government policy. Economists are the experts who give economic advice to decision-makers.

**LAWYER**
*Page 110*

Whether working for individuals or organizations, lawyers advise and represent clients on all sorts of legal matters, both inside and outside the courtroom.

**JUDGE**
*Page 112*

Combining an expert knowledge of the law and strong decision-making skills, judges ensure the legal process is upheld in the courtroom and during legal negotiations.

**POLITICIAN**
*Page 114*

Representing the interests of their political party and voters, politicians campaign to win support for their policies in order to achieve social and political change.

# BANK MANAGER

## JOB DESCRIPTION

Managers in retail banks provide banking and financial services to individuals and businesses. They supervise the day-to-day work of the branch's staff and ensure that procedures are followed. Bank managers are also responsible for attracting new clients, generating sales of financial products, such as mortgages and credit cards, assessing applications for loans, and reporting to the bank's head office.

### SALARY

Assistant branch manager ★★★☆☆
Regional bank manager ★★★★★

### INDUSTRY PROFILE

Opportunities available worldwide • Competitive sector, but pay levels good and bonuses common • Branch closures among certain banks due to recent economic events

## ▼ RELATED CAREERS

▶ **INVESTMENT ANALYST** *see pp. 100–101*

▶ **ACCOUNTANT** *see pp. 102–103*

▶ **FINANCIAL ADVISOR** *see pp. 106–107*

▶ **INVESTMENT BANKER** Provides advice to companies about strategic issues, such as taking over businesses or merging existing ones. They raise money from investors to fund the growth and expansion of companies.

According to the American Bankers Association, more than 2 million people are employed by banks in the United States.

## AT A GLANCE

**YOUR INTERESTS** Financial services • Accounting • Business studies • Economics • Mathematics • Statistics • Information Technology (IT)

**ENTRY QUALIFICATIONS** Bank managers are typically expected to hold a bachelor's degree in business administration, finance, or accounting.

**LIFESTYLE** Working hours are normal, although some branches remain open in the evenings and on Saturday mornings.

**LOCATION** Bank managers work at a specific branch or at a bank call center. Some travel is needed to meet business clients and liaise with the head office.

**THE REALITIES** New managers often have to work long hours to gain promotion and may be under pressure to meet strict sales targets.

## CAREER PATHS

Aspiring bank managers may consider earning professional credentials as a Certified Public Accountant (CPA) or Certified Financial Analyst (CFA). These certifications may help with securing a senior-level position at a bank.

**GRADUATE** With a bachelor's degree and experience working in a bank as a teller, loan officer, or mortgage officer, you may progress to senior roles.

**POSTGRADUATE** Some banks will require you to hold an advanced degree, such as a master's degree in finance or economics, before becoming a branch manager.

## SKILLS GUIDE

 Commercial awareness and a strong interest in economic affairs and financial markets.

 Excellent communication skills for handling customers and managing staff.

 Strong leadership skills and the ability to guide staff and help them meet targets.

 Good organizational skills to manage a high workload and lead a large team.

 The ability to use computerized systems and banking-specific software efficiently.

**BANK MANAGER** To become a manager, you must work in a range of banking areas—from personal loans for individuals and families to business accounts. Most managers go on to senior or specialized roles.

**PRODUCT DEVELOPMENT MANAGER** Conducts research and analyzes data about the needs of bank customers in order to develop and target new products, such as loans, credit cards, and mortgages.

**REGIONAL MANAGER** Takes responsibility for a number of bank branches, devising and implementing a regional business plan, and ensuring that branch staff follow company policies.

**BANK CALL CENTER MANAGER** Leads and supervises staff at telephone and online banking centers, and makes decisions about staff targets, lending, and day-to-day operations.

**RISK MANAGER** Identifies potential threats to the bank's profitability, such as fraud or risky lending practices, and recommends solutions. There are growing opportunities in this area.

# TRADER

## JOB DESCRIPTION

Traders are employed by financial institutions—such as investment banks—to trade investments by buying and selling them on the world's financial markets. These trades are made on behalf of individuals, companies, or institutional investors, such as pension funds and banks. Traders work in a fast-paced environment, using their judgment and experience to create a profit for their clients.

## AT A GLANCE

 **YOUR INTERESTS** Economics • Finance • Mathematics • Financial markets • Accounting • Information Technology (IT) • Languages

 **ENTRY QUALIFICATIONS** A degree or higher is required; employers favor subjects related to business, finance, or mathematics.

 **LIFESTYLE** Traders work long hours every day to track movements in markets around the world. Much of the work is screen-based.

 **LOCATION** Traders work in an office. Most job opportunities exist in the world's major financial centers, such as New York, London, and Tokyo.

 **THE REALITIES** The job can be very demanding and stressful. Traders must excel in a fiercely competitive and pressurized work environment.

## CAREER PATHS

Prospective traders must pass a rigorous recruitment process that may include aptitude and personality tests. Most entrants then spend two years working in a junior trading role and studying for professional qualifications. With experience, they may manage a team of traders in a particular type of financial market, or specialize in a specific trading area.

**GRADUATE** Due to strong competition for jobs, you need high grades in an undergraduate degree in a technical, financial, or business-related subject when applying for jobs as a trader.

**POSTGRADUATE** You can increase your chances of becoming a trader by gaining a higher degree in a subject such as economics, finance, mathematics, or business.

## SKILLS GUIDE

 Excellent communication skills and high levels of confidence to negotiate trading options.

 Strong numerical skills to manipulate financial data when compiling and analyzing reports.

 Strong computer skills for using computerized financial systems to conduct efficient financial trades.

 In-depth knowledge and awareness of issues that might affect financial markets.

 Attention to detail and the ability to react swiftly and decisively to market changes.

## ▼ RELATED CAREERS

▶ **INVESTMENT ANALYST** *see pp. 100–101*

▶ **FINANCIAL ADVISOR** *see pp. 106–107*

▶ **ECONOMIST** *see pp. 108–109*

▶ **INVESTMENT BANK ACTUARY** Conducts research to assess the potential risks of investment decisions, such as buying or selling particular shares. Investment bank actuaries are among the most influential and best-paid professionals in the world of finance.

▶ **STOCKBROKER** Buys and sells stocks and other investments on behalf of businesses and individual clients, rather than for large financial institutions, taking a percentage of clients' fees.

**PROPRIETARY TRADER** Working as an employee of a bank or other financial institution, a proprietary trader increases profits for an employer by using the company's money—rather than that of a client—to buy and sell on the financial markets.

 **SALES TRADER** Works to create new business for banks by identifying and talking to potential clients, and liaising between the client and the traders who will handle the investments.

 **COMMODITY BROKER** Buys and sells contracts for physical commodities—such as oil, gas, metals, and foods—on behalf of companies.

**STRUCTURER** Develops, models, and sets the pricing structure for sophisticated financial products, such as derivatives, the price of which may vary according to the value of a linked asset, such as a share.

**TRADER** You will need to gain professional qualifications before you can perform all the functions of a trader. With experience, you can progress into specialized roles.

 **QUANTITATIVE ANALYST (QUANT)** A "quant" develops and runs complex mathematical formulae, or algorithms, that determine the prices of shares or other financial products and assess risks. Also identifies profitable trading opportunities.

# INVESTMENT ANALYST

## JOB DESCRIPTION

Working in the world's financial markets, analysts research the economic, business, and market conditions that affect the value of investments, such as stocks and bonds. They then advise their clients, which may be companies or individuals or funds, on which investments to buy or sell to make the highest profit.

### SALARY

Graduate trainee ★★★★★
Senior analyst ★★★★★

### INDUSTRY PROFILE

Intense competition for entry-level roles • Long working hours • Increase in jobs with expanding range of financial products • Emerging global markets creating opportunities to work abroad

## CAREER PATHS

Analysts work for buyers or sellers of investments, such as pension funds, hedge funds, banks, insurance companies, stock brokers, and traders. There are many opportunities for experienced analysts who could, for example, specialize in a specific type of investment or region, or choose to manage an investment firm.

**ACCREDITED ANALYST**
Advises high-profile clients. An industry-recognized accreditation is necessary to qualify for the position, which may take several years of study.

**GRADUATE TRAINEE** You will need a college degree in a major such as finance, mathematics, or economics. Your employer may sponsor your training while you work under a senior analyst. To move into senior positions, you may need a graduate degree such as a Master of Business Administration.

**INVESTMENT ANALYST** In this role you research the past and project the future performance of a company to forecast its value on a stock exchange. You may produce reports that guide clients on their investment decisions.

# SKILLS GUIDE

 Acute commercial awareness and maturity to make judgments about complex markets.

 Excellent communication skills to develop working relationships with people at all levels.

 Good organizational and research skills to gather relevant, time-sensitive information.

 Strong mathematical skills and the ability to interpret statistical data.

 The ability to work under pressure and to deadlines, within and outside business hours.

 **STOCK BROKER** Acts as an agent for businesses or personal clients, and buys and sells shares and other financial products in markets around the world.

 **WEALTH MANAGER** Guides individuals on how to invest their money to maximize returns, and also advises them on tax payments.

 **FUND MANAGER** Looks after specialty investment funds that focus on buying and selling shares in a particular type of company, such as firms working in mining or pharmaceuticals.

## AT A GLANCE

 **YOUR INTERESTS** Financial management or accounting • Business studies • Economics • Mathematics • Statistics

 **ENTRY QUALIFICATIONS** A degree is required. A graduate degree in mathematics or business is usually necessary to progress to senior positions.

 **LIFESTYLE** The job can bring big financial rewards but it is very pressurized. Employers expect analysts to work very long hours.

 **LOCATION** Investment analysts mostly work from the offices of large financial institutions, but travel to visit investors and companies.

 **THE REALITIES** The work is closely scrutinized—mistakes can be very costly. Progress to senior positions demands lengthy periods of study.

## ▼ RELATED CAREERS

▶ **BANK MANAGER** see pp. 96–97

▶ **TRADER** see pp. 98–99

▶ **ACTUARY** see pp. 104–105

▶ **FINANCIAL MANAGER** Works within a business to guide its financial affairs. Financial managers monitor activities, produce financial statements, and develop plans based on business objectives.

 Annual bonuses for analysts tend to be between 70 and 100 percent of their base salaries.

# ACCOUNTANT

## JOB DESCRIPTION

Accountants play a vital role in the operation of virtually every business and organization, ensuring that financial systems run smoothly and that tax laws and other regulations are followed. They calculate annual accounts and produce financial reports, and may specialize in other areas, such as fraud detection. Increasing automation of accounting processes requires accountants today to have excellent IT skills.

### SALARY

Associate ★★★☆☆
Senior partner ★★★★★

### INDUSTRY PROFILE

Consistent demand for industry professionals • Highest salaries in banking and finance accountancy • Fierce competition for positions in large firms

## AT A GLANCE

**YOUR INTERESTS** Finance • Accounting • Economics • Mathematics • Statistics • Information Technology (IT) • Business studies

**ENTRY QUALIFICATIONS** Applicants can join accounting firms as assistants and learn on the job, or as associates after completing their bachelor's degree.

**LIFESTYLE** Regular office hours are the norm, although some overtime may be required to complete reports or financial audits to tight schedules.

**LOCATION** Hybrid working is becoming commonplace. Travel to meet clients and conduct audits—an official examination of accounts—is a vital part of the job.

**THE REALITIES** Although the financial rewards can be high, evening and weekend work is often required to meet deadlines during busy periods.

## CAREER PATHS

There are two main types of accounting: public practice, in which accounting services are provided to clients, and management accounting, in which accountants work in-house for a public- or private-sector organization or business. Career progression may follow a structured path, from accreditation, to gaining experience in different sectors—such as tax or corporate finance—leading to promotion to management, and eventually, partnership in a firm.

**HIGH SCHOOL OR SOME COLLEGE**
You may be taken on as a trainee after leaving school or college. Once qualified, you can enter a program to become an accredited accountant. Accounting apprenticeships are also highly sought after.

**GRADUATE** With a degree in accounting or a related discipline, you can apply for entry-level positions, which are offered by many large accountancy firms, public-sector organizations, and commercial businesses in all sectors of industry.

## ▼ RELATED CAREERS

▶ **MANAGEMENT CONSULTANT** *see pp. 84–85*

▶ **ACTUARY** *see pp. 104–105*

▶ **ACCOUNTING TECHNICIAN** Assists qualified accountants by preparing accounting figures, tax reports, and helping in all other areas of business finance.

▶ **COMPANY SECRETARY** Works with a company's senior management to ensure that legal, financial, and regulatory requirements are followed.

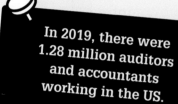

In 2019, there were 1.28 million auditors and accountants working in the US.

## SKILLS GUIDE

 Excellent numerical skills and the ability to interpret complex financial data.

 Precision and attention to detail in order to perform repeated calculations accurately.

 Strong communication skills for explaining financial information to clients and senior managers.

 The ability to analyze financial problems and identify the most appropriate solution.

Honesty, integrity, and discretion for dealing with sensitive financial information appropriately.

**CORPORATE FINANCE ACCOUNTANT** Works in a company's corporate finance division, performing functions such as analyzing accounts to identify money that can be used for growing the business, through acquiring firms or merging existing ones.

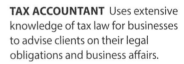 **TAX ACCOUNTANT** Uses extensive knowledge of tax law for businesses to advise clients on their legal obligations and business affairs.

 **BUSINESS INSOLVENCY ACCOUNTANT** Provides specialized advice to companies in financial trouble, helping them to close their businesses in a controlled manner.

 **FORENSIC ACCOUNTANT** Studies the financial dealings of companies to detect fraud, enabling insurance companies and corporate lawyers to resolve financial disputes.

**ACCOUNTANT** You will need to pass a number of exams to become a certified accountant. You can then choose to train further to specialize in one area of accountancy.

**AUDITOR** Reviews the financial accounts of companies and organizations to ensure that they are valid and meet legal guidelines. Auditors may also assess the health of clients' businesses and advise on working practices.

# ACTUARY

## JOB DESCRIPTION

Actuaries assess the probability of a particular event occurring and then calculate the possible financial risks to a company. Many actuaries work for insurance companies, at which they calculate the likelihood of a loss, such as the chances of a ship sinking at sea, and set the amount to be paid by the ship's owners. Others work in banks, monitoring the levels of risk when buying and selling investments.

### SALARY

Actuary ★★★☆☆
Senior director ★★★★★

### INDUSTRY PROFILE

Jobs available worldwide, although competition for places is strong • Opportunities within a wide range of businesses and organizations • High salary

## AT A GLANCE

**YOUR INTERESTS** Mathematics • Statistics • Economics • Risk management • Business studies • Information Technology (IT) • Science

**ENTRY QUALIFICATIONS** A degree in a numerate subject—such as mathematics, statistics, or actuarial science—is required.

**LIFESTYLE** Actuaries usually work regular hours, although evening or weekend working may be required to meet deadlines.

**LOCATION** Actuarial work is office-based and firms are mostly found in large cities. Business travel to visit clients is occasionally required.

**THE REALITIES** This mathematical, intellectually challenging field requires a determined mindset. The exams to achieve accreditation can be grueling.

## ▼ RELATED CAREERS

▶ **INVESTMENT ANALYST** *see pp. 100–101*

▶ **ACCOUNTANT** *see pp. 102–103*

▶ **AUDITOR** Checks the financial accounts of companies and organizations to ensure that they are accurate and follow legal guidelines. Auditors also assess the health of clients' businesses and advise on ways to avoid risk.

▶ **INSURANCE UNDERWRITER** Works for an insurance company assessing applications for the insurance cover of individuals and businesses. Underwriters decide if insurance cover should be given and set the terms and price of the insurance policy.

> Employment of actuaries is projected to grow 18 percent from 2019 to 2029, faster than the average for most other occupations.

## CAREER PATHS

Graduates with a degree in a numerate subject can apply to train as an actuary. Training involves several years of on-the-job study, during which time trainees need to take a series of exams to gain professional accreditation.

**GRADUATE** To be taken on as a trainee, you will need a degree in mathematics, statistics, or a similar subject, and will then have to pass a series of selection tests.

**POSTGRADUATE** You can increase your chances of being taken on by studying actuarial science at the graduate level, which may also count toward your future accreditation.

### SKILLS GUIDE

 Strong communication and presentation skills for explaining complex findings.

 A logical and analytical approach to make sense of complex information.

 Advanced numerical skills to analyze and interpret large amounts of data.

 A thorough knowledge of issues affecting financial markets when pricing products and services.

 Precision and attention to detail to ensure mathematical calculations are correct.

**ACTUARY** Traditionally employed by insurance firms, actuaries now work for a range of organizations, from consulting firms and health authorities to government departments. After qualifying, you can specialize in a particular sector or work toward senior roles.

**CHIEF RISK OFFICER** Coordinates a team of actuaries and other professionals who assess and take action to avoid potential risks. This is a senior position in a large company.

**INVESTMENT BANK ACTUARY** Conducts research to identify the financial costs and potential risks of investment decisions, such as investing in a new business.

**CONSULTANT ACTUARY** Advises on business activities, such as large companies' pension or health plans, complying with legal requirements.

**LIFE INSURANCE ACTUARY** Analyzes statistical information on risk factors—such as existing health conditions—to set the prices that customers pay for their life insurance policies.

**ENTERPRISE RISK MANAGER** Identifies risks that may affect the operation of a business, and then assesses the impact these risks might have. Also devises strategies to avoid these risks or to minimize their effects on the business.

# FINANCIAL ADVISOR

## JOB DESCRIPTION

Financial advisors help people plan their financial futures. They meet with clients, usually in person, to provide informed advice on a range of financial products and services, from pensions and investments to mortgages and tax-efficient savings. Taking into account a client's income and circumstances, they recommend products and strategies to help them meet their financial goals.

### SALARY

New financial advisor ★★☆☆☆
Senior financial advisor ★★★★☆

### INDUSTRY PROFILE

Employers include investment firms, banks, financial-services companies, and insurance companies • Demand for financial advice, particularly on retirement, is growing rapidly

## AT A GLANCE

**YOUR INTERESTS** Economics • Law • Mathematics • Business studies • Accountancy • Finance • Information Technology (IT)

**ENTRY QUALIFICATIONS** Experience working in a sales, customer service, or finance role, and/or a degree in a related subject, is typically required.

**LIFESTYLE** Many advisors work office hours, and may need to meet clients during evenings and weekends. For some, however, their schedule is flexible.

**LOCATION** Advisors work from an office or from home. Traveling to meet with clients in their homes is a regular feature of the job.

**THE REALITIES** Dealing with multiple clients can be stressful, especially in hard economic times. It can take years to build a client base.

## CAREER PATHS

To enter this career, applicants must pass a series of professional examinations and be registered by a regulatory body that ensures they give high-quality, unbiased advice. Qualified advisors can choose to provide general guidance to their clients or to specialize in one type of product, such as retirement or insurance.

**TRAINEE** New hires may enter on-the-job programs where they work directly under senior advisors, providing administrative and research support. Training may culminate in a certification, offering entry into a field.

**GRADUATE** You will need a degree, preferably in finance or accounting, to apply for entry-level financial advisor jobs with banks and independent financial advice firms.

## ▼ RELATED CAREERS

▶ **MANAGEMENT CONSULTANT** *see pp. 84–85*

▶ **BANK MANAGER** *see pp. 96–97*

▶ **INSURANCE BROKER** Helps people decide on the best insurance policy to meet their individual needs, whether they require home, travel, car, or life insurance.

▶ **INSURANCE UNDERWRITER** Works for an insurance company assessing applications for the insurance coverage of individuals and businesses.

▶ **PENSION ADMINISTRATOR** Performs administrative tasks relating to a pension program, such as dealing with inquiries from program members, or calculating pension forecasts.

# SKILLS GUIDE

 The ability to explain complicated financial matters in simple terms, and to understand a client's needs.

 Good interpersonal skills for building relationships and establishing trust with clients.

 Sharp analytical skills to analyze financial information and identify the best product for a client.

 Determination and self-motivation for maintaining high levels of service and meeting sales targets.

 Understanding and awareness of financial markets in order to offer accurate advice to clients.

**WEALTH MANAGER**
Helps individuals invest their money to bring as high a return on their investment as possible. Wealth managers also advise on regulatory matters, such as inheritance tax rules.

**SPECIALIZED FINANCIAL ADVISOR** Provides specialized advice in one type of product or to one type of client—for example, property investment or financial planning for farmers.

**COMPLIANCE MANAGER** Works for a company of financial advisors, inspecting premises and reviewing financial records and policies to ensure legal and industry standards are met. This is a senior role.

**FINANCIAL ADVISOR** You will likely choose between two types of practice: independent (offering unbiased advice on all the products available to a client) and restricted (offering advice on your company's products alone). Financial advisors often specialize in a client group—such as wealthy clients—or a type of product.

**GENERAL MANAGER** Supervises the work of financial advisors and oversees areas such as recruitment and training, as well as a firm's marketing strategy. Managers in financial firms are often former financial advisors who have been promoted into the role.

# ECONOMIST

## JOB DESCRIPTION

Economists research and analyze how people and businesses spend their money and make use of resources, such as labor, energy, and capital. They produce reports and forecasts for companies and governments, who use the information in various ways, such as shaping their policies on matters such as wages and taxation, or making them more competitive in comparison to their rivals.

### SALARY

Junior economist ★★★☆☆
Senior finance economist ★★★★★

### INDUSTRY PROFILE

Varied opportunities for employment in sectors such as government, banks, businesses, and academia • Excellent salaries available for highly qualified individuals

## AT A GLANCE

 **YOUR INTERESTS** Economics • Mathematics • Statistics • Business studies • Information Technology (IT) • Philosophy • Politics • Social science

 **ENTRY QUALIFICATIONS** A relevant bachlor's degree is required. A graduate qualification may be required for high-level positions.

 **LIFESTYLE** Economists typically keep regular office hours, although preparing for conferences or writing for publications may demand extra work.

 **LOCATION** Economists typically work in an office, with some from home, but travel may be required to present findings or meet clients.

 **THE REALITIES** Economists need to be motivated to carry out independent research. They are expected to learn new skills throughout their career.

## ▼ RELATED CAREERS

▶ **INVESTMENT ANALYST** *see pp. 100–101*

▶ **FINANCIAL ADVISOR** *see pp. 106–107*

▶ **POLITICIAN** *see pp. 114–115*

▶ **MATHEMATICIAN** Uses advanced mathematics to analyze or solve difficult problems. This may include calculating risks in the insurance industry, analyzing statistics to examine the effectiveness of a new drug, or investigating the way that air flows over the wing of an aircraft.

Economists held about 20,500 jobs in 2019, with the largest employer being the Federal Government.

## CAREER PATHS

All economists require a bachelor's or graduate degree in economics. They continue learning throughout their career, becoming an expert in one or more fields—such as health care or taxation—and publish papers and reports to build their reputation. Many economists also hold teaching or research jobs in colleges or universities at some stage of their career.

### SKILLS GUIDE

 A strategic understanding of politics and business to help with leading teams and solving complex issues.

 The ability to interpret complex consumer data, identify economic trends, and forecast accurately.

 Strong mathematical skills for analyzing key data and assessing the state of the economy.

 A good working knowledge of specialized software programs to conduct statistical analyses.

 Sound business knowledge and understanding of financial systems in the public and private sectors.

 An eye for detail to interpret quantitative and qualitative data and produce accurate reports.

**RESEARCHER** With a degree in economics or finance, you may find an entry-level job as a researcher at a financial organization. With experience and higher-level degrees, you can progress to more senior roles.

**ECONOMIST** Works in government or public-sector organizations or in academic, managerial, and various other consultancy roles. Increasingly relies on computerized data analysis and mathematical modeling techniques.

**STATISTICIAN** Collects, analyzes, and interprets statistics. Statisticians work in a number of sectors, including health, education, government, finance, the environment, and market research.

**POLICY ADVISOR** Works in government, for political parties, or for private research groups to develop new policies.

**INVESTMENT BANKER** Raises money from individual and corporate investors on behalf of businesses that need funds to get started, grow, or develop.

**FINANCIAL DIRECTOR** Oversees the financial activities of a business or other organization. Financial directors are responsible for producing financial statements, monitoring budgets and spending, and developing new business objectives.

# LAWYER

## JOB DESCRIPTION

Lawyers provide advice and numerous legal services to their clients, from drawing up contracts and wills to representing their clients in court. Lawyers are hired by individuals, nonprofit organizations, corporations, and government agencies. From prosecutors and defense attorneys to environmental lawyers, family lawyers, and tax attorneys, lawyers have a a vast range of specializations from which they can choose.

### SALARY

Associate ★★★☆☆
Partner ★★★★★

### INDUSTRY PROFILE

Highly regulated profession • Intense competition for position at law firms • Private-sector law firms are biggest employers • Global opportunities in multinational businesses of all kinds

## CAREER PATHS

Once qualified, lawyers can begin practicing as an associate, working under the supervision of a senior partner at a law firm. With experience and ability, they can rise to become a partner in the firm. Lawyers can choose from a range of specialties, such as serving nonprofit organizations or military services, or dealing with the legal matters of individuals or the government.

**CORPORATE LAWYER** Serves as a full-time staff member of a corporation, advising and representing the company in all law-related matters.

**GRADUATE** After completing an undergraduate program, you will need to take the Law School Admission Test (LSAT) and apply to accredited law schools.

**LAW SCHOOL GRADUATE** Law school programs typically last three years. At their completion, you will need to study for and pass a state's bar exam in order to qualify for a license.

**LAWYER** Once you have obtained your license, you may start your career as a lawyer. It is important for lawyers to keep up to date with changing practices through continuing education.

# SKILLS GUIDE

 Excellent verbal and written skills and the ability to understand complex legal language.

 Strong problem-solving skills for identifying the best course of action for clients.

 The ability to follow detailed legal procedures correctly in order to maintain professional integrity.

 Sensitivity for dealing with a range of clients, and the ability to explain legal matters to nonexperts.

 Dedication and perseverance to press your client's interests from start to finish of a legal case.

**CRIMINAL DEFENSE LAWYER**
Represents defendants in the criminal court system, offering legal counsel and appearing in court if their client's case goes to trial.

**INTELLECTUAL PROPERTY LAWYER**
Takes on copyright infringement or intellectual property rights cases for the music, film, news, and publishing industries.

**FAMILY PRACTICE LAWYER**
Specializes in family-related issues, such as divorce and child custody disputes. May also advise and represent clients who are looking to adopt a child.

**ENVIRONMENTAL LAWYER** Advises on issues related to the environment, ensuring companies and organizations comply with state and national laws.

## ▼ RELATED CAREERS

▶ **JUDGE** *see pp. 112–113*

▶ **ARBITRATOR** Helps resolve legal conflicts outside of the court system. Arbitrators are often retired attorneys. They meet with the disputing parties and assist them in their negotiations.

▶ **FORENSIC SCIENCE TECHNICIAN** Collects, analyzes, and reports on evidence found at crime scenes. Many forensic science technicians choose to specialize in either crime scene investigation or laboratory work.

▶ **PARALEGAL** Works on legal matters, but is not a lawyer. Paralegals are responsible for many tasks ranging from conducting research and preparing reports to contacting clients and witnesses and gathering and organizing evidence.

## AT A GLANCE

**YOUR INTERESTS** Law • Criminology • Psychology • Sociology • History • Business studies • Debating • Research and writing

**ENTRY QUALIFICATIONS** Lawyers must complete an accredited law school program and pass a state's bar exam in order to practice.

**LIFESTYLE** Lawyers work regular office hours, but evening and weekend work is not uncommon. On-call work can take place any time of day or night.

**LOCATION** The work is predominantly office-based, but traveling to meet clients, or to attend court proceedings, is a common feature of the job.

**THE REALITIES** This profession is intellectually demanding, and involves long working hours. Experienced lawyers are very well paid.

# JUDGE

## JOB DESCRIPTION

With infallible knowledge of the law and excellent research, writing, and decision-making skills, judges preside over and ensure fairness within courtrooms. Judges are employed by local, state, and federal governments to oversee a variety of cases, both civil and criminal. A highly sought-after role in the law profession, most judges are elected or appointed into their positions.

### SALARY

Administrative law judge ★★★★★
Supreme Court justice ★★★★★

### INDUSTRY PROFILE

Fierce competition for open positions • Most jobs open only after a current judge finishes his or her term or retires • Length of appointments vary

## AT A GLANCE

**YOUR INTERESTS** Law • Research and writing • English • History • Psychology • Sociology • Criminology • Politics • Decision-making

**ENTRY QUALIFICATIONS** A law degree is required for most judgeships. Some appointments are available for non-lawyers, but opportunities are scarce.

**LIFESTYLE** Judges typically work regular office hours, depending on the requirements of the court. Overtime hours spent researching are common.

**LOCATION** Judges spend the majority of their working hours in an office, at law libraries or research centers, or in the courtroom.

**THE REALITIES** Research hours are long. The work is often intellectually demanding, requiring a very thorough understanding of the details.

## CAREER PATHS

**GRADUATE** There are some hearing officer and administrative law judge positions available to those without a law degree. However, these opportunities are scarce and often filled by candidates with higher law qualifications.

**LAW SCHOOL GRADUATE** The most common route to becoming a judge is to graduate from an accredited law school and pass a state's bar exam, qualifying you to practice as a lawyer.

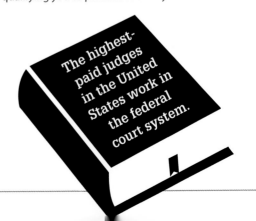

The highest-paid judges in the United States work in the federal court system.

## ▼ RELATED CAREERS

▶ **LAWYER** *see pp. 110–111*

▶ **POLITICIAN** *see pp. 114–115*

▶ **COLLEGE PROFESSOR** *see pp. 270–271*

▶ **ARBITRATOR** Resolves legal conflicts between two parties outside of the court system. Arbitrators meet with and listen to the disputing parties, then determine the outcome.

▶ **MEDIATOR** Facilitates legal discussions outside of the court system. Mediators, often also practicing lawyers, help the disputing parties to negotiate effectively until they reach a mutually agreeable decision.

# SKILLS GUIDE

Excellent written and verbal skills and the ability to speak in court under high-pressure situations.

The ability to communicate clearly with lawyers, defendants, members of a jury, and others.

Good organizational skills for following multiple cases at once and managing court room staff.

Strong attention to detail for ensuring court room proceedings are carried out correctly.

Patience, perseverance, and mental stamina to preside over lengthy court sessions.

**LAWYER** Through years of practicing as a lawyer, you will gain the knowledge, courtroom experience, and professional contacts necessary to begin submitting your name to a judicial nomination commission for consideration as a judge.

**JUDGE** Newly appointed judges can expect to undergo specific orientation and training to ensure they are ready to serve. Typically, advancing as a judge means being appointed to judgeships within a larger jurisdiction. Career paths vary.

**LOCAL/STATE COURT JUDGE** Reviews cases at either the local or state level, serving as impartial deciders for the majority of civil and criminal cases. May preside over a small claims court.

**DISTRICT/FEDERAL COURT JUDGE** Hears cases involving the federal government or parties from different states. Federal judges must be nominated by the President and approved by a two-thirds majority Senate vote.

**SUPREME COURT JUSTICE** The highest-ranking judges in the country. The nine US Supreme Court justices review only a very small number of cases each year, all of which are determined to be of national importance.

# POLITICIAN

## JOB DESCRIPTION

Politicians are public servants elected by voters to make decisions that shape society and affect their communities on all levels—local, state, and national. They aim to improve citizens' lives by pressing for changes in society and the laws that govern it. In this role, you will hold face-to-face sessions in your community, debate and vote on issues, and campaign for yourself and your political party.

### SALARY

Political aide ★★★★★
Politicians' salaries vary

### INDUSTRY PROFILE

Entry into the field is competitive • Opportunities to work at a local, state, and/or national level • Career prospects and pay rates vary depending on the role

## CAREER PATHS

Entry into—and advancement within—this career is largely down to self-motivation. Some politicians work in local government, while others represent their voters at the state or national levels. In politics, perhaps even more so than in other fields, career paths vary according to the type of politician you want to be.

**NON-GRADUATE** You can run for office as long as you meet certain basic qualifications, such as age and residency.

**GRADUATE** You can earn a degree in political science or public administration. Experience working for political campaigns or interning with an elected official's office is helpful.

**LAWYER** Though it is not a requirement, many politicians at the higher levels of government hold law degrees.

**DIPLOMAT** Represents the United States in foreign affairs. Job responsibilities vary from negotiating treaties to managing staff at an overseas embassy.

**POLITICIAN** As a politician, you work at every level of government, from town council membership all the way up to the presidency. Once elected, you can choose to focus on specific areas of policy. There are a vast amount of career options and specializations for you to choose from.

## SKILLS GUIDE

Excellent public speaking skills for presenting political arguments and winning support for policies.

The ability to work as part of a team in order to reach a consensus on legislation and policies.

Interpersonal skills for relating to members of the public and understanding their concerns.

Good problem-solving skills for devising political solutions to economic and social problems.

Perseverance and integrity to press for political change and inspire others to adopt the party's cause.

**MAYOR** Leads a town or city council and presides over local government, taking responsibility for its major departments—including police, fire, housing, education, and transportation.

**GOVERNOR** Serves as a state's chief executive officer, ensuring all state laws are implemented properly by the state's executive branch. The responsibilities of a governor vary from state to state.

**SENATOR** Represents his or her state in the senate. This job is part of the legislative branch of government, and it includes writing and voting on bills. State senators serve six-year terms.

**PRESIDENT** Leads the US government. Serves as Commander in Chief of the federal armed forces, travels extensively to represent the US around the world, and has the power to sign a bill into law.

## ▼ RELATED CAREERS

▶ **CHARITY FUNDRAISER** *see pp. 90–91*

▶ **LAWYER** *see pp. 110–111*

▶ **POLITICAL SCIENTIST** Uses expertise in areas such as law, politics, and history to research and advise on public policy. Political scientists must stay up to date with political ideas and trends.

In 2021, a record 143 women served as members of US Congress, an increase of 13 percent from 2019.

## AT A GLANCE

**YOUR INTERESTS** Politics • Political science • Debating • Current affairs • Law • Economics • Business studies • Sociology • History • Public relations

**ENTRY QUALIFICATIONS** Evidence of past political activity is vital. Many politicians hold advanced degrees in law, economics, or political science.

**LIFESTYLE** Long working hours are common. Debates and campaigning or networking events are often held during evenings. Privacy is difficult.

**LOCATION** Politicians typically work out of an office in their community, but national—and, sometimes, overseas—travel is required.

**THE REALITIES** Campaigning during elections can require frequent overnight stays away from home. Politicians' lives are often very public.

# INFORMATION TECHNOLOGY AND COMPUTING

Today's business world depends on the availability and flow of high-quality data. Information Technology (IT) and computing are key, so the range of careers in this field—from maintaining computer networks to designing websites— is increasing all the time.

# SOFTWARE ENGINEER

## JOB DESCRIPTION

Software engineers plan, analyze, design, develop, test, and carry out maintenance work on a wide variety of computer software products. These can range from games, apps, and home entertainment systems, to programs that run a computer's operating system or control network communications between computers.

### SALARY

Junior engineer ★★★★★
Senior engineer ★★★★★

### INDUSTRY PROFILE

High demand • Many jobs in software and telecommunication companies • Highly paid contract-based roles available for experienced engineers

## AT A GLANCE

**YOUR INTERESTS** Computer science • Information Technology (IT) • Mathematics • Physics • Engineering • New technologies

**ENTRY QUALIFICATIONS** A degree or a postgraduate qualification in software engineering or a related discipline is the best way to get a job.

**LIFESTYLE** Working hours are flexible, but tight deadlines demand long hours. Work is usually office-based; travel to meet clients is possible.

**LOCATION** Most jobs are office-based, but many people work remotely from home or take a hybrid approach so that they can minimize distractions.

**THE REALITIES** The market is highly competitive. However, it is very well compensated and there are many opportunities for job advancement.

## CAREER PATHS

Software engineers start their careers supporting a team that is developing or modifying computer code. After gaining experience and knowledge of multiple computer systems and languages, they can progress to lead their own development teams or enter specialized areas of the industry.

**GRADUATE** You will need a degree in an analytical or technical subject—but not necessarily in computer science or Information Technology (IT)—and some experience in computer coding.

**POSTGRADUATE** If you hold a degree in a nontechnical discipline, you may take an IT conversion course at postgraduate level. It is increasingly popular to learn to write software through online and independent study.

## SKILLS GUIDE

 Good team-working skills and the ability to work with people from all over the globe.

 Strong analytical and problem-solving skills to work through the many challenges of a project.

 A creative approach to solving what can often be extremely complex problems.

 Excellent computer skills and the resourcefulness to stay up to date with new technologies.

 Attention to detail and the patience to code and test new software products.

## ▼ RELATED CAREERS

▶ **SYSTEMS ANALYST** *see pp. 120–121*

▶ **FULL STACK DEVELOPER** Handles databases, servers, and clients. This professional must be highly skilled in a wide range of computer software development.

▶ **MACHINE LEARNING ENGINEER** Performs sophisticated programming—working with complex data sets and algorithms—to train Artificial Intelligence (AI) machines and systems that can learn and apply knowledge.

From 2017 to 2026, there is expected to be a 24 percent increase in software jobs.

**LEAD SOFTWARE ENGINEER**
Runs a team and sets the specific project requirements. This person requires experience in order to mentor new recruits and manage their development of technical skills. This is a common role for someone who wants to become a Chief Technology Officer (CTO).

**QUALITY ASSURANCE TESTER** Tests software to understand the quality of a potential product. A person may take on a role as a software tester before becoming a software engineer in some companies.

**GAME DEVELOPER** Writes and tests the code used to run games on computers, consoles, and handheld devices, such as tablets and mobile phones.

**SOFTWARE RESEARCHER**
Conceives new ideas, individually or for a company, and develops them as software prototypes. Coding skills are required for this role.

**SOFTWARE ENGINEER** Experienced software engineers have numerous options for career development. You can progress to a lead engineer or specialize in a variety of areas.

# SYSTEMS ANALYST

## JOB DESCRIPTION

Information Technology (IT) lies at the heart of most businesses and organizations, so a poorly designed computer system can make a company less efficient. Systems analysts identify potential problems in a computer system by working closely with its users and programmers. They provide recommendations for how the system may be redesigned, and plan and manage ways of achieving these goals.

### SALARY

Junior systems analyst ★★☆☆☆
Senior systems analyst ★★★☆☆

### INDUSTRY PROFILE

Healthy jobs market • Employers range from large corporations to small enterprises • Growth in employment in the public and financial services sectors

## AT A GLANCE

 **YOUR INTERESTS** Information Technology (IT) • Computer science • Business information technology • Electronic engineering • Mathematics

 **ENTRY QUALIFICATIONS** A degree in a computing-based subject is preferred. A postgraduate degree (MBA) in business administration is desirable.

 **LIFESTYLE** Systems analysts usually work regular hours, but they may have to work overtime to meet project deadlines.

 **LOCATION** The work is usually office-based, but employees are increasingly adopting hybrid working practices using online technologies.

 **THE REALITIES** The fast-paced nature of work and tight deadlines can be stressful. Systems analysts need to keep up to date with fast-evolving technology.

## ▼ RELATED CAREERS

▶ **SOFTWARE ENGINEER** *see pp. 118–119*

▶ **DATABASE ADMINISTRATOR** *see pp. 122–123*

▶ **NETWORK ENGINEER** *see pp. 124–125*

▶ **DATA SCIENTIST** Analyzes the huge volume of computer data companies collect to identify patterns that may help make a business more profitable. Data analysts then present these findings to senior management.

▶ **IT RISK MANAGER** Scrutinizes a company's IT systems, and identifies and fixes security weaknesses that could lead to the theft or damage of computer-based information.

Systems analysts are increasingly involved in setting up cloud storage technologies for companies.

## CAREER PATHS

Once qualified, systems analysts can specialize in a particular type of computer system, such as an accounting or health-care system. If they work for a big company, they may be able to move into management or a strategic planning role.

## SKILLS GUIDE

Good team-working skills, and the ability to work with people in all parts of a company.

Strong leadership skills to motivate technicians, instruct developers, and influence managers.

An analytical and logical approach to designing and testing complex systems.

Highly developed IT skills across a wide range of hardware, software, and networks.

Sound commercial awareness to provide clients with cost-effective system solutions.

**TRAINEE** After graduating high school, you can become a trainee IT technician while studying part-time or via distance learning for a relevant degree.

**GRADUATE** To become a systems analyst, you need a degree in computer science, mathematics, business studies, or a related area.

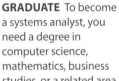

**SYSTEMS ANALYST**
Analysts work closely with business managers to develop effective IT systems. As an analyst, you may recommend and install new hardware or software, test the system, and teach staff how to use it. With experience, you may choose to specialize.

**SENIOR ANALYST** Heads up a team of IT professionals or takes on a management role, advising the directors of a company on IT strategy, such as implementing the use of databases.

**TECHNICAL ARCHITECT**
Makes decisions about the types of hardware and software products to be used. A technical architect is sometimes called a systems designer.

**IT SYSTEMS PROJECT MANAGER** Oversees an IT project from start to finish. You will develop plans, manage teams, study risks, and track project budgets.

**SOFTWARE ANALYST**
Diagnoses problems with business software. May develop and write code for new applications when necessary.

**IT CONSULTANT**
Provides advice on IT matters to a range of businesses and government bodies for a management consultancy firm.

# DATABASE ADMINISTRATOR

010101

## SALARY

Graduate ★★☆☆☆
Experienced DBA ★★★★★

## INDUSTRY PROFILE

Worldwide job opportunities • Possibility of working in a variety of sectors, from publishing to finance • Linking smart devices using cloud technologies is an ongoing challenge

## JOB DESCRIPTION

Companies in almost every sector, from engineering to marketing, rely on accurate data to make business decisions. Database administrators (DBAs) store and organize data in databases that recognize patterns in the information. They ensure that the databases run efficiently, providing users with data when they need it.

## SKILLS GUIDE

 Good communication skills to understand and supply accurate data as it is requested.

 Efficient time management skills for dealing with constant data-processing requests.

 Problem-solving skills to ensure that data is backed up reliably, easy to retrieve, and secure.

 A strong interest in, and a good understanding of, software and coding.

 Attention to detail to fix—or avoid—computer bugs that can cause problems in a database.

## ▼ RELATED CAREERS

▶ **SOFTWARE ENGINEER** *see pp. 118–119*

▶ **SYSTEMS ANALYST** *see pp. 120–121*

▶ **NETWORK ENGINEER** *see pp. 124–125*

▶ **WEB DEVELOPER** *see pp. 128–129*

▶ **FINANCIAL PROGRAMMER** Combines finance and technology to write programs and develop software for banks and financial institutions to offer mobile banking apps, trade cryptocurrencies, or design chatbots in a growing sector called "Fintech."

▶ **INFORMATION SCIENTIST** Manages an organization's information resources, such as databases, online services, books, and paper-based records.

▶ **IT CONSULTANT** Advises a business on how to improve its IT infrastructure. They must have a good knowledge of databases, networks, and all different kinds of software.

## AT A GLANCE

 **YOUR INTERESTS** Computer science • Coding • Information Technology (IT) • New technologies • Data security • Mathematics

 **LOCATION** Work is office-based. Some administrators may be able to work from home, even though they deal with staff from all parts of a company.

 **ENTRY QUALIFICATIONS** A technical degree, such as in software engineering, computer science, or mathematics, is desirable but not required.

 **THE REALITIES** This is a high-pressure role. DBAs are expected to respond quickly and accurately to all sorts of problems, from hard-drive failure to servers not functioning.

 **LIFESTYLE** Working after-hours is likely. You may be expected to field round-the-clock requests from members of your company.

> Security and data recovery are important aspects of this job.

## CAREER PATHS

Large companies with complex data requirements provide the best opportunities for career progression. A DBA can specialize in one area of technology.

**TRAINEE** If you have an interest in IT, you may be able to train on the job within a company's IT department.

**DATABASE ADMINISTRATOR**
Increasing data needs and advances in technology mean that you will have several potential options for career development in this field.

**GRADUATE** Graduates with degrees in IT, computer science, or another related major will be able to find entry-level positions.

**NETWORK MANAGER**
Ensures that networks are secure and synchronized across the globe, and also implements the latest technologies.

**PROJECT MANAGER**
Oversees a project from start to finish, liaising with a range of people across the business.

**DATABASE ARCHITECT**
Designs the underlying structure of a database, based on the client's needs and goals.

**DATA WAREHOUSE SPECIALIST** Manages and analyzes data (both current and historical) collected from different parts of an organization.

# NETWORK ENGINEER

## JOB DESCRIPTION

Network engineers set up and maintain the networks that carry information between computers. These networks use a range of technologies to work. They may connect computers located either in a single office or computers separated by huge distances. Network engineers also diagnose and fix problems with network software and check the cables, radio links, and even satellites that carry the information. They also provide on-site help to a company's staff.

## SALARY

Junior network engineer ★★★★★
Senior network engineer ★★★★★

## INDUSTRY PROFILE

Growing job market • Opportunities available in almost every area of business or industry • Growing number of opportunities in healthcare information technology

## CAREER PATHS

Career progress as a network engineer depends on the type and size of the company you work for. If the company is small, you will be called upon to deal with a variety of computer issues, from slow Internet speeds to virus infections. However, if you work for a large global company, you are more likely to specialize in one particular area, such as network architecture or cybersecurity.

**NETWORK ARCHITECT** Designs an organization's computer network. This involves analyzing how the business works and planning a network that can meet its needs both now and in the future.

**TRAINEE** A person with a good general education and strong Information Technology (IT) skills may find work as a trainee technician. On-the-job learning and taking college-level courses may put you on the path to becoming a network engineer.

**GRADUATE** If you have an undergraduate or graduate degree in computer science or systems engineering, you can find work with companies that run large and complex networks.

**NETWORK ENGINEER** The role requires continual learning to keep up to date with changing technologies. Many companies require you to learn and be certified in the products they use, such as Microsoft or Cisco. With experience, you can move into a number of different roles.

# SKILLS GUIDE

 Excellent communication skills to be able to work with non-technical staff in an organization.

 The ability to work as part of a team of software developers and other IT professionals.

 The efficient management of IT technicians and an ability to support senior managers.

 The ability to identify and solve technical problems within urgent time frames.

 Patience and perseverance to resolve problems and restore a company's network function.

 Knowledge and expertise across a wide range of IT software, hardware, and networks.

**NETWORK CONTROLLER** Manages the staff who maintain the network, and ensures the network operates reliably.

**IT CONSULTANT** Works for an IT consultancy or sets up their own business to provide networking advice and services to a range of clients.

**HELP DESK PROFESSIONAL** Provides telephone and online support and advice to a company's network users.

## AT A GLANCE

 **YOUR INTERESTS** Information Technology (IT) • Computer science • Electronic or electrical engineering • Computer networks • Mathematics

 **ENTRY QUALIFICATIONS** A technical degree in computer-systems engineering or another related subject is useful but not required.

 **LIFESTYLE** Network engineers work shifts or are on call to resolve issues outside normal hours, as companies rely on their networks 24 hours a day.

 **LOCATION** Much of the work is office-based, but some network engineers operate remotely from home, depending on the type of project.

 **THE REALITIES** Technological advances mean this is a growth area with many new fields of work opening up. Skills need to be regularly updated.

## ▼ RELATED CAREERS

▶ **SOFTWARE ENGINEER** *see pp. 118–119*

▶ **SYSTEMS ANALYST** *see pp. 120–121*

▶ **DATABASE ADMINISTRATOR** *see pp. 122–123*

▶ **CYBERSECURITY ANALYST** *see pp. 132–133*

Network engineers are in high demand in the United States, with a projected growth rate of 6½ percent through 2030.

# IT SUPPORT EXECUTIVE

## JOB DESCRIPTION

Information Technology (IT) support executives provide technical assistance or help to computer users in an organization. They aim to solve common problems, such as forgotten passwords or lost data, maintaining computer hardware and networks to ensure that they work efficiently and function continuously.

### SALARY

Newly qualified executive ★★★★★
Experienced executive ★★★★★

### INDUSTRY PROFILE

Varied opportunities with a wide range of employers, from large corporations to small firms • Growing demand for IT support in public and financial services sectors

## AT A GLANCE

**YOUR INTERESTS** IT • Mathematics • Physics • Business studies • Business information technology • English • Computer programing

**ENTRY QUALIFICATIONS** A degree in an IT-related subject is desirable, but entry with suitable vocational training is also possible.

**LIFESTYLE** Most IT support companies operate 24 hours a day, so shift work is common. Part-time opportunities are offered by many employers.

**LOCATION** Increasingly, the work can be performed remotely via online technologies. Hybrid working is common, with occasional travel to work sites.

**THE REALITIES** This work can be fast-paced and target-driven, with pressure to resolve calls quickly. Dealing with clients can be stressful.

## CAREER PATHS

IT support jobs are found across a wide range of industries, in public sector organizations, and in IT consultancies providing support services to clients. Support executives are computer "all-rounders" with a good knowledge of hardware and software, and so may move into related IT jobs, such as network engineering or database administration.

**HIGH SCHOOL OR SOME COLLEGE** You can enter IT support by studying for certifications from technology companies such as Microsoft, CompTIA, or Cisco. This will qualify you to maintain their systems or software products.

**GRADUATE** You need a degree in a subject such as business information technology, systems engineering, or software engineering to apply for graduate IT support jobs.

## ▼ RELATED CAREERS

▶ **PROJECT MANAGER** *see pp. 82–83*

▶ **SYSTEMS ANALYST** *see pp. 120–121*

▶ **DATABASE ADMINISTRATOR** *see pp. 122–123*

▶ **NETWORK ENGINEER** *see pp. 124–125*

▶ **CALL CENTER MANAGER** Manages the daily operation of telephone call-center staff, who deal with client and customer queries and complaints, and sell products or services over the telephone.

▶ **SOCIAL MEDIA MANAGER** Creates and leads an organization's social media strategy by producing good content, managing online campaigns, and analyzing user data.

# SKILLS GUIDE

 Excellent communication skills to ensure problems are understood and resolved efficiently.

 The capacity to work well in a team and identify serious issues for managers and IT specialists.

 Good management skills to guide IT support staff, and the ability to influence senior managers.

 The application of technical skills and a logical approach for effective problem-solving.

 Expertise in IT programs, systems, and networks, and the capacity to learn quickly on the job.

**NETWORK SUPPORT ENGINEER** Provides hardware and software support for users of telephone and computer networks, both in person and on the telephone.

**DESKTOP SUPPORT EXECUTIVE** Delivers IT user support across a particular business area, such as retail or banking, to resolve systems faults and user problems.

**WEBSITE HOSTING EXECUTIVE** Works for a website hosting firm, providing 24-hour IT support for users who have purchased server space from the company for their website or email services.

**IT SUPPORT EXECUTIVE** Working in this role gives insight into all the IT functions of an organization, so sideways moves into related IT jobs are common. You can also specialize in a technical area, such as network support, or industry.

**SERVICE DESK MANAGER** Manages a team of staff who are responsible for delivering support for IT applications and business services, ensuring that targets and client expectations are met or exceeded.

# WEB DEVELOPER

## JOB DESCRIPTION

Building an effective website requires a blend of technical and creative skills. Web designers take into account the appearance and usability of the website as well as its back end—the software that delivers the information to the user and makes the site run smoothly. Web designers also build apps for organizations, so consumers can view and buy products or services using their mobile devices.

### SALARY
Junior web developer ★☆☆☆☆
Experienced web developer ★★★★☆

### INDUSTRY PROFILE
Fast-moving environment • Opportunities in small or large development and design agencies • Freelancing common • Global market

## CAREER PATHS

Web developers and designers typically work as part of a team, developing or testing a website. With experience, they may progress to leading a team or working with clients through a website-creation agency.

**WEB PROGRAMMER** Specializes in writing the code that makes a website work. Code is written using languages, such as HTML, Javascript, and PHP.

**ASSISTANT** If you have strong computer skills, you may be able to find work with an agency as an assistant. You will need to prove yourself on the job to progress.

**GRADUATE** You can become a web developer or designer if you have a bachelor's degree or a master's degree in IT or web design, along with a good knowledge of current web technologies.

**WEB DEVELOPER** You will continue to update your skills and adapt designs to new technologies such as mobile apps and websites with animation and video, as well as keep up to date with emerging design trends.

# SKILLS GUIDE

 Creativity and innovation to stay ahead in the competitive world of website development.

 Clarity of thought and strong analytical skills to handle complexities in the design.

 The ability to analyze the design of a website, then identify and solve problems with it.

 Confidence with technology and a willingness to keep up to date with new software developments.

 An eye for detail when planning and/or designing the content of complex websites.

## ▼ RELATED CAREERS

▶ **SOFTWARE ENGINEER** *see pp. 118–119*

▶ **DATABASE ADMINISTRATOR** *see pp. 122–123*

▶ **GAME DEVELOPER** *see pp. 130–131*

▶ **MULTIMEDIA PROGRAMMER** Creates interactive features for products, such as websites, using photographs, animation clips, sounds, and text.

▶ **SEO SPECIALIST** Combines technical and marketing skills to generate extra traffic to websites. This can increase sales and raise the profile of brands.

▶ **VIRTUAL REALITY DESIGNER** Exploits cutting-edge virtual reality (VR) technologies to simulate the real environment. They create applications for many industries, from gaming to aeronautics.

 **GRAPHIC DESIGNER** With a focus on design, uses images, colors, and type to create layouts to express information and messages for print or electronic media in a visual way.

 **USER-EXPERIENCE DESIGNER** Specializes in improving the function and layout of a website to make it as user-friendly as possible.

 **CREATIVE DIRECTOR** Combines extensive design experience and excellent organizational skills to manage a team. Responsible for the overall look and feel of the website.

## AT A GLANCE

 **YOUR INTERESTS** Information Technology (IT) • Computer science • Design • Internet security • New technologies • Multimedia • Graphics

 **ENTRY QUALIFICATIONS** A degree in computer science or graphic design is useful, but many web developers are self-taught.

 **LIFESTYLE** Working hours are flexible, but tight deadlines often mean working into the evening or weekend. Freelance contracts are common.

 **LOCATION** Hybrid working approach and remote working are becoming common. Clients can discuss work and see designs via online platforms.

 **THE REALITIES** A web developer's reputation is the key to success. It is essential to ensure you keep up to date with regularly changing technologies.

# GAME DEVELOPER

## JOB DESCRIPTION

A game developer produces games for different platforms, including personal computers (PCs), game consoles, smartphones, tablets, and websites. As a game developer, you could be involved in a variety of roles, from developing the game's initial concept or writing the code for it, to creating audio and video files, to writing instructions for animators and other members of their team.

### SALARY

Junior developer ★★☆☆☆
Lead developer ★★★★☆

### INDUSTRY PROFILE

Huge expansion in recent years, and set to grow further • Many freelance contracts available • Growing market in Virtual Reality (VR) and Augmented Reality (AR) games

## AT A GLANCE

**YOUR INTERESTS** Computer science • Graphics • 3-D design • Animation and illustration • Gaming • Coding • Mathematics • Physics

**ENTRY QUALIFICATIONS** A degree in computer science or a media-related discipline is useful, although not required, for becoming a developer.

**LIFESTYLE** Teams are close-knit and may work extra hours together to prepare a new game for an upcoming launch date.

**LOCATION** Game developers work mainly in an office, where the atmosphere is informal and creative. Some do operate remotely from home.

**THE REALITIES** Entry to the field is highly competitive. Strict deadlines drive the work, and spending long periods on a computer can be tiring.

## CAREER PATHS

There is no formal career structure for game developers. Progress depends largely on which path is taken—for example, focusing on programming graphics or the user interface. In this young and dynamic industry, success depends on performance, and on the sales and critical acclaim of the games.

**PLAY TESTER** You may be able to find work with a gaming company testing their products for playability and flaws (bugs). This can provide an entry route into the industry.

**GRADUATE** Having a degree in computer science gives you the best chance of employment. Some colleges offer specialty game-programming courses or modules.

## ▼ RELATED CAREERS

▶ **SOFTWARE ENGINEER** *see pp. 118–119*

▶ **WEB DEVELOPER** *see pp. 128–129*

▶ **ANIMATOR** Brings to life the characters in cartoons, advertisements, and video games by modeling the movement of a character or object on-screen. An animator needs good artistic and design skills.

▶ **FORENSIC COMPUTER ANALYST** Investigates computer hacking and other illegal computer-related activities. Forensic computer analysts may be hired by the police or large companies.

▶ **STORYBOARD ARTIST** Illustrates how a character progresses in a computer game using a series of drawings or animations. Storyboard artists have good storytelling and drawing skills.

## SKILLS GUIDE

 Good cooperation skills to work smoothly with people from all different educational backgrounds.

 Imagination to develop new products, and the flexibility to handle a wide range of tasks.

 A logical approach to problem-solving and strong mathematical and analytical skills.

 An in-depth knowledge of computer games and excellent computer skills.

 Attention to detail to ensure bug-free codes; the ability to work under pressure and meet deadlines.

**SENIOR DEVELOPER**
Leads a team of specialists to complete an entire game or part of a larger digital product. This role could go to a person with either a programming or design background.

**PROJECT MANAGER**
Oversees a project, ensuring that all of the resources and personnel required to complete the work on time are in place.

**GAME DEVELOPER** Can follow one of two routes: programming (building the game) or designing (creating the graphics).

**GAME DESIGNER** Devises the look of the characters, levels, and the game's storyline. Some may have a programming background, but many come from a design discipline.

 In 2020, the global revenue from the video gaming industry was $159 billion.

# CYBERSECURITY ANALYST

## JOB DESCRIPTION

The computerized data that organizations and government agencies hold needs constant protection. With a high-level knowledge of computing and networks, cybersecurity analysts work toward preventing counter-security breaches by identifying and fixing weaknesses in the computer code and hardware of an organization.

### SALARY

Newly qualified analyst ★★★★★
Senior consultant ★★★★★

### INDUSTRY PROFILE

Increased reliance on computer systems has seen a growing demand for skilled cybersecurity analysts • Employment is expected to grow 31 percent in this area by 2029

## AT A GLANCE

**YOUR INTERESTS** Information Technology (IT) • Software engineering • Database design • Computer networks • Mathematics • Physics • Law

**ENTRY QUALIFICATIONS** A degree in software engineering or computer science is required. A higher qualification in cybersecurity is useful.

**LIFESTYLE** Regular office hours are the norm, but cybersecurity analysts often work extra hours if there is a threat to their employer's system.

**LOCATION** This job is normally office-based, but hybrid working is increasing. Some travel to client premises may be necessary.

**THE REALITIES** Cybersecurity analysts must keep up to date with new systems, technologies, and threats. The high level of responsibility can be stressful.

## ▼ RELATED CAREERS

▶ **SOFTWARE ENGINEER** *see pp. 118–119*

▶ **NETWORK ENGINEER** *see pp. 124–125*

▶ **POLICE OFFICER** *see pp. 240–241*

▶ **CYBER-CRIME LAWYER** Specializes in the legal aspects of data security and online crime.

▶ **IT CONSULTANT** Advises businesses on how to improve their IT infrastructure. An IT consultant needs an extensive knowledge of databases, IT networks, and software.

More than 60 percent of Americans who went online received at least one online scam offer.

## CAREER PATHS

Most entrants have a relevant computing degree. With experience, cybersecurity analysts can move into a management role or choose to specialize in areas such as research into new threats or computer forensics.

**TECHNICIAN** If you are a computing enthusiast with good IT skills, you may be able to find work as an IT technician or intern while studying for your bachelor's degree.

**GRADUATE** You will usually need at least an undergraduate degree in a computing, security, or IT subject to enter this field.

### SKILLS GUIDE

 Creative thinking to spot new ways in which systems could be attacked.

 Logical and analytical skills to understand how systems have been put together.

 The ability to think quickly and to respond to threats to avert any potential damage.

 A thorough knowledge of a variety of computer-programing languages, networks, and areas of vulnerability.

 Attention to detail when checking for fraud and while conducting research.

**CYBERSECURITY ANALYST**
Working under one of a company's chief executives, you will check systems for vulnerabilities, monitor unusual activity on networks, install security software, and take other measures to neutralize the threats of a cyber attack.

 **SECURITY TRAINER** Trains staff and network users on how to keep valuable electronically stored data secure and confidential.

**FORENSIC ANALYST**
Examines computers, smartphones, and other digital devices to identify and investigate their contents for illegal material. Forensic analysts typically work with the police and other law enforcement agencies.

**RISK MANAGER**
Analyzes security risks that could potentially affect an organization's IT systems. They also work with senior management to update and organize systems to ensure their reliability.

**SECURITY INVESTIGATOR**
Conducts research to identify the location, motives, and methods of cyber criminals, often working with the authorities to prevent illegal activities and provide evidence in prosecutions.

**PEN TESTER** Tests the resistance of computer networks by attempting to penetrate their defenses. Also called "ethical hackers," pen testers identify vulnerabilities in security that could be exploited by malicious computer hackers, and then fix them.

# SCIENCE AND RESEARCH

The scientific sector comprises a broad range of specializations suited to people with an inquiring mind, an analytical approach, and an excitement for making new discoveries. The Covid-19 pandemic has highlighted the importance of jobs that involve researching viruses to create treatments and vaccines.

## BIOTECHNOLOGIST
*Page 136*

Biotechnologists use scientific methods—from genetics to biochemistry—to develop new materials, organisms, and products for use in a range of sectors, such as agriculture.

## MICROBIOLOGIST
*Page 138*

Research carried out by microbiologists into viruses, bacteria, and other microorganisms is critical in preventing infectious diseases and protecting public health.

## PHARMACOLOGIST
*Page 140*

Conducting research into new drugs, existing medicines, and other chemical substances, pharmacologists use their scientific knowledge to improve human health.

## FOOD SCIENTIST
*Page 142*

Employed by regulatory bodies and the food and drink industry, food scientists develop new products and check the safety and health effects of existing products.

## MARINE BIOLOGIST
*Page 144*

Marine biologists study sea life, find new species, and analyze the effects that human activity and climate change have on ocean ecosystems.

## FORENSIC SCIENTIST
*Page 146*

Conducting scientific analysis of crime scenes and gathering evidence for criminal cases, forensic scientists help to solve crimes by bringing hidden facts to light.

## GEOSCIENTIST
*Page 148*

Exploring the natural riches of Earth through fieldwork and research, geoscientists enhance our knowledge of the oil, gas, and mineral resources that lie beneath the ground.

## MATERIALS SCIENTIST
*Page 150*

At the forefront of technology, materials scientists create the substances of tomorrow by researching the properties and behaviors of natural and human-made materials.

## METEOROLOGIST
*Page 152*

Conducting climate research, and creating and presenting weather forecasts, meteorologists study and interpret the atmospheric conditions that shape the world around us.

## ASTRONOMER
*Page 154*

Studying the stars, planets, and space through observation and research, astronomers work in an academic discipline to help us understand the universe.

## ASTRONAUT
*Page 156*

Space science is a niche discipline that contributes greatly to scientific understanding. Astronauts are the celestial explorers who conduct research in outer space.

# BIOTECHNOLOGIST

## JOB DESCRIPTION

Biotechnologists use their knowledge of how living organisms function to find solutions to problems and develop new products. Their work includes developing new medicines and vaccines against diseases, improving animal feed, growing crops that are more resistant to drought and pests, and improving everyday products, such as cheese and bread, and fuels.

## SALARY

Biotechnologist ★★☆☆☆
Senior biotechnologist ★★★★☆

## INDUSTRY PROFILE

Many global opportunities • Wide range of potential employers • Best job prospects in industrial and medical specialty areas

## AT A GLANCE

 **YOUR INTERESTS** Laboratory work • Scientific investigation • Biology • Chemistry • Physics • Mathematics • Engineering

 **ENTRY QUALIFICATIONS** A degree or graduate qualification in a biological- or chemical-related discipline is required for this career.

 **LIFESTYLE** Work hours are regular, but biotechnologists may have to work in the evenings, on weekends, or in shifts to check on research experiments.

 **LOCATION** For the most part, biotechnologists work in sterilized laboratories in research or industrial buildings, and sometimes in offices.

 **THE REALITIES** Ground-breaking discoveries can be exciting, but the work can also be repetitive and frustrating. Many hours are spent in the laboratory.

## ▼ RELATED CAREERS

▶ **MICROBIOLOGIST** *see pp. 138–139*

▶ **FOOD SCIENTIST** *see pp. 142–143*

▶ **CHEMICAL ENGINEER** *see pp. 180–181*

▶ **BIOCHEMIST** Conducts scientific research into chemical reactions that take place in living organisms. Biochemists analyze the effects of drugs, foods, allergies, and disease on cells, proteins, and DNA.

▶ **BIOMEDICAL RESEARCH SCIENTIST** Performs clinical trials and lab tests to research methods of treating disease and other health-related conditions.

The Human Genome Project was completed in 2003; before then, no one knew all the genes in a human.

## CAREER PATHS

Biotechnology encompasses many roles, from high-level research to manufacturing. Having a solid understanding of how one process works makes the transition into different fields much easier if you want to change jobs down the road, including sales and marketing roles.

**TECHNICIAN** You may be able to begin as a trainee laboratory technician while studying for a degree or industry qualification.

**GRADUATE** A degree in biology, chemistry, plant sciences, or biochemistry is required if you want to become a biotechnologist.

### SKILLS GUIDE

 Innovation and a willingness to learn new technologies as they emerge.

 Logical and analytical approach to performing experiments and conducting research.

 Problem-solving skills and the ability to formulate ideas, plan experiments, and interpret results.

 Good computer skills to record and analyze experimental and product data.

 The perseverance and motivation to rethink and restart experiments that may not work.

 The ability to handle scientific equipment and take measurements very carefully.

**BIOTECHNOLOGIST**
There are various opportunities to specialize, but each of these strands of biotechnology require further study.

**BREWING BIOTECHNOLOGIST**
One example of a specific foods application. Discovers methods of brewing and storing fermented products.

**BIOPHARMACEUTICAL ANALYST**
Applies advanced techniques, such as genetic engineering, to develop new drugs used for treating diseases, such as arthritis and high blood pressure.

**CLINICAL SCIENTIST**
Works in a hospital carrying out clinical studies and analyzing data to develop new therapies, or providing diagnoses for medical staff.

**FUELS AND CHEMICALS BIOTECHNOLOGIST** Conducts research into the manufacture of cleaner fuels, such as bioethanol, or novel materials, such as biodegradable plastics, which are far more eco-friendly than many of the current products in use.

# MICROBIOLOGIST

## JOB DESCRIPTION

A microbiologist studies tiny organisms, such as bacteria and viruses, which can cause disease, pollution, and crop destruction, but which may also be used to produce vaccines to prevent diseases. They collect organisms from the environment or from patients, and study and conduct experiments on them. Their work benefits a number of sectors, from medicine to agriculture.

### SALARY

Junior microbiologist ★★☆☆☆
Senior consultant ★★★★★

### INDUSTRY PROFILE

A fast-growing sector • Opportunities in research, production, quality control, and government • Some research at the cutting edge, such as public health and environmental science

## AT A GLANCE

**YOUR INTERESTS** Laboratory work • Health and medicine • Research and development • Food technology • Biology • Physics • Chemistry

**ENTRY QUALIFICATIONS** A degree in microbiology or a related subject is required. Many employers require a PhD and academic research experience.

**LIFESTYLE** Most microbiologists work regular hours, but they may need to supervise laboratory experiments during evenings and weekends.

**LOCATION** Much of the work is laboratory-based, although experienced microbiologists may need to gather samples at a variety of locations.

**THE REALITIES** Laboratory work can be repetitive, especially for junior microbiologists. Competition for senior roles is intense.

## CAREER PATHS

Qualified microbiologists can find jobs in many areas, including the health care, pharmaceutical, food, water, and agricultural industries. They will be expected to publish research papers to build their academic reputation and gain promotion.

**LABORATORY TECHNICIAN** After leaving high school, you can start working as a laboratory technician, while studying for a degree part-time.

**GRADUATE** You will need a degree in life sciences, such as microbiology, applied biology, biomedical science, or molecular biology. A graduate-level degree will help you to progress to more responsible positions.

## ▼ RELATED CAREERS

▶ **BIOTECHNOLOGIST** *see pp. 136–137*

▶ **PHARMACOLOGIST** *see pp. 140–141*

▶ **BIOINFORMATICIAN** Supports scientists by developing computerized modeling systems to manage and analyze data from experiments.

▶ **CLINICAL BIOCHEMIST** Carries out experiments to analyze samples of blood, urine, and body tissue.

▶ **IMMUNOLOGIST** Studies the immune system and helps devise new diagnostic tools, therapies, and treatments.

▶ **TOXICOLOGIST** Conducts experiments to find out the impact of toxic and radioactive materials on people, animals, and the environment.

## SKILLS GUIDE

 Good team-working skills for collaborating with other scientists and manufacturers.

 An innovative approach to scientific experiments. A desire to challenge existing ideas.

 Good organizational skills for managing complex experiments and large amounts of data.

 The ability to solve difficult problems using logic and a sound experimental approach.

 The perseverance to continue searching for solutions, even in the face of repeated failures.

 Attention to detail when taking measurements, making calculations, or studying data.

**RESEARCH MICROBIOLOGIST** Studies the effects and uses of microorganisms in a wide range of areas. They usually combine research with teaching undergraduates.

**CLINICAL MICROBIOLOGIST** Works on identifying disease-causing microbes and developing ways to treat disease and prevent its spread. They are usually based at a hospital or clinic.

**PATENT EXAMINER** Assesses an application for a patent, which are granted to inventors to give them the right to prevent other people from using, selling, or making their inventions.

**MICROBIOLOGIST** You conduct experiments on microorganisms to gain a better understanding of why they can be harmful to humans and crops and to see whether they can be used for human benefit.

**PHARMACEUTICAL SALESPERSON** Uses specialized knowledge to work in sales for pharmaceutical companies. They sell their products to doctors, researchers, and other companies in the medical field.

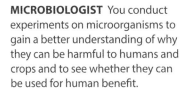

# PHARMACOLOGIST

## JOB DESCRIPTION

Pharmacologists conduct experiments on chemicals that have medicinal properties in order to research their effects on people, animals, and the environment. Working for pharmaceutical companies, universities, hospitals, or government laboratories, they study the beneficial and possible harmful effects of these substances, using their data to develop new drugs and treatments that are safe to use.

### SALARY

Newly qualified ★★☆☆☆
Senior pharmacologist ★★★★★

### INDUSTRY PROFILE

Highly competitive field • Growing sector due to advances in research and increased human life expectancy • Opportunities in pharmaceutical industry, hospitals, and universities

## CAREER PATHS

An advanced degree is required to enter this scientific profession; many senior researchers hold a PhD and have experience of conducting related research at college level. Pharmacologists usually specialize in developing drugs in a specific area, such as those that work on the heart, or the nervous or digestive systems.

**TOXICOLOGIST** Carries out clinical and laboratory studies to identify toxic chemicals and substances for a range of purposes such as new product development in the pharmaceutical or petrochemical industries.

**GRADUATE** While having a degree in pharmacology is preferable, other subjects such as biochemistry, biomedical sciences, physiology, and toxicology can provide an entry into this career. Work experience with a pharmaceutical company during your studies is also an advantage.

**POSTGRADUATE** Many pharmacologists hold both a PhD and a PharmD—a doctor of pharmacy degree.

**PHARMACOLOGIST** As a pharmacologist, you might be involved in nonlaboratory work such as sales and marketing or product licensing for new drugs. With experience, you can expect to move into more senior roles with increased managerial responsibilities.

# SKILLS GUIDE

Good communication skills for preparing reports and presenting the results of experiments.

The ability to lead and motivate others in a team, and supervise or train junior team members.

Sharp analytical skills to interpret data from experiments and peer-reviewed publications.

Strong problem-solving skills for improving medicines during the drug-development phase.

Excellent computer skills to record test results and analyze complex data.

Acute observational skills and an attention to detail in carrying out precise scientific work.

**NEUROPHARMACOLOGIST** Studies how nerve cells and human behavior are affected by drugs, and develops new medicines to treat health issues ranging from chronic pain to mental health conditions.

**CLINICAL PHARMACOLOGIST** Drafts guidelines for how and when medicines should be prescribed, and runs clinical trials of new drugs. This highly specialized role requires a medical degree.

**UNIVERSITY RESEARCHER** Works in a university pharmacology department, leading teams undertaking research projects and experiments, teaching and supervising students, and performing administration and management tasks.

## ▼ RELATED CAREERS

▶ **MICROBIOLOGIST** *see pp. 138–139*

▶ **FORENSIC SCIENTIST** *see pp. 146–147*

▶ **MEDICAL DOCTOR** *see pp. 276–277*

▶ **PHARMACIST** *see pp. 284–285*

▶ **PHARMACEUTICAL SALESPERSON** Uses specialized knowledge to work in sales for pharmaceutical companies. They sell their products to doctors, researchers, and other companies in the medical field.

▶ **BIOMEDICAL RESEARCH SCIENTIST** Performs clinical trials and laboratory tests to research new treatments for diseases and other health issues.

## AT A GLANCE

**YOUR INTERESTS** Chemistry • Biology • Physics • Mathematics • Information Technology (IT) • Health and medicine

**ENTRY QUALIFICATIONS** An advanced degree, such as a doctor of pharmacy degree, is required in order to work as a pharmacologist.

**LIFESTYLE** Working hours are regular, but weekend or shift work may be required to monitor experiments. Part-time hours may be available.

**LOCATION** Pharmacological work is primarily laboratory- or office-based, but traveling to scientific conferences is a common part of the job.

**THE REALITIES** Laboratory analysis may be repetitive and involve working with hazardous chemicals. Some roles involve animal testing.

# FOOD SCIENTIST

## JOB DESCRIPTION

Food scientists research and develop a wide range of food-related products, making sure they are safe and palatable for consumption. They develop new ingredients, test the quality of food items, check labeling for accurate nutritional information, and design or improve food manufacturing machinery to find ways of producing food more safely and efficiently.

### SALARY

Junior scientist ★★★★★
Experienced scientist ★★★★★

### INDUSTRY PROFILE

Many job opportunities worldwide • Primary employers include food manufacturers, retailers and supermarket chains, and government research establishments

## CAREER PATHS

A food scientist may find work with large food- and drink-manufacturing companies, retail chains, government food-inspection departments, public health laboratories, and academic research organizations. To gain seniority and responsibility, you can advance within large companies or move between organizations.

**FOOD DEVELOPMENT TECHNOLOGIST**
Specializes in creating and developing new food products for manufacturing companies, supermarkets, and other food retailers.

**LABORATORY TECHNICIAN**
You can start your career as an intern or part-time lab technician and train on the job while studying for a degree in a relevant subject.

**GRADUATE** To become a food scientist, you need an undergraduate or graduate degree in food science, food technology, or another related science subject.

**FOOD SCIENTIST** Once you are qualified as a food scientist, you can move into many different areas—such as food production, research, quality, and environmental health.

# SKILLS GUIDE

 An innovative approach to researching new food products and production techniques.

 Good analytical skills to assess products for quality and to develop new processes.

 Strong computer skills for recording and analyzing research and development.

 The perseverance to conduct multiple experiments and produce numerous sample products.

 Attention to detail and precision in handling tasks, such as labeling food and checking hygiene.

## AT A GLANCE

 **YOUR INTERESTS** Food science and technology • Food production • Consumer research • Engineering • Chemistry • Biology

 **ENTRY QUALIFICATIONS** A degree in a food-related subject, such as food technology, biology, or chemistry, is required.

 **LIFESTYLE** Food scientists usually work normal hours, but they may also work shifts to check food manufacturing production lines.

 **LOCATION** As well as working in laboratories, food scientists may have to travel to factories and production lines, and to meet suppliers.

 **THE REALITIES** As the work involves repetitive quality checks and experiments, food scientists may spend many hours in a laboratory.

 **FOOD PRODUCTION MANAGER** Sets and monitors quality standards in processed food and oversees food production, ensuring that the items leaving a factory or processing plant meet the appropriate standards.

 **FOOD MARKETING MANAGER** Presents and markets food products to the public. The job involves close collaboration with market researchers, packaging designers, and advertising teams.

 **ACADEMIC FOOD RESEARCHER** Conducts research into areas such as food production, storage, and processing. Academic food researchers may also teach at colleges and universities.

## ▼ RELATED CAREERS

▶ **BIOTECHNOLOGIST** *see pp. 136–137*

▶ **MICROBIOLOGIST** *see pp. 138–139*

▶ **BIOCHEMIST** Conducts scientific research into chemical reactions in living organisms in order to study the effects of drugs, foods, and disease on cells, protein, and DNA.

▶ **CONSUMER SCIENTIST** Conducts research and advises companies on consumer preferences. Consumer scientists work with industries dealing in food, marketing, advertising, and publishing, and also with government departments.

▶ **DIETICIAN** Diagnoses and treats diet-related health conditions, advising on nutrition, weight loss or gain, and general eating habits.

# MARINE BIOLOGIST

## JOB DESCRIPTION

Marine biologists study life within the world's seas and oceans, conducting research in both the water and in the laboratory to analyze how plants and animals are affected by changes in the environment, some of which are caused by human activities. They often specialize in studying one species of animal or plant and may travel the world to study its habitats and feeding patterns.

### SALARY

Junior marine biologist ★★★★★
Senior marine biologist ★★★★★

### INDUSTRY PROFILE

Growth opportunities in sectors including pollution control, biotechnology, and aquaculture • Work available across the world • Competitive job market

## ▼ RELATED CAREERS

▶ **MICROBIOLOGIST** *see pp. 138–139*

▶ **ECOLOGIST** *see pp. 172–173*

▶ **BIOCHEMIST** Investigates chemical reactions that take place in living organisms. Areas of research include DNA, proteins, drugs, allergies, and disease.

▶ **ENVIRONMENTAL CONSERVATIONIST** Works to protect and manage the natural environment in locations such as forests, deserts, and coastal areas.

▶ **OCEANOGRAPHER** Conducts scientific research related to the oceans and seas, and how they interact with rivers, glaciers, and the atmosphere. Oceanographers work in waste management, offshore wind farms, coastal construction, and for oil and water companies.

Our oceans are still a mystery: more than 80 percent remains unmapped and unexplored.

## AT A GLANCE

**YOUR INTERESTS** Marine life • Oceanography • Paleontology • Conservation • Biology • Geography • Geology • Chemistry

**ENTRY QUALIFICATIONS** A degree in a relevant subject, such as marine biology, zoology, or oceanography, is required.

**LIFESTYLE** Work hours are often irregular. Field trips are commonplace and may require long-distance travel, often at short notice.

**LOCATION** Long days at sea are normal when collecting data on field trips, but much of the work is based in a laboratory or an office.

**THE REALITIES** Activities such as diving and working on board ships are exciting but also physically demanding, and may be dangerous at times.

# CAREER PATHS

Many marine biologists aspire to work for the conservation of species and ecosystems, but employment in this area is scarce. You are more likely to find work with government agencies or industries concerned with pollution control, fisheries management, and environmental monitoring.

**GRADUATE** You will need a bachelor's degree, and usually a graduate degree, to become a marine biologist. Following school, you can improve your job prospects by working as an intern in marine research or conservation.

**MARINE BIOLOGIST** The job of a marine biologist is varied. Early in your career, you may spend time collecting samples, analyzing data in a laboratory, and writing reports. With experience, you may lead a research team or give advice to government or industry.

## SKILLS GUIDE

 The ability to work well in a team, especially when spending long periods away at sea.

 Flexibility to handle a variety of tasks, from setting up experiments to planning trips.

 Good organizational skills for coordinating research and experiments effectively.

 The motivation and perseverance to continue research in difficult and challenging conditions.

 Physical endurance, resilience, and stamina while undertaking work in the oceans.

 Attention to detail, as the results of oceanic experiments must be reported accurately.

**MARINE CONSERVATIONIST** Specializes in protecting animals, plants, and the oceans from harmful pollutants, overfishing, and other human-influenced changes to biodiversity.

**MARINE BIOTECHNOLOGIST** Investigates marine animals and plants, which contain chemicals that can be developed into drugs or other useful products.

**FISHERIES AND AQUACULTURE SCIENTIST** Works to increase fish production and improve the health of marine life at commercial fish farms or in the wild, using their in-depth knowledge of fish and crustacean biology.

**RESEARCHER AND LECTURER** Researches marine biology at a university. This can be purely scientific or applied to real-world problems. This role also involves teaching students marine-related subjects.

# FORENSIC SCIENTIST

## JOB DESCRIPTION

Forensic scientists work with the police and other law enforcement agencies to help solve crimes. Collecting samples, such as body fluids, hair, fibers, or fragments from the scene of a crime, they then process and examine the samples for evidence that may help in the identification of a suspect or victim, or provide other valuable information about the incident.

### SALARY

Assistant forensic scientist ★☆☆☆☆
Senior forensic scientist ★★★★☆

### INDUSTRY PROFILE

New techniques in forensics, such as DNA fingerprinting, have opened specialized job opportunities • Fierce competition for jobs, but demand is expected to grow in the next decade

## CAREER PATHS

A degree in a scientific subject is the most common first step in this career. You begin as a trainee, supporting forensic scientists in the lab. With experience, you can go on to manage teams of scientists, or move into private consultancy, where you may investigate the causes of industrial fires or accidents.

**GRADUATE** Although you may be able to find work as a lab assistant with only a high school diploma, the most common route into the profession is to earn a degree. Graduates in chemistry, biology, or other related majors are the usual recruits. Some states require workers to have licenses for each type of hazardous waste they remove.

**DNA ANALYST** Analyzes human genetic material, DNA. This lab-based job in a fast-growing, cutting-edge specialty of forensics demands an in-depth knowledge of DNA sequencing techniques and how to interpret genetic data.

**POSTGRADUATE** You may stand a better chance of getting a job with graduate training in a specialty such as ballistics (firearms) or fingerprint examination.

**FORENSIC SCIENTIST** Most of your training will be on the job. After a few years' experience, you may be called as an "expert witness" to give evidence in court. You will have opportunities to specialize in areas such as firearms and ballistics or drugs and poisons.

## SKILLS GUIDE

 Good communication skills for presenting complex scientific evidence to legal experts.

 The ability to work as part of an investigative team made up of scientists and police.

 Excellent analytical skills and absolute attention to detail when examining evidence.

 A logical and methodical approach to build a probable sequence of events in a crime case.

## ▼ RELATED CAREERS

▶ **CYBERSECURITY ANALYST** *see pp. 132–133*

▶ **POLICE OFFICER** *see pp. 240–241*

▶ **INTELLIGENCE OFFICER** *see pp. 246–247*

▶ **BIOCHEMIST** Investigates chemical reactions that take place inside living organisms. Research areas include DNA, proteins, drugs, and disease.

▶ **PATHOLOGY TECHNICIAN** Supports doctors during postmortem examinations to identify the cause of a person's death.

▶ **TOXICOLOGIST** Conducts experiments to determine the impact of toxic and radioactive materials on people, animals, and the environment.

 **PUBLIC HEALTH FORENSIC SCIENTIST** Works with health or government organizations to locate the sources of environmental contamination or investigate the causes of disease epidemics.

 **FORENSIC EXPLOSIVES SPECIALIST** Uses chemical analysis to establish both the cause of an explosion and the origin of the chemicals involved in it.

Fingerprint evidence has been used in court for over a century.

## AT A GLANCE

 **YOUR INTERESTS** Chemistry • Biology • Mathematics • Physics • Information Technology (IT) • Research and laboratory work

 **ENTRY QUALIFICATIONS** A degree in a relevant science subject is usually required, while a graduate degree in forensic science is useful.

 **LIFESTYLE** Hours of work are variable because call-outs to crime scenes can come at any time, including evenings and weekends.

 **LOCATION** Most work is carried out in a laboratory, although visits to crime scenes and courts to present evidence are also a crucial part of the role.

 **THE REALITIES** Visiting accident or crime scenes can be distressing. Forensic scientists have to keep up to date with the changing technology.

# GEOSCIENTIST

## JOB DESCRIPTION

This is the perfect career for those who love to study our planet, its structure, and how the oceans, atmosphere, and living things interact. Geoscientists use their knowledge of physics, chemistry, and mathematics to study a variety of issues in the world—from predicting volcanic activity, to ensuring clean water supplies, to finding the best way to extract natural resources (such as oil and gas) from the ground.

### SALARY

Newly qualified geoscientist ★★☆☆☆
Experienced geoscientist ★★★★☆

### INDUSTRY PROFILE

Job opportunities worldwide • Industry demands highly technical skills • Higher salaries offered by oil and gas companies • Growing number of roles in finding clean energy sites

## AT A GLANCE

**YOUR INTERESTS** Geology • Physics • Scientific exploration • Mathematics • Engineering • Chemistry • Biology • Computers

**ENTRY QUALIFICATIONS** A bachelor's degree is required. Employers may look for candidates with higher degrees in geology, geophysics, or Earth science.

**LIFESTYLE** Geoscientists usually work regular office hours, but they also may have to do field work, which can lead to extremely varied schedules.

**LOCATION** When not in the office, geoscientists may work from various locations, such as oil rigs, earthquake zones, quarries, and nuclear waste sites.

**THE REALITIES** Traveling to sites across the world and working with equipment, such as drilling machines, can be physically demanding.

## CAREER PATHS

Geoscientists may work in research, focusing on issues such as climate change, or in government, advising on policy. Most jobs are in either mineral and extraction industries or in consultancies that advise on the impact of developments, such as dams and waste-treatment projects. Government-related geoscience jobs are the most likely to include volcanic studies and watershed studies.

**GRADUATE** A degree in geoscience or a related subject is required. Accreditation from a professional body may be required as well, and field experience is highly regarded.

**POSTGRADUATE** Most employers expect you to have a master's degree or PhD, combined with some academic research experience.

## ▼ RELATED CAREERS

▶ **METEOROLOGIST** *see pp. 152–153*

▶ **ARCHAEOLOGIST** Excavates and explores ancient sites. The role may involve working in museums or research organizations.

▶ **GEOGRAPHICAL INFORMATION SYSTEMS OFFICER** Uses maps, photos, and satellite images to produce detailed images showing a range of information, from location of roads to population density, to help with planning and development.

▶ **HYDROLOGIST** Researches the movement, distribution, and quality of water on Earth.

▶ **SEISMOLOGIST** Studies earthquakes, volcanoes, and geological faults and evaluates how they may impact the environment.

## SKILLS GUIDE

 The ability to communicate effectively and use diplomacy to address sensitive issues

 A logical, methodical, and organized approach to solving problems.

 Knowledge of mathematics and statistics to handle detailed measurements and calculations.

 Competence in technology to work with scientific equipment and interpret results.

 Attention to detail for precise measurements and making accurate calculations.

**MINING GEOSCIENTIST**
Works for mining companies, exploring and evaluating production sites and making recommendations about extraction techniques.

**PETROLEUM GEOSCIENTIST**
Specializes in the exploration and extraction of oil and gas, usually working for large multinational petrochemical companies.

**GEOSCIENTIST** Specializes in a specific area once they are qualified. The areas include geology, mining, petroleum, and energy resources.

**ENVIRONMENTAL GEOSCIENTIST**
Applies scientific knowledge to environmental issues, such as pollution and waste disposal, and to issues concerned with large-scale construction projects.

Demand for geoscientists may grow 5 percent by 2029.

# MATERIALS SCIENTIST

## JOB DESCRIPTION

Materials scientists study the composition and structure of matter at microscopic level. Using this specialized knowledge, they develop materials with new properties. The silicon chips used in computers, the carbon fiber frames of racing bikes, and the concrete used in skyscrapers have all been developed and tested by materials scientists.

### SALARY

Newly qualified scientist ★★☆☆☆
Senior materials scientist ★★★★☆

### INDUSTRY PROFILE

Good opportunities across a wide range of industries • Industry currently facing a skills shortage • Most jobs with large companies with over 1,000 employees

## CAREER PATHS

Material scientists usually specialize in working with one type of material, which will govern their career direction. You could, for example, develop lightweight composite materials for the aerospace industry or environmentally-friendly plastics for food packaging. You can usually focus on research or manufacturing, or move into a management role later in your career.

**RESEARCH SCIENTIST**
Uses an advanced knowledge of physics and chemistry to study the structure of solids, and to design, produce, and test new materials.

**MATERIALS TECHNICIAN** With a high-school degree and strong understanding of science and mathematics, you may find work as a materials technician with a large company. You can then study for a degree while on the job.

**GRADUATE** You will need a degree in a relevant subject, such as chemistry, physics, or materials engineering. Some employers will expect a higher degree in your chosen area of specialization.

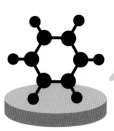

**MATERIALS SCIENTIST**
As a qualified materials scientist, you can work in diverse industries, from metal foundries to nanotechnology—the design and engineering of machines on a microscopic scale.

# SKILLS GUIDE

 Strong communication skills to articulate new ideas and proposals, and to report findings.

 An ability to collaborate with scientists and engineers of various disciplines.

 Strong analytical skills to investigate the properties of materials in the laboratory.

 Good mathematics and chemistry skills to develop materials.

 Practical problem-solving skills to address engineering and manufacturing issues.

 **PROJECT MANAGER** Leads a team of scientists and engineers to develop new materials or the processes for their manufacture. They also monitor progress, assign resources, and liaise with the client.

 **PRODUCTION SPECIALIST** Ensures that materials are made to agreed quality and safety standards at manufacturing plants, and resolves any production problems on site.

 Manufacturing companies employ about 33 percent of all material scientists.

## ▼ RELATED CAREERS

▶ **GEOSCIENTIST** *see pp. 148–149*

▶ **CHEMICAL ENGINEER** *see pp. 180–181*

▶ **AEROSPACE ENGINEER** *see pp. 190–191*

▶ **ENVIRONMENTAL SCIENTIST** Researches ways of protecting the environment, and reducing pollution and waste.

▶ **INDUSTRIAL ENGINEER** Devises efficient ways of making a product through the best use of materials, machines, workers, and energy resources.

▶ **METALLURGIST** Studies the chemical and physical behavior of metals under different conditions. Metallurgists help to test existing products and develop new technologies.

## AT A GLANCE

 **YOUR INTERESTS** Engineering • Physics • Chemistry • Mathematics • Information Technology (IT) • Mineralogy • Geology

 **ENTRY QUALIFICATIONS** A degree-level qualification in a subject such as materials science or applied chemistry is required.

 **LIFESTYLE** Researchers work normal office hours; production staff may need to work shifts to supervise costly manufacturing processes.

 **LOCATION** Material scientists may work in a laboratory, an office, or at an industrial plant. They may also have to travel to visit clients.

 **THE REALITIES** Degree programs are demanding and ongoing study is required to keep up with fast-changing technologies.

# METEOROLOGIST

## JOB DESCRIPTION

Meteorologists study Earth's weather, climate, and atmospheric conditions. In this role, you will use weather data from observation stations, satellite images, and radar to produce short- and long-range weather forecasts for the general public, commercial clients, government agencies, or the military. Meteorologists also play a key role in research into global climate change.

### SALARY

Junior meteorologist ★★☆☆☆
Senior meteorologist ★★★★☆

### INDUSTRY PROFILE

Competitive field • Employers include national weather services, the armed forces, and media and research organizations • Predicted growth in private-sector weather services

## ▼ RELATED CAREERS

▶ **ENERGY ENGINEER** Designs machines and implements processes for the energy industry, from oil and gas production to clean-energy projects, including solar and wind.

▶ **HYDROLOGIST** Monitors, studies, and promotes the sustainable management of water resources, such as lakes, reservoirs, and domestic pipelines.

▶ **OCEANOGRAPHER** Conducts research into oceans, studying how the seas interact with rivers, ice sheets, and the atmosphere. Also provides advice on currents and tides, marine pollution, and underwater mineral resources.

Meteorologists can track weather and make predictions that can help to save lives by warning people dangerous approaching weather.

## AT A GLANCE

**YOUR INTERESTS** Earth sciences • Geography • Mathematics • Physics • Chemistry • Biology • Information Technology (IT)

**ENTRY QUALIFICATIONS** A relevant degree is needed to enter the field, while a postgraduate qualification is necessary to conduct research.

**LIFESTYLE** Forecasters work in shifts to provide 24-hour cover. Researchers work regular hours, with occasional overtime if necessary.

**LOCATION** A meteorologist is based in an office at a regional weather station or commercial weather-service provider, at a television studio, or on a military base.

**THE REALITIES** Meteorologists have a responsibility for accurate forecasting, particularly when severe weather threatens property or lives.

## CAREER PATHS

National weather services are the largest employers of meteorologists, but there are also recruitment opportunities with private-sector firms, research institutes, environmental consultancies, and utility companies.

**GRADUATE** To enter this profession you will need a degree in meteorology, environmental science, physics, mathematics, or a related subject.

**POSTGRADUATE** If you have a postgraduate degree in a related subject, you can apply for research posts. A degree will also help if you are applying for forecasting jobs.

**METEOROLOGIST** You will need to stay up to date with scientific and technological advances throughout your career, in areas such as climate change or mathematical modeling. You can move between a variety of roles, including research, forecasting, training, and consultancy.

## SKILLS GUIDE

Effective verbal and written communication skills to explain weather forecasts clearly.

Good team-working skills to interact with groups, from the general public to technical staff.

Strong analytical skills for studying and interpreting complex meteorological data.

Excellent numerical skills for using advanced mathematical models to process weather data.

Advanced computer skills to use modeling software for simulating weather scenarios.

Attention to detail to spot unexpected weather events so that future forecasts can be revised.

**FORECAST METEOROLOGIST**
Prepares weather forecasts using real-time observations and data from computerized models. Forecasters also compile rolling weather reports that are shared with international weather organizations.

**BROADCAST METEOROLOGIST**
Presents forecasts that are televised, broadcast on radio stations, or accessed via the Internet, using maps to show aspects such as temperature and rainfall.

**FORENSIC METEOROLOGIST**
Usually works in a consultancy capacity, analyzing and reconstructing past weather events to help insurance companies or lawyers determine the impact of the weather conditions on a particular claim or legal case.

**ENVIRONMENTAL METEOROLOGIST**
Conducts research into areas including severe weather patterns, air pollution, or how weather affects the spread of disease.

# ASTRONOMER

## JOB DESCRIPTION

Astronomers are scientists who study the Universe. They rely on ground- or space-based telescopes, spacecraft, and other advanced instruments to make their observations. Using mathematical techniques to interpret data, they investigate the properties and behavior of planets, stars, and galaxies, and then propose and test theories about the nature and makeup of the Universe.

**SALARY**

Graduate student ★★★★★
Astronomy professor ★★★★★

**INDUSTRY PROFILE**

Academic profession with few employment opportunities • Entry to research posts is competitive • Jobs found in government departments, laboratories, and observatories

## AT A GLANCE

 **YOUR INTERESTS** Astronomy • Mathematics • Physics • Chemistry • Geology • Engineering • Information Technology (IT) • Exploration

 **ENTRY QUALIFICATIONS** Entrants to this profession usually hold an advanced degree in astronomy, space science, astrophysics, or geophysics.

 **LIFESTYLE** Studying the sky and collecting data can involve long, irregular hours. Weekend and evening work is a crucial part of the job.

 **LOCATION** Astronomers work mainly in space laboratories, observatories, and research departments. They are likely to work on an international team.

 **THE REALITIES** This is a highly demanding, theoretical field. Entry is competitive, and many graduates are not able to find work as astronomers.

## CAREER PATHS

Because astronomy is a highly academic field, aspiring astronomers need a degree in physics or astronomy and usually a PhD to progress. Most professional astronomers carry out research and hold teaching posts at universities, but some move into related fields, such as instrument engineering, computer programming, or space science, where they provide support for space missions.

 **GRADUATE** If you have an astronomy degree, you can apply for support roles in planetariums, research laboratories, and science museums. You can also gain relevant work experience before moving to graduate study.

 **POSTGRADUATE** You will require the highest level of academic qualifications to progress in this field; a master's or PhD in astronomy will improve your prospects.

## ▼ RELATED CAREERS

▶ **SOFTWARE ENGINEER** *see pp. 118–119*

▶ **ELECTRONICS ENGINEER** Designs and creates electronic equipment for use in industry, from telecommunications to manufacturing.

▶ **GEOPHYSICIST** Studies physical aspects of Earth, analyzing data on phenomena such as earthquakes, volcanoes, and the water cycle.

▶ **RESEARCH PHYSICIST** Investigates and proposes theories about the nature and properties of matter and energy. Physicists may work in academic or industrial research, or in government laboratories.

▶ **SATELLITE SYSTEMS ENGINEER** Uses a knowledge of electronics, computer science, and astronomy to design and build space satellites.

# SKILLS GUIDE

 A logical approach to solving complex problems and analyzing abstract astronomical ideas.

 Mathematical skills for computer modeling, data analysis, and conducting theoretical research.

 Excellent computer skills for generating theoretical models and interpreting observational data.

 Perseverance to study infrequent and slowly occurring astronomical phenomena patiently.

 Attention to detail and the ability to make precise measurements and keep meticulous records.

**THEORETICAL ASTRONOMER** Creates complex computer models to develop and test theories, and presents findings in reports, scientific journals, and at conferences around the world.

**OBSERVATIONAL ASTRONOMER** Uses radio, infrared, and optical telescopes to gather data from spacecraft and satellites, then records and analyzes that data to test theories and predictions.

**PLANETARIUM DIRECTOR** Develops exhibitions and film shows on the subject of planetary science to educate and entertain visitors, and hosts and liaises with different visitor groups, from tourists to schools.

**ASTRONOMER** This is an inherently academic career, so you will be expected to carry out original research, publish papers, and continue learning, as well as teach others.

**ASTRONOMY PROFESSOR** Teaches astronomy at undergraduate and postgraduate levels, and conducts research to contribute to our understanding of the universe.

# ASTRONAUT

## JOB DESCRIPTION

Astronauts are highly trained individuals who pilot spacecraft or carry out specialized missions in space. These may include launching or repairing satellites, or carrying out scientific experiments in low-gravity conditions. Astronauts are employed by national space agencies, and only a select few ever end up actually traveling into space, making this one of the world's most exclusive careers.

### SALARY

Astronaut ★★★★★

### INDUSTRY PROFILE

Very few openings—there have been just over 500 astronauts in total since space flight began • Highly competitive selection process • Many other opportunities in the growing space industry

## CAREER PATHS

To be selected as an astronaut, you usually need to be a citizen of the country running a manned space program. You must be physically fit, and meet the space agency's height, weight, and age criteria. Almost all astronauts also hold degrees or higher qualifications in science or engineering, or are skilled and experienced jet pilots. You will undergo multiple rounds of interviews to determine if you are physically and psychologically suited to the role.

**INSTRUCTOR** Provides training in the skills required to fly and maintain a spacecraft. They use flight simulators to teach new astronauts how to deal with routine operations and potential emergencies.

**JET PILOT** You could begin your career by joining your country's military and specializing as a test pilot. You may then be able to apply to join a space program. Most space agencies will require you to hold a degree as a minimum qualification.

**SCIENTIST OR ENGINEER** You can apply to train as an astronaut if you have a degree—and preferably a postgraduate qualification—in science or engineering, plus flight-related work experience.

**ASTRONAUT** Basic astronaut training takes about two years. If selected for flight, you have a choice of roles, from fixing equipment in Earth's orbit to conducting research on a space station.

# SKILLS GUIDE

The ability to work well with crew members and the many staff who support missions on the ground.

Creativity for solving unexpected and complex problems using limited resources.

The flexibility to adapt to extreme environments and to deal with challenging living conditions.

A logical and analytical approach when handling critical and challenging situations.

The physical endurance to train for live missions, which can be hugely demanding.

An eye for detail and constant vigilance to successfully complete missions in space.

**COMMANDER OR PILOT** Takes responsibility for the flight of the spacecraft, as well as the safety of the crew, and the overall success of a mission. They may also perform other duties, such as helping with onboard experiments or carrying out extravehicular activity, or space walks.

**FLIGHT ENGINEER** Does a variety of jobs on the mission including conducting scientific experiments under micro-gravity conditions, performing routine maintenance on board space stations, and operating robotic arms to accomplish external maintenance tasks.

## AT A GLANCE

**YOUR INTERESTS** Space • Flight • Mathematics • Physics • Mechanical engineering • Electrical engineering • Materials science

**ENTRY QUALIFICATIONS** As a minimum, you need at least a degree in science or engineering, or extensive experience in flying fast jets.

**LIFESTYLE** Working hours are irregular. Training missions involve long periods away from home, and space flights can last many months.

**LOCATION** Astronauts often work in remote, high-security locations, and may have to travel widely for training purposes.

**THE REALITIES** Working hours are long and conditions are tough and dangerous. Extensive training is both physically and mentally challenging.

## ▼ RELATED CAREERS

▶ **MECHANICAL ENGINEER** *see pp. 182–183*

▶ **ELECTRICAL ENGINEER** *see pp. 186–187*

▶ **ARMED FORCES PILOT** *see pp. 232–233*

▶ **ASTROBIOLOGIST** Investigates how life may be able to exist in space and extreme environments.

▶ **ASTROPHYSICIST** Studies the Universe—from planets to stars—using sophisticated equipment, such as satellites and telescopes.

▶ **SATELLITE ENGINEER** Designs and builds space satellites used for relaying electronic communication, monitoring Earth, or studying the Universe.

# ANIMALS, FARMING, AND THE ENVIRONMENT

If you enjoy working with animals or plants, or on the land, you could consider some of the careers in this sector. From grooming horses and caring for sick animals to researching crop-cultivation techniques, the number of available career options is growing all the time.

## VETERINARIAN
*Page 160*

Protecting the health of animals in zoos, farms, and homes, vets use their knowledge of physiology and anatomy to treat sick and injured animals.

## ANIMAL CARE WORKER
*Page 162*

Providing hands-on care in a range of locations —from rescue centers to pet shops—animal care workers clean, feed, and look after the animals in their care.

## ZOOKEEPER
*Page 164*

Working in zoos and wildlife parks, zookeepers ensure that the animals under their care are well looked after and have a suitable living environment.

## FARM MANAGER
*Page 166*

Modern-day agriculture makes use of large machinery, scientific methods, and biotechnology, so farmers are skilled in both business management and farming.

## HORTICULTURAL WORKER
*Page 168*

Horticulture is a growing industry. Workers in this area may be responsible for planting seeds, taking cuttings, pruning plants, and preventing disease.

## LANDSCAPE ARCHITECT
*Page 170*

With a passion for designing outdoor spaces, landscape architects use their creative skills to produce visually stunning yet practical designs for their clients.

## ECOLOGIST
*Page 172*

Working in universities, government departments, and field stations, ecologists help us understand living things and the environments in which they live.

# VETERINARIAN

## JOB DESCRIPTION

Veterinarians, commonly known as vets, treat and operate on sick or injured animals. They train to work with many species, including animals in zoos and in the wild—but in general practice, vets focus mostly on domestic and farm animals. As a vet, you may control standards of care and hygiene in animal care environments, such as veterinary hospitals, and also research the diagnosis and prevention of animal diseases.

### SALARY

Newly qualified vet ★★★☆☆
Senior practitioner ★★★★★

### INDUSTRY PROFILE

Half of vets self-employed in general practice • Opportunities in public health, zoos, animal charities, and hospitals • Employment is expected to grow 19 percent by 2026

## CAREER PATHS

After qualifying, most vets begin their careers as employees in a general veterinary practice. With experience and further study, they can specialize in a wide range of fields, such as surgery, nutrition, or parasitology (the study of parasites). Some go on to start their own practices, or to work in research or for the government.

**DOMESTIC ANIMALS' VET**
Works in a veterinary practice that deals with domestic animals such as cats, dogs, gerbils, rabbits, caged birds, and others.

**GRADUATE** You will need a Doctorate of Veterinary Medicine (DVM) accredited by a professional body. Courses can take between four and six years.

**VET** Provides general health care treatment to animals. As an experienced vet, you can choose to specialize in a specific area, such as emergency care.

In 2020, 67 percent of US households, or about 85 million families, owned a pet.

# SKILLS GUIDE

Excellent verbal and written communication skills to advise owners on the best care practices for their animals.

Good team-working skills in order to work closely with practice support staff to ensure animals receive the best health care.

Strong organizational skills, particularly when running a practice that involves accurate billing and record-keeping.

The ability to solve problems quickly, make difficult decisions, and take prompt action when treating ill or injured animals.

**FARM VET** Works with animals that are reared on farms, such as sheep, pigs, cattle, and chickens. Farm vets spend a lot of their time traveling to farms, checking livestock, and advising farmers.

**ZOO VET** Works specifically with wild animals that are kept in captivity in zoos and wildlife parks. They can work wtih some rare and unusual species.

**EQUINE VET** Specializes in working with horses in riding schools, farms, or polo clubs, and other similar locations. Some also care for high-value racehorses.

## AT A GLANCE

**YOUR INTERESTS** Animal welfare • Biology • Chemistry • Zoology • Scientific research • Mathematics

**ENTRY QUALIFICATIONS** Vets need to complete a degree at a veterinary college, pass a national exam, and apply for licensure.

**LIFESTYLE** The job involves long days and being on call at odd hours. Vets often work outdoors and in all kinds of weather.

**LOCATION** Vets can work at varied locations—from farms, zoos, and stables to wildlife hospitals—in order to treat sick animals.

**THE REALITIES** The job can be physically and emotionally stressful, and requires assertiveness yet sensitivity when making decisions.

## ▼ RELATED CAREERS

▶ **ANIMAL CARE WORKER** *see pp. 162–163*

▶ **ZOOKEEPER** *see pp. 164–165*

▶ **MEDICAL DOCTOR** *see pp. 276–277*

▶ **NURSE** *see pp. 278–279*

▶ **EQUINE NUTRITIONIST** Formulates foods and diets for horses. May work in research, manufacturing, or as an advisor to horse owners.

▶ **VETERINARY PHYSICAL THERAPIST** Treats dogs and horses, including both pets and "working animals," such as greyhounds and racehorses. Veterinary physical therapists can work with farm or zoo animals. A degree in veterinary physiotherapy is essential to qualify in this profession.

# ANIMAL CARE WORKER

## JOB DESCRIPTION

Animal care workers provide the essentials of life—from food and water to exercising, cleaning, grooming, and administering medical care—to ensure that pets or domesticated animals are healthy. They work in a range of places, such as kennels, stables, pet stores, rescue centers, and animal hospitals.

### SALARY

Animal care worker ★★★★★
Animal care manager ★★★★★

### INDUSTRY PROFILE

Job tasks can vary greatly from one position to another • Public interest in treatment of domestic and captive animals has tightened standards

## AT A GLANCE

**YOUR INTERESTS** • Animal welfare • English • Chemistry • Mathematics • Biology • Physical education

**ENTRY QUALIFICATIONS** Formal qualifications are not always required; some vocational training in animal care is desirable.

**LIFESTYLE** Since animal care is an all-day job, working hours often involve shifts over evenings, weekends, or public holidays.

**LOCATION** The work is often outdoors, and may involve a range of domesticated or wild animals. Travel is often required, either to move animals or visit sites.

**THE REALITIES** Salaries are modest and the work often physically exhausting. Some situations can be emotionally upsetting.

## ▼ RELATED CAREERS

▶ **VETERINARIAN** *see pp. 160–161*

▶ **ZOOKEEPER** *see pp. 164–165*

▶ **ANIMAL TECHNOLOGIST** Cares for laboratory animals used for research in the medical, veterinary, and dental industries.

▶ **FARRIER** Specializes in equine hoof care, making and fitting shoes on horses and donkeys.

▶ **RIDING SCHOOL COACH** Teaches students in horsemanship and prepares them for competitions, from beginners to professionals.

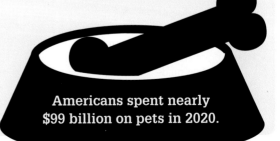

Americans spent nearly $99 billion on pets in 2020.

## CAREER PATHS

A formal degree is not always necessary to enter this career, but a vocational course or experience through volunteering will improve your job prospects. Career progression is usually achieved through specialization.

**ASSISTANT** If you have prior experience of working with animals, you can apply for work-based trainee jobs straight out of high school.

**GRADUATE** You will need an undergraduate degree in animal care management or animal sciences to enter this sector in a professional or managerial role.

### SKILLS GUIDE

 Excellent communication skills for interacting with colleagues, vets, customers, and visitors.

 Good observation skills to monitor animals for different behavioral patterns and signs of any disease.

 Physical resilience for working outdoors in all weathers and for lifting animals and bags of feed.

 The ability to organize and prioritize routine tasks, and to manage time effectively.

 Good computer skills for maintaining records and accessing the correct information for clients.

**ANIMAL CARE WORKER** Many animal care workers specialize in a particular type of care, such as rehabilitation through hydrotherapy—exercising animals in a pool of water—or massage. With experience and qualifications, you could move into training or managerial roles.

**STABLEHAND** Provides daily care for horses at a yard or farm to ensure that they are healthy, happy, and in good condition. Duties include feeding, cleaning, and preparing horses for exercising and events.

**ANIMAL TRAINER** Trains animals to respond to cues and commands. Trainers work with performing or working animals, such as guide dogs, or with rescue dogs and animals that have behavioral problems.

**ANIMAL THERAPIST** Treats animals with joint or muscular problems by massaging muscles or flexing and stretching affected areas. Animal therapists need further qualifications for practicing.

**PET GROOMER** Keeps a pet's coat in good condition, advising owners on care of pet hair, grooming, and nutrition. Groomers can be employed by pet salons or may run their own business.

**PET STORE MANAGER** Cares for animals, birds, and reptiles prior to their sale as pets, and provides advice to customers on the feeding, housing, exercising, and general welfare of their pets.

# ZOOKEEPER

## JOB DESCRIPTION

A zookeeper looks after wild, rare, and exotic animals in zoos, animal parks, or aquariums. In this active, often outdoor job, duties range from feeding, washing, and grooming animals to designing and maintaining enclosures, assisting with the delivery of medical care to animals, and record-keeping. Zookeepers may also guide and educate zoo visitors, and collect data that may be useful in conservation research.

### SALARY

Zookeeper ★★★★★
Head keeper ★★★★★

### INDUSTRY PROFILE

Strong competition for entry-level positions • More applicants than vacancies • Higher salaries offered in larger zoos

## CAREER PATHS

Experience working with animals is required in order to become a zookeeper. Prospective zookeepers can pick up useful skills by joining volunteer programs, offered by most zoos and animal parks, or through voluntary or paid work in a pet store, stable, or farm. Senior roles are rare, so progression usually requires moving to another zoo.

**GRADUATE** You will need a degree in zoology, biology, or a related field in order to progress to a senior or more specialized position in this profession.

**VOLUNTEER** Although you will not always have direct contact with animals as a volunteer, you can still gain valuable experience of working in a zoo environment. These opportunities are very popular, so you may have to join a waiting list.

**APPRENTICE** You can gain useful experience by taking a related college course or applying for an apprenticeship, both of which may involve direct contact with animals.

**ZOOKEEPER** Once you have gained experience you may be able to join— or apply for promotion at—a larger zoo, where there may be good prospects for progression. Opportunities also exist in education and conservation research.

## SKILLS GUIDE

 Excellent observational skills for spotting physical and behavioral signs of injury or illness in animals.

 The ability to keep detailed records in a diary or on a computer for monitoring and research purposes.

 Physical strength for lifting and handling equipment and working in wet and dirty conditions.

 Strong team-working skills to interact with other keepers, vets, and animal specialists.

 Good communication skills to give demonstrations and educational talks to visitors.

 **SENIOR KEEPER** Leads a team of zookeepers and volunteers, overseeing the care and welfare of the animals at the zoo.

 **KEEPER** Specializes in the care of one type or group of animals, such as reptiles or primates. Keepers may travel widely, giving advice to zoos and animal collections around the world.

 **ANIMAL CURATOR** Sources and acquires new animals for zoos to maintain their populations and help with breeding programs.

 **ANIMAL PARK MANAGER** Runs the daily operations and services of an animal park. A park manager also guides tourists and is responsible for the care and welfare of the animals.

## ▼ RELATED CAREERS

▶ **ECOLOGIST** *see pp. 172–173*

▶ **ENVIRONMENTAL EDUCATION OFFICER** Develops and promotes educational programs for schools, families, and communities.

▶ **PET STORE ASSISTANT** Cares for mammals, birds, reptiles, and fish to be sold as pets.

▶ **SAFARI TOUR LEADER** Guides parties of tourists on safari-park tours so that they can see wild animals and birds in their natural habitat.

▶ **WILDLIFE REHABILITATOR** Rescues sick and abandoned wild animals, and nurses them back to health with the ultimate aim of releasing them back into their natural environments.

## AT A GLANCE

 **YOUR INTERESTS** Wildlife and animal behavior • Biology • Geography • Animal welfare • Information Technology (IT)

 **ENTRY QUALIFICATIONS** A good general education, work experience, and commitment are required. A degree is needed for specialized roles.

 **LIFESTYLE** Shift-work is the norm, but part-time working may be possible. Head keepers will often work evenings while on call.

 **LOCATION** The job is usually based at public and private zoos, animal parks, or aquariums. Travel may be necessary when transporting animals.

 **THE REALITIES** Outdoor work in all weathers is often required. Some jobs may aggravate allergies to animals or plants. Some animals pose safety risks.

# FARM MANAGER

## JOB DESCRIPTION

Farm managers are responsible for ensuring that livestock, dairy, crops, or mixed farms are run smoothly and at a profit. From using machinery and moving animals, to planning crop rotations and managing the business, the job involves a range of duties that varies according to the local climate, soil conditions, the public's demand for produce, and contracts with supermarkets, food companies, and other customers.

## SALARY

Assistant farm manager ★★★★★
Experienced farm manager ★★★★★

## INDUSTRY PROFILE

Industry is changing due to precision techniques, such as GPS-guided crop sowing • Opportunities with estates, farm-management firms, and food companies, and for self-employment

## AT A GLANCE

**YOUR INTERESTS** Agriculture • Animal welfare • The natural world • Environmental science • Biology • Technology

**ENTRY QUALIFICATIONS** Although it is possible to secure work as a farm manager based on experience alone, a degree in a related subject is preferred.

**LIFESTYLE** Work patterns are seasonal and farm managers are expected to put in very long hours at harvest or lambing times, for example.

**LOCATION** Managers carry out practical work on a farm and administrative tasks in an office. Travel to other sites or to agricultural shows is common.

**THE REALITIES** The work can be relentless at busy times of year. Profitability may be affected by external factors, such as poor weather.

## CAREER PATHS

Farming is a diverse industry that offers good career prospects. Farm managers may be employed by landowners or work their own land. Many farms specialize in a single type of farming, so it may be necessary to move to broaden your experience.

**FARM APPRENTICE** You may be able to find work as a farm apprentice right after high school, gaining the necessary experience to apply for management training.

**TRAINEE MANAGER** You must have some prior experience of agricultural work to join a management-training program.

**GRADUATE** With a bachelor's degree in agriculture or farm management and experience of a farm apprenticeship, you can apply to join a graduate management-training program.

## ▼ RELATED CAREERS

▶ **ECOLOGIST** *see pp. 172–173*

▶ **FISH FARMER** Breeds and rears fish and shellfish for profit, for the food industry, for recreational angling, or as stock for ornamental pools.

▶ **FOREST OFFICER** Supervises activities that develop and protect forest environments. Forest officers also oversee the ecological conservation and recreational use of forests, as well as managing commercial aspects of forestry.

▶ **GROUNDS MAINTENANCE WORKER** Ensures that the grounds of houses, businesses, and parks are attractive and healthy.

▶ **PARKS OFFICER** Manages parks and green spaces for the benefit of local residents and visitors.

# SKILLS GUIDE

 High levels of stamina and resilience to meet the physical demands of the job.

 Good organizational skills for arranging the operation and business management of the farm.

 Strong computer skills for monitoring supply levels and keeping accurate records.

 The ability to form a strong team of farm workers, and to oversee the activities of apprentices.

 Business expertise to manage finances, plan budgets, and ensure that production targets are met.

 **ESTATE MANAGER** Supervises and manages the maintenance of grounds and outbuildings, as well as overseeing the financial and legal affairs of farms and country estates.

 **AGRONOMIST** Carries out field research into the breeding, physiology, production, yield, and management of crops and agricultural plants.

**AGRICULTURAL CONSULTANT** Solves agricultural problems and provides technical advice and support to farmers, growers, and government agencies.

**AGRICULTURAL SALES EXECUTIVE** Sells, promotes, and sometimes trains farmers in the use of agricultural products, such as machinery or fertilizer. Practical experience of farming is useful.

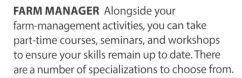 **FARM MANAGER** Alongside your farm-management activities, you can take part-time courses, seminars, and workshops to ensure your skills remain up to date. There are a number of specializations to choose from.

# HORTICULTURAL WORKER

## JOB DESCRIPTION

If you enjoy working outdoors, you may want to explore opportunities in horticulture—the business of growing, harvesting, and selling flowers, plants, shrubs, and trees. You can find work in nurseries, botanical gardens, landscaping companies, and with the authorities who maintain green spaces in towns and cities.

### SALARY

Horticultural worker ★☆☆☆☆
Horticulturist ★★★★☆

### INDUSTRY PROFILE

Majority of work in the production of high-value crops • Diverse industry dominated by small- to medium-sized companies

## CAREER PATHS

Entry-level jobs in horticulture require only a high school education. You may need a degree or vocational training to progress into managerial roles, or to find jobs in landscape design or horticultural science as a botanist, plant breeder, or soil scientist.

**GRADUATE** Some colleges offer courses in gardening and horticultural skills. Although not essential for entry into this career, an official qualification may help you in the job market

**ASSISTANT** You can begin your career as an assistant, learning on the job as you work within a team at a plant nursery or in gardens.

### ▼ RELATED CAREERS

▶ **ARBORICULTURALIST** Cultivates, manages, and protects trees, hedges, and large shrubs. Arboriculturalists also provide information and advice on tree-related issues.

▶ **FLORIST** Cuts, arranges, and dries flowers to create pleasing visual displays for gifts, weddings, and funerals. Florists may work in a shop or from home.

**HORTICULTURAL WORKER** In this role, you carry out gardening duties, including plant care, and looking after playing fields or golf courses. You can choose to specialize in working with food crops or ornamental plants in nurseries or farms, or sell plants and advise on plant care.

## AT A GLANCE

**YOUR INTERESTS** Gardening • Botany (plant science) • Plants and natural history • Biology • Chemistry • Health and fitness • Geography

**ENTRY QUALIFICATIONS** A high school education is required; a degree or higher is needed for more specialized roles.

**LIFESTYLE** The hours are generally regular, but shift work may be required at some nurseries where delicate plants are grown under intensive conditions.

**LOCATION** Working bases may be plant nurseries, greenhouse complexes, garden centers, public or private parks, or open spaces in towns or cities.

**THE REALITIES** The work can be repetitive and uncomfortable in poor weather. There is little rest, so physical stamina is necessary.

## SKILLS GUIDE

Physical strength and stamina for labor-intensive outdoor work, sometimes in bad weather.

Manual dexterity for planting seedlings and handling gardening equipment.

Organizational skills for planning tasks, including unloading supplies, digging soil, and pruning plants.

Problem-solving skills to examine and care for plants and flowers that need specific treatments to thrive.

Creativity and imagination to make town spaces, gardens, and nurseries look vibrant and appealing.

**LANDSCAPE DESIGNER** Uses a detailed knowledge of plants and horticulture to plan, plant, and maintain gardens and landscapes surrounding homes and businesses.

**BOTANIST** Studies plant life and its interactions with soils, the atmosphere, and other living things. Botanists hold degrees, and may work on plant cultivation and growth, and document diverse and exotic plant species.

**HORTICULTURAL TECHNICIAN** Specializes in technical areas of horticulture, such as installing irrigation systems, pest control in greenhouses, or laboratory work.

**HORTICULTURIST** Studies plant disease, genetics, and nutrition in order to improve the quality and productivity of commercial crops.

**HORTICULTURAL THERAPIST** Uses practical gardening to promote well-being in people recovering from illness or suffering from long-term conditions.

# LANDSCAPE ARCHITECT

## JOB DESCRIPTION

Landscape architects design, create, and manage open spaces in both man-made and natural environments. In this role, you work with other construction and engineering professionals to plan and manage projects as diverse as parks and recreational sites, pedestrian areas, sports venues, and urban regeneration.

### SALARY

Junior landscape architect ★☆☆☆☆
Senior landscape architect ★★★★☆

### INDUSTRY PROFILE

Growing demand for sustainably designed open spaces and buildings • Salaries higher in private practice • Around 50 percent of professionals are self-employed

## AT A GLANCE

**YOUR INTERESTS** Design • Art • Environmental science • Architecture • Town planning • Information Technology (IT) • Geography

**ENTRY QUALIFICATIONS** A degree from a landscape architecture program is required for most jobs. State licensure may also be required.

**LIFESTYLE** Regular office hours are the norm, but the job is deadline driven, so evening and weekend work may sometimes be required.

**LOCATION** The work is office-based, although it features regular travel to survey projects, visit sites, and present plans to clients or the public.

**THE REALITIES** Improving urban and natural spaces for the benefit of the community and the environment is highly rewarding.

## CAREER PATHS

A bachelor's degree or certification in a relevant subject is usually required to find work as a landscape architect. Local authorities and private practices are the biggest employers, but jobs may also exist with environmental agencies, utility companies, construction firms, and voluntary organizations. With experience, you can also work on a self-employed basis.

**GRADUATE** You will need a professionally accredited degree in a subject such as garden design, landscape architecture, planning, or environmental conservation.

**POSTGRADUATE** You can take a postgraduate-level conversion course in landscape architecture if you have a prior degree in a related subject, such as architecture, horticulture, or botany.

## SKILLS GUIDE

 Effective communication skills for liaising with clients and construction staff.

 A flair for design and an awareness of the future need for creating aesthetic, sustainable spaces.

 The ability to understand client requirements and incorporate them into the site's design.

 The ability to use Computer-aided Design (CAD) software to create designs and presentations.

 Commercial awareness, combined with an understanding of social and environmental issues.

### ▼ RELATED CAREERS

▶ **HORTICULTURAL WORKER** *see pp. 168–169*

▶ **CIVIL ENGINEER** *see pp. 176–177*

▶ **ARCHITECT** *see pp. 194–195*

▶ **COST ENGINEER** *see pp. 198–199*

▶ **TOWN PLANNER** *see pp. 200–201*

▶ **LANDSCAPER** Works to a landscape architect's designs and specifications to build features such as garden paving, patios, walls, and borders.

▶ **LAND SURVEYOR** Carries out survey work to gather data for mapping an area of land, in advance of building or engineering projects.

**LANDSCAPE CONTRACTOR** Works to realize a landscape architect's designs by hiring and overseeing construction staff and the machinery required to complete the job.

**LANDSCAPE PLANNER** Advises on land development proposals with the aim of protecting natural resources and historic or cultural sites in urban and rural settings.

**LANDSCAPE MANAGER** Helps to plan new landscapes and maintain existing ones, supervising and directing the work of landscape architects, monitoring progress, and advising on legal aspects of the planning process.

**LANDSCAPE ARCHITECT** To progress in this career, you will need to achieve professional status. You can then choose to specialize in a particular type of work—such as ecological design or highways landscaping—or become a partner or owner of a private practice.

**LANDSCAPE SCIENTIST** Carries out surveys of ecologically valuable habitats and advises on how to manage them in order to improve their long-term viability and enhance biodiversity.

# ECOLOGIST

## JOB DESCRIPTION

An ecologist studies the relationship between plants and animals, and their interaction with their physical environment. They may specialize in a particular habitat (such as a rain forest) or groups of species (such as lions). Their work could range from conducting research on global issues to developing plans for local land management. A deep passion to protect the environment and biodiversity drives most ecologists.

### SALARY

Newly qualified ecologist ★★☆☆☆
Experienced ecologist ★★★★☆

### INDUSTRY PROFILE

Many potential employers, especially in government and environmental agencies • Fierce competition for higher-level posts • Freelance work is becoming more common

## CAREER PATHS

To work as an ecologist, you need a degree or graduate qualification in ecology or biological science. Opportunities exist with national and local government agencies, environmental consultancies, and Non-Governmental Organizations (NGOs) that campaign for the environment and wildlife.

**MARINE ECOLOGIST** Studies marine organisms and ecosystems to protect biodiversity, conserve habitats, and help preserve commercially important fish stocks and other marine life.

**VOLUNTEER** Volunteering for a conservation NGO and gaining experience in the field will improve your chances of employment once you obtain a relevant degree.

**GRADUATE** You should hold a relevant degree, and be experienced in carrying out field research and data analysis. Graduate degrees are becoming increasingly sought after.

**ECOLOGIST** Early in your career, you will carry out field surveys, write reports, and provide advice to various organizations. With experience, you could move into management roles or work on environmental policy in a government department or with an NGO, before specializing in a number of different fields.

## SKILLS GUIDE

 Good written and verbal skills to write and present reports and academic papers.

 A methodical approach to gathering data and using lab equipment for analysis of samples.

 Dedication and patience, as global projects may take many years to research and complete.

 Good team-management skills for advising and leading a team on a large project.

 Strong computer skills for the analysis, presentation, and accurate reporting of data.

**CONSERVATION ECOLOGIST**
Plans and carries out programs to preserve natural resources and encourage wildlife to flourish in a variety of environments.

**BIODIVERSITY OFFICER**
Works to protect endangered plant species and key habitats. Performs fieldwork in order to advise NGOs and government authorities.

## ▼ RELATED CAREERS

▶ **FOREST AND CONSERVATION WORKER**
Oversees environmental and forestry issues, including management of conservation activities. The role may include making presentations for education or publicity.

▶ **OCEANOGRAPHER** Studies the seas and oceans. Also conducts research into the effects of climate change, and explores the impact of pollution on marine life.

▶ **WASTE MANAGEMENT OFFICER** Coordinates waste disposal and recycling services.

▶ **ZOOLOGIST** Observes and studies animals and their behavior in their natural habitats. This job usually requires a degree in zoology, animal ecology, animal behavior, or conservation.

## AT A GLANCE

 **YOUR INTERESTS** Wildlife and environmental conservation • Botany • Biology • Zoology • Chemistry • Geography • Mathematics • Statistics

 **ENTRY QUALIFICATIONS** A degree in a subject such as ecology, geography, or environmental science is required. Postgraduate study is useful.

 **LIFESTYLE** Ecologists tend to be highly committed to wildlife and the environment. The job often requires long working hours.

 **LOCATION** Ecologists can work in an office, laboratory, or in the field. Travel to sites may mean being away from home for extended periods.

 **THE REALITIES** Long periods of field work and research can be physically exhausting. Site-to-site travel can become extensive.

# ENGINEERING AND MANUFACTURING

If you enjoy learning how things work and improving them, there is a vast range of potential career options in this sector. Whether you are building new machines, conducting experiments, or analyzing the science behind it all, you will need to be creative, methodical, and organized.

### CIVIL ENGINEER
*Page 176*

By drawing up and following construction designs, civil engineers shape our environment. They oversee and deliver building projects on time and to budget.

### DRILLING ENGINEER
*Page 178*

At the cutting edge of fossil fuel exploration and extraction on land and at sea, drilling engineers design and install the wells that open up oil and gas fields.

### CHEMICAL ENGINEER
*Page 180*

Researching ways of using raw materials through new chemical processes, chemical engineers develop new substances and products for commercial profit.

### MECHANICAL ENGINEER
*Page 182*

Anything with moving parts—from a watch to a train— has been designed by a mechanical engineer, making this the broadest of all the engineering disciplines.

### MOTOR VEHICLE TECHNICIAN
*Page 184*

Using their practical skills and knowledge, motor vehicle technicians diagnose and fix problems and replace worn parts to keep our vehicles on the road.

### ELECTRICAL ENGINEER
*Page 186*

Designing, building, and maintaining a range of electrical systems and components, electrical engineers are the specialists whose job it is to keep the power on.

### TELECOM ENGINEER
*Page 188*

Working with telephones, mobile networks, radio, and the Internet, these engineers ensure that telecommunications networks stay connected across the globe.

### AEROSPACE ENGINEER
*Page 190*

Specializing in aircraft and space technology, aerospace engineers design, build, test, and maintain the vehicles that fly in—and beyond—our skies.

# CIVIL ENGINEER

## JOB DESCRIPTION

Civil engineers design and manage a wide range of infrastructure projects, both large and small, such as roads, bridges, and pipelines. A civil engineer's role is challenging and varied. It includes talking to clients, surveying sites, preparing designs (called blueprints), budgeting, assessing a project's environmental impact, and making sure a site meets health and safety standards.

### SALARY
Newly qualified graduate ★★★☆☆
Senior engineer ★★★★★

### INDUSTRY PROFILE
Worldwide sector • Steadily growing market • Many engineering jobs in the construction industry • Growing number of renewable-energy projects, such as wind and solar farms

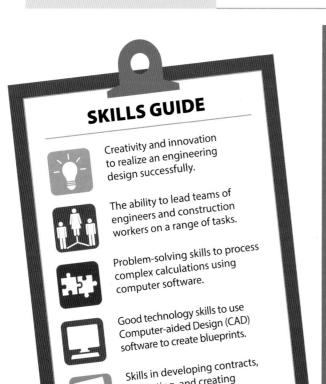

## SKILLS GUIDE

Creativity and innovation to realize an engineering design successfully.

The ability to lead teams of engineers and construction workers on a range of tasks.

Problem-solving skills to process complex calculations using computer software.

Good technology skills to use Computer-aided Design (CAD) software to create blueprints.

Skills in developing contracts, budgeting, and creating proposals for new projects.

## AT A GLANCE

**YOUR INTERESTS** Engineering • Construction • Physics • Mathematics • Computer-aided Design (CAD) • Geology • Materials science

**ENTRY QUALIFICATIONS** Most entrants hold an engineering degree, but it is possible to combine work and study to qualify as an engineer.

**LIFESTYLE** Civil engineers usually work regular hours. However, most roles will require frequent travel to work sites.

**LOCATION** Depending on the nature of a project, civil engineers work at home, offices, or building sites. They may need to travel both locally or overseas.

**THE REALITIES** Projects may require you to be away from home for periods of time. On-site environment is usually hazardous, and you may be working at great heights.

## CAREER PATHS

Civil engineers can choose from a number of specializations, including transportation, planning and designing roads and ports, working on dams and pipelines, dealing with waste and pollution, disaster prevention, and others.

The giant roller coasters in theme parks have all been designed by civil engineers.

**GRADUATE** A degree in civil engineering is the most common route into this career. Some employers offer graduate training programs.

**ENGINEERING TECHNICIAN**
Although higher education is required for a career in civil engineering, you can gain practical experience as an engineering technician while you work toward your degree.

**CIVIL ENGINEER** After gaining experience, you can study for further qualifications and seek professional accreditation. This will allow you to progress to more senior positions and specialized roles.

**CONTRACTING CIVIL ENGINEER** Implements the designs of consulting engineers on site, overseeing the work of contractors, checking quality and progress, and buying in appropriate materials and equipment.

**CONSULTING CIVIL ENGINEER** Plans and advises on engineering projects, working closely with clients and architects. They produce detailed designs and oversee the entire project.

**PROJECT MANAGER** Is in charge of an engineering project and makes sure the solutions are delivered to the highest possible standards, on time, and on budget.

### ▼ RELATED CAREERS

▶ **MECHANICAL ENGINEER** see pp. 182–183

▶ **STRUCTURAL ENGINEER** see pp. 196–197

▶ **COST ENGINEER** see pp. 198–199

▶ **ENGINEERING GEOLOGIST** Primarily analyzes the earth of a chosen site to ensure that a man-made structure will sit safely upon it.

▶ **MARINE ENGINEER** Designs and develops offshore structures, such as oil platforms, wind farms, and tidal barriers.

# DRILLING ENGINEER

## JOB DESCRIPTION

Drilling engineers are responsible for planning, coordinating, and managing oil and gas drilling operations. In this role, you will use a combination of geology, physics, and engineering to design, plan, and oversee the drilling of an oil and gas well. The majority of drilling engineers work for oil and gas companies, while others may work for consultant drilling contractors.

## SALARY

Drilling engineer ★★★☆☆
Senior drilling engineer ★★★★★

## INDUSTRY PROFILE

Most jobs in international companies and specialized consulting firms • First jobs can be highly paid and are currently in high demand • Number of jobs depends on economic conditions

## AT A GLANCE

**YOUR INTERESTS** Geology • Physics • Chemistry • Mathematics • Engineering • Geography • Languages • Information Technology (IT)

**ENTRY QUALIFICATIONS** A degree in a subject such as engineering, physics, or geology, or a related postgraduate degree, is required.

**LIFESTYLE** Most drilling engineers work long hours. Extended periods away from home and travel to drilling sites, possibly overseas, are common.

**LOCATION** Drilling engineers should expect to shuttle between the office and the wellsite (either an offshore or land-based drilling rig).

**THE REALITIES** Working on rigs may require travel by helicopter or boat. The work is physically challenging, and may involve dangerous conditions.

## ▼ RELATED CAREERS

▶ **GEOSCIENTIST** see pp. 148–149

▶ **MECHANICAL ENGINEER** see pp. 182–183

▶ **ENERGY ENGINEER** Researches and develops methods of generating energy from different sources, including renewable forms, such as wind, wave, geothermal, and solar power.

▶ **MARINE ENGINEER** Designs, builds, and tests oil rigs, pipelines, remotely operated vehicles, ships, boats, and support vessels for the oil, gas, and marine-leisure industries.

▶ **MINING ENGINEER** Plans, designs, and monitors new and existing mining and quarrying sites. Mining engineers are also responsible for ensuring that sites are safe and working efficiently.

Drilling engineers have extracted more than 43 billion barrels of oil from UK waters since the 1970s.

## CAREER PATHS

Drilling engineers typically gain on-the-job responsibility quickly, moving from managing small projects to larger, multi-million-dollar projects in a relatively short space of time. Training programs typically last for five years, and may include several changes of project and location.

**GRADUATE** You can apply for graduate training programs with a degree in subjects such as geology, natural sciences, or petroleum engineering.

**POSTGRADUATE** You may improve your chances of entry into this career if you have a higher-level degree. You may also begin your career in a area of drilling.

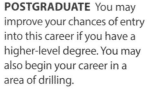

**DRILLING ENGINEER** Since some firms operate overseas, you may need to be fluent in a foreign language. With experience you can choose a particular specialty, or seek promotion to senior roles.

**DIRECTIONAL DRILLING ENGINEER** Specializes in techniques that enable wells to be drilled at an angle, in order to extract more oil and gas.

**DEEP WATER DRILLING ENGINEER** Specializes in drilling wells under the sea floor from floating or fixed platforms. These wells may be for the exploration of new gas or oil reserves, or for extraction.

**OIL COMPANY WELLSITE MANAGER** Oversees every aspect of the drilling project from the wellsite, on behalf of the oil company.

**HIGH-PRESSURE HIGH-TEMPERATURE DRILLING ENGINEER** Drills wells under high pressures and temperatures, which require advanced drilling equipment and technique.

**WELL TEST ENGINEER** Conducts technical checks to ensure the optimum conditions for production of oil and gas. Also monitors operations, equipment, and staff to ensure health and safety standards are met.

# CHEMICAL ENGINEER

## JOB DESCRIPTION

Chemical engineers develop the technologies that turn raw materials into useful products, such as paints, glues, textiles, and plastics. Some work in laboratories, designing new—or improving existing—products, while others specialize in developing efficient manufacturing processes—the machinery and techniques used to produce the products while meeting quality and safety standards.

### SALARY
Graduate industrial chemist ★★★☆☆
Senior engineer ★★★★☆

### INDUSTRY PROFILE
Huge global industry • Rising energy costs driving innovation • Manufacturing often based in countries with lower labor and resource costs

## AT A GLANCE

**YOUR INTERESTS** Chemistry • Mathematics • Physics • Biology • Technology • Project Management • Computing

**ENTRY QUALIFICATIONS** A degree in chemical, process, or biochemical engineering, as well as some practical experience, is required.

**LIFESTYLE** Working hours are regular in research and development, but shiftwork may be necessary in some processing and manufacturing fields.

**LOCATION** The work is usually based in an office, laboratory, or chemical plant. Chemical engineers may have to travel sometimes overseas to visit sites.

**THE REALITIES** This is a high-pressure job demanding swift problem-solving skills. Chemical engineers may be in charge of operating expensive facilities.

## SKILLS GUIDE

Good interpersonal skills to interact with a range of people across the industry.

Problem-solving and analytical skills to manage complex projects and large budgets.

Mathematical skills and an ability to apply scientific principles to real-world problems.

Expertise in specialized computer software, used to process data and control production lines.

The ability to predict and analyze the commercial results of scientific applications.

Creativity and innovation to define manufacturing processes that make industrial products.

## ▼ RELATED CAREERS

▶ **ENERGY ENGINEER** Researches and develops ways to generate energy from fossil fuels, such as coal and oil, as well as from renewable sources, such as wind, waves, and sunlight.

▶ **ENVIRONMENTAL ENGINEER** Uses knowledge of engineering, biology, and chemistry to help solve environment-related issues.

▶ **NUCLEAR ENGINEER** Designs and maintains facilities in the nuclear energy industry. Nuclear engineers are also responsible for decommissioning nuclear facilities when they shut down.

▶ **PROCESS ENGINEER** Uses chemical and mechanical engineering knowledge to develop efficient manufacturing and production processes.

Chemical engineers are expected to work in growing fields, such as alternative energies and biotechnology.

## CAREER PATHS

After completing a degree and obtaining experience in the industry, an engineer may need to study further to gain professional accreditation. You can then choose to specialize in production, research and development, or the sales and marketing of your company's products, or you may decide to move into management.

**GRADUATE** You need a degree or postgraduate certification in chemical engineering or a related subject. Larger employers in the field usually offer a graduate training plan, through which it is possible to gain valuable experience across different areas of the business.

**CHEMICAL ENGINEER** Once qualified, you have the option of focusing on researching new products, improving industrial products already in use, or managing activity at a manufacturing plant.

**PROCESS ENGINEER** Designs, maintains, and optimizes the processes used in the mass production of chemicals and other products. Works in areas as diverse as pharmaceuticals and oil refineries, and oversees the running of a manufacturing plant.

**RESEARCH ENGINEER** Specializes in the development of new products and manufacturing techniques. Some of this work is at the cutting edge of science, such as advancing new medicines or treatments.

**PROJECT MANAGER** Applies engineering, problem-solving, and organizational skills to lead technical projects. Manages timelines and costs while coordinating the efforts of a team.

# MECHANICAL ENGINEER

## JOB DESCRIPTION

As part of a production team, mechanical engineers design, build, test, and repair machinery that operates in many products, from dishwashers to automobiles to power stations. They use computer software—and increasingly 3-D printers—to create and test working prototypes of mechanical devices.

### SALARY

Junior mechanical engineer ★★★★★
Lead mechanical engineer ★★★★★

### INDUSTRY PROFILE

Broadest engineering discipline, covering high-tech areas to everyday technologies • Excellent job opportunities overseas • Focus on sustainable designs

## CAREER PATHS

Once qualified, a mechanical engineer is expected to join a professional engineering body and continue learning throughout their career. They may choose to specialize in one area of engineering or work on large-scale projects. Opportunities in sales and marketing, or a role in an independent consultancy, offer a path into the business side of the profession.

**BUSINESS MANAGER** Manages people and commercial activities in the engineering sector. These engineers usually have an interest in business, leading them to more corporate roles.

**TECHNICIAN** As a high school graduate, you may be able to find work as a trainee technician. This may involve installing and maintaining mechanical systems, but you will normally need to study part-time for a degree if you wish to qualify as a mechanical engineer.

**GRADUATE** After completing an engineering degree, you can join a graduate training program at a large company or take an entry-level position in a smaller firm.

**MECHANICAL ENGINEER** You will have many choices in this field, from working on the design of aircraft engines to developing wind turbines or improving the performance of cutting-edge medical technologies, such as prosthetic limbs or artificial hearts.

## SKILLS GUIDE

 Excellent communication skills for collaborating with colleagues on a range of projects.

 The creativity and innovation necessary to find working solutions to engineering problems.

 The ability to handle pressure while maintaining good working relationships.

 Good computer skills to work with Computer-aided Design (CAD) programs.

 A strong eye for detail and the ability to build and test working prototypes.

**MATERIALS ENGINEER** Develops and tests the properties of materials, such as their strength or resistance to corrosion, to see if they're fit for a specific purpose.

**INDUSTRIAL PRODUCTION MANAGER** Refines mechanical systems and deals with on-site problems that may arise at manufacturing facilities and production lines.

**MINING ENGINEER** Manages the safe operation of mechanized wells and mines for the efficient extraction of oil and minerals.

## ▼ RELATED CAREERS

▶ **PRODUCT DESIGNER** *see pp. 18–19*

▶ **AEROSPACE ENGINEER** *see pp. 190–191*

▶ **AUTOMOTIVE ENGINEER** Works in production plants, designing and manufacturing road vehicles. An automotive engineer may also build race cars or other specialized vehicles.

▶ **MECHATRONIC ENGINEER** Develops products by combining mechanical, electronic, and computer components. These products include home appliances, cameras, and computer hard drives.

▶ **ROBOTIC ENGINEER** Plans, builds, and maintains robots for use in a variety of sectors, from drilling engineering to motor vehicle manufacturing.

## AT A GLANCE

**YOUR INTERESTS** Engineering • Science • Mathematics • Physical sciences • Design • Computers

**ENTRY QUALIFICATIONS** A degree in mechanical engineering is usually required, although a higher degree may also be useful.

**LIFESTYLE** Regular hours are the norm, though engineers in some sectors may need to travel or work overnight to meet project deadlines.

**LOCATION** Although the work is mainly office based, engineers may need to make frequent visits to manufacturing and testing sites.

**THE REALITIES** Higher education in mechanical engineering is notoriously tough. Ongoing learning is essential to keep up to date with new technologies.

# MOTOR VEHICLE TECHNICIAN

## JOB DESCRIPTION

Motor vehicle technicians inspect faults and use computer-based tests to diagnose problems with a vehicle's mechanical or electrical systems, then repair, service, or replace any worn parts. This is a good profession for those who enjoy the challenge of dismantling, fixing, and maintaining mechanical systems.

## AT A GLANCE

**YOUR INTERESTS** Motor vehicles • Mechanical systems • Engineering • Electronics • Physics • Mathematics • Information Technology (IT)

**ENTRY QUALIFICATIONS** Good school grades in science and mathematics are usually required for trainee positions and vocational courses.

**LIFESTYLE** Most employees work full-time, but shift-work, overtime, and on-call hours—for breakdown services especially—are often required.

**LOCATION** The job is usually based in a workshop. Breakdown work requires travel as well as performing repairs outdoors and in all weather conditions.

**THE REALITIES** The job can be physically tiring, messy, and potentially dangerous due to the heavy, dirty, and hazardous nature of vehicle parts.

## CAREER PATHS

Technicians may specialize in a particular type of vehicle, such as electric or hybrid cars, or a particular make. Some build their expertise in suspension, steering, or wheels, for example. Options for progression include senior technician, workshop supervisor, or garage manager.

**TRAINEE** You can work as a trainee or apprentice motor vehicle technician, combining paid work with practical, on-the-job training.

**COLLEGE GRADUATE** You can gain a qualification before finding a job by taking a vocational course in motor vehicle technology. This will combine classroom instruction with workshop experience.

## SKILLS GUIDE

 Strong communication skills to explain faults to clients who have limited technical knowledge.

 Strength for lifting and reaching inaccessible parts, and stamina to concentrate for long periods.

 Good problem-solving skills for investigating, diagnosing, and fixing mechanical faults.

 Manual dexterity to use a wide variety of tools and handle complex vehicle components.

 Precision and attention to detail to disassemble parts and reassemble them correctly.

## ▼ RELATED CAREERS

▶ **MECHANICAL ENGINEER** *see pp. 182–183*

▶ **AUTO DAMAGE APPRAISER** Inspects vehicles that have been damaged in accidents to estimate the cost of repair.

▶ **AUTO PARTS ADVISOR/SALESPERSON** Orders and sells vehicle parts and accessories in addition to providing advice to customers on vehicle faults and other troubleshooting issues.

▶ **MOTOR VEHICLE BODY REPAIRER** Fixes, restores, and refinishes damaged vehicle parts. Repairers also inspect vehicles for damage, replace or repair affected body panels, and refinish paintwork.

**The number of vehicles is expected to rise, and technicians will still be needed to perform repairs.**

**FITTER** Also known as a "fast fitter," this specialized role involves repairing, testing, and fitting vehicle parts, including tires, brakes, exhausts, and batteries.

**MOTOR VEHICLE TECHNICIAN**
You perform preventative and repair work to make vehicles roadworthy. With experience, you could move into a senior workshop role or maintain a fleet of vehicles for a commercial firm.

**MOBILE TECHNICIAN** Assists drivers whose vehicles have broken down. Mobile technicians drive to the motorist's location, inspect the vehicle for faults, and make any necessary repairs or tow the vehicle to a repair center or to the driver's home.

**AIR-CONDITIONING/ REFRIGERATION TECHNICIAN** Specializes in the repair and maintenance of air-conditioning systems, handling any refrigerants in a manner that meets statutory safety requirements.

# ELECTRICAL ENGINEER

## SALARY

Engineering technician ★★★★★
Experienced engineer ★★★★★

## INDUSTRY PROFILE

Growing profession due to pace of technological innovation • New developments in solar energy and communication technologies are leading to range of career prospects

## JOB DESCRIPTION

Electrical engineers are employed in a wide range of sectors to design, install, and maintain electrical systems and components. In this role, you might work on infrastructure projects (such as developing low-energy street lighting), power-generation networks, construction projects, or consumer goods manufacturing. A key aspect of the job is ensuring equipment meets relevant safety and design standards.

## CAREER PATHS

Qualifying as an electrical engineer usually requires accreditation by a professional body. You can choose to specialize in one area, such as telecom or research. Alternatively, you can become a self-employed consultant or seek a senior role within the management team of an engineering firm.

**RELIABILITY ENGINEER** Finds reliability risks that could cause a process or product to falter. May test components, subsystems, and systems to assess product reliability.

**TECHNICIAN** You can find employment as an entry-level technician straight from high school, and then train on the job to achieve the necessary qualifications to become an accredited electrical technician.

**GRADUATE** With a degree in electrical engineering or a related subject, you can apply for graduate school to pursue an advanced degree in engineering or a related field.

**ELECTRICAL ENGINEER** Often working with experts in other disciplines, you may carry out studies, oversee the work of junior engineers and technicians, or conduct the testing and analysis of new systems. With experience, you can specialize or seek senior roles.

# SKILLS GUIDE

 Innovation and creativity for designing parts and equipment that fulfill the client's brief.

 Strong leadership skills to ensure that colleagues work to relevant electrical safety standards.

 Good analytical skills to understand complex technical problems and devise cost-effective solutions.

 High-level mathematical skills for recording, analyzing, and interpreting product test data.

 Proficiency in using computer software and hardware when installing and fixing equipment.

**TELECOMMUNICATIONS ENGINEER** Specializes in the design and maintenance of electronic telecommunications technology, such as broadband, wireless networks, fiber-optic cabling, and satellite systems.

**CONSULTING ENGINEER** Provides advice to clients on the design and build of electrical systems and components, from power distribution to fire safety systems and interior lighting.

**RESEARCH ENGINEER** Works at a college or corporate research facility, carrying out research into emerging areas, such as nanoelectronics—electrical engineering on a molecular scale.

## AT A GLANCE

 **YOUR INTERESTS** Electrical circuitry • Engineering • Mathematics • Computing • Science • Physics • Optics • Technical drawing

 **ENTRY QUALIFICATIONS** A degree in electrical engineering or a related subject is required. Internships or apprenticeships may be available.

 **LIFESTYLE** Most electrical engineers work regular office hours, but evening, weekend, or on-call work may be required in some sectors.

 **LOCATION** The work is based in an office or workshop, but visits to service equipment, monitor installations, or oversee manufacturing are common.

 **THE REALITIES** Continual learning is required to keep pace with fast-changing technologies. Numerous career options are available.

## ▼ RELATED CAREERS

▶ **SYSTEMS ANALYST** see pp. 120–121

▶ **NETWORK ENGINEER** see pp. 124–125

▶ **MECHANICAL ENGINEER** see pp. 182–183

▶ **BROADCAST ENGINEER** Operates systems used in television, radio, and new-media broadcasts.

▶ **INFORMATION TECHNOLOGY (IT) CONSULTANT** Advises businesses on how to use IT systems to resolve operational issues.

▶ **ROBOTIC ENGINEER** Plans, builds, and maintains robots for use in a variety of sectors.

▶ **SOLAR ENERGY ENGINEER** Designs solar arrays that harness sunlight to generate electricity.

# TELECOM ENGINEER

## JOB DESCRIPTION

A telecommunications—or telecom—engineer works with a variety of technologies that enable the exchange of data and communications. These include cell and fixed-line telephones, radio, cable or wireless broadband Internet, fiber optics, and satellite-based systems. As a telecom engineer, you design, install, test, or repair these systems for clients that may range from large organizations to individual customers.

### SALARY

Graduate trainee engineer ★★★★★
Senior telecom engineer ★★★★★

### INDUSTRY PROFILE

Growing sector due to increase of technologies • Employers include manufacturers of communications systems and devices, government departments, and telecom providers

## AT A GLANCE

**YOUR INTERESTS** Electronics • Information Technology (IT) • Electrical engineering • Software engineering • Mathematics • Physics

**ENTRY QUALIFICATIONS** A degree in telecommunications, electrical engineering, computer science, or a related subject is required.

**LIFESTYLE** Full-time office hours are the norm, but telecom engineers may have to work overtime to meet deadlines. Self-employed contract work is common.

**LOCATION** Engineers mostly work in an office, but travel is required for site visits, meetings, or conferences. Hybrid working is also possible.

**THE REALITIES** Meeting delivery deadlines can be stressful. However, working at the forefront of developing technologies can be rewarding.

## CAREER PATHS

Telecommunications engineering is a broad field. Following a degree, most telecom engineers join a graduate training program and specialize in an area, such as broadcast technology or computer networks. You must continue learning throughout your career to keep pace with fast-changing technologies.

**TECHNICIAN** Studying at a vocational school will enable you to work as a technician, testing and maintaining telecom equipment. You can then study for a degree while employed.

**GRADUATE** With a degree in a technical subject, you can enter a company's graduate training program. You can increase your chances of entry with previous work experience, such as an industrial placement.

## ▼ RELATED CAREERS

▶ **SYSTEMS ANALYST** *see pp. 120–121*

▶ **ELECTRICAL ENGINEER** *see pp. 186–187*

▶ **AEROSPACE ENGINEER** *see pp. 190–191*

▶ **TELECOMMUNICATIONS RESEARCHER** Studies new forms of telecommunications technology.

The introduction and growth of 5G technology will lead to many new job opportunities for telecom engineers.

# SKILLS GUIDE

 Good communication skills to explain complex design solutions to technicians and customers.

 Strong team-working skills to collaborate with other specialists on multidisciplinary projects.

 The ability to find creative, innovative, and cost-effective solutions to design challenges.

 Strong analytical skills for understanding a vast and evolving range of technologies.

 The ability to multitask and prioritize jobs while managing several projects at once.

**BROADCAST ENGINEER** Operates and maintains hardware and software systems for broadcasting content via television, radio, and new-media channels, ensuring that the content is transmitted on time and to a high standard of quality.

**SATELLITE ENGINEER** Specializes in installing, configuring, and repairing satellite communications equipment used in areas including television services for home users or videoconferencing to remote sites.

**NETWORK ENGINEER** Installs and maintains IT networks—such as fiber-optic, wired, and wireless systems—used by businesses and Internet Service Providers (ISPs).

**TELECOM ENGINEER** As a telecom engineer, you must possess technical expertise to understand and design telecom systems, and management skills to ensure that your projects are run efficiently. You can choose to work freelance or as a company employee.

**INTEGRATION/TEST ENGINEER** Writes, modifies, and tests the computer code that underpins most telecommunications technologies.

# AEROSPACE ENGINEER

## JOB DESCRIPTION

Aerospace engineers design, build, and maintain a range of aircraft and spacecraft, from passenger airliners and military jets to satellites and space vehicles. In this role, you might work on the parts that make up the aircraft's fuselage, wings, or undercarriage, or the instruments and electronic systems that enable the pilot and crew to operate the craft.

### SALARY

Junior aerospace engineer ★★★★★
Senior aerospace engineer ★★★★★

### INDUSTRY PROFILE

Global opportunities • Diverse industry shaped by technological advances • Jobs in aircraft manufacturing firms, airline operators, armed forces, and government research agencies

## ▼ RELATED CAREERS

▶ **MECHANICAL ENGINEER** see pp. 182–183

▶ **ELECTRICAL ENGINEER** see pp. 186–187

▶ **DESIGN ENGINEER** Works in a range of industries, developing ideas for the design of new products and researching ways to improve existing ones.

In 2019, the US aerospace and defense industry employed more than 2.5 million people.

## AT A GLANCE

**YOUR INTERESTS** Aviation, aircraft, and flight technology • Mathematics • Physics • Information Technology (IT) • Engineering • Chemistry • Robotics

**ENTRY QUALIFICATIONS** A degree in aerospace engineering or similar, such as mechanical engineering or physics, is a minimum requirement.

**LIFESTYLE** Working hours are regular, but evening or weekend work may be necessary to meet project deadlines, or to deal with repairs and emergencies.

**LOCATION** Engineers usually carry out design work in an office, but may also visit aircraft hangars, production sites, or aeronautical laboratories.

**THE REALITIES** The job bears great responsibility as the work has a direct impact on the functioning of aircraft and the safety of passengers and crew.

# CAREER PATHS

Aerospace engineering offers good prospects for career development. Specializing in a particular area—such as aerodynamics—is common, and training courses to improve professional skills are possible throughout one's career.

**TRAINEE** You can find work as an aerospace technician or trainee apprentice without a degree, but further qualifications are required to become an engineer.

**GRADUATE** You need a degree in engineering or a related field, such as physics or mathematics. Some firms offer graduate training programs.

**AEROSPACE ENGINEER** In this sector, you may specialize in research and development, aircraft systems testing, or maintenance and production. You can advance into senior project management positions or specialize in a particular technical area, such as aerodynamics or aircraft engines.

**ROTORCRAFT ENGINEER** Designs and develops helicopter components such as engines, electrical systems, and blade technology.

## SKILLS GUIDE

 Excellent verbal and written communication skills to explain complex designs clearly.

 The ability to work in a team to coordinate the designs for the numerous parts of an aircraft.

 Creativity and innovation to develop designs in keeping with technological advances.

 Good problem-solving skills for finding effective solutions to technical design issues.

 The capacity to use advanced mathematical methods to assist designing and problem-solving.

**ASTRONAUTICAL ENGINEER** Specializes in the research, design, and development of vehicles for space exploration, including rockets and satellites.

**AVIONICS AND SYSTEMS ENGINEER** Designs electronic equipment used in civil and military aircraft, such as flight-control and weapon-combat systems.

**AERODYNAMICIST** Researches the effect of airflow on the speed and performance of vehicles in order to improve stability and fuel-efficiency, and reduce the environmental impact of aircraft.

**MATERIALS AND STRUCTURES ENGINEER** Designs and builds the body and framework of an aircraft, before testing it to ensure that the structure is strong and durable.

# CONSTRUCTION

A vast sector with global opportunities, the construction industry requires a steady supply of skilled personnel to keep up with demand from domestic and commercial customers. If you enjoy being practical and hands-on, there is a range of career options available.

# ARCHITECT

## JOB DESCRIPTION

An architect plans and designs buildings for a range of clients, from companies developing healthcare or sports facilities to individuals erecting their own homes. Architects may design new buildings, work on existing structures, or specialize in the restoration and conservation of historic sites. They are responsible for budgeting a project, making sure it runs on time, and for managing the workflow of the people involved.

### SALARY

Newly qualified architect ★★✩✩✩
Senior architect ★★★★★

### INDUSTRY PROFILE

Employment opportunities linked to the state of construction industry • Rising demand for architects due to growth in housing market • Growth in sustainable ("green") architecture

## AT A GLANCE

**YOUR INTERESTS** Art • Design • Construction • Design technology • Materials science • Engineering • Physics • Mathematics

**ENTRY QUALIFICATIONS** A degree followed by at least a two-year apprenticeship and licensing exams are required for entry.

**LIFESTYLE** Architects may work regular office hours, but more often than not, project deadlines demand longer hours.

**LOCATION** Architects spend much of their time in offices, where they meet with clients. Some architects work from home offices.

**THE REALITIES** Markets can be affected by changes in the economy. Pay can vary greatly between the public and private sectors.

## CAREER PATHS

There are typically three main steps to becoming a licensed architect: completing a bachelor's degree in architecture, gaining relevant experience through an internship, and passing exams to earn professional accreditation. Large architectural practices offer opportunities for promotion, but many architects choose to set up their own business or to take jobs with property developers or local authorities.

**DISTANCE EDUCATION STUDENT** Some universities offer online courses in architecture. For most of these degrees, you first need an accredited undergraduate degree.

**GRADUATE** An architecture degree can take up to five years, after which you will need to work and learn under professional supervision before registering as a qualified architect.

## ▼ RELATED CAREERS

▶ **PRODUCT DESIGNER** *see pp. 18–19*

▶ **LANDSCAPE ARCHITECT** *see pp. 170–171*

▶ **CIVIL ENGINEER** *see pp. 176–177*

▶ **STRUCTURAL ENGINEER** *see pp. 196–197*

▶ **QUANTITY SURVEYOR** *see pp. 198–199*

▶ **TOWN PLANNER** *see pp. 200–201*

▶ **CONSTRUCTION MANAGER** *see pp. 204–205*

▶ **BUILDING INFORMATION MODELER** Produces 3-D images and photo-realistic animations to aid the design and building process.

# SKILLS GUIDE

 Strong communication skills and the ability to liaise with clients and the construction team.

 A willingness to work in a team of construction personnel of varying skills and abilities.

 Artistic flair and the creativity to generate unique and innovative design ideas.

 Efficient management skills for running design projects, both on a large and small scale.

 Good technical knowledge and a logical, analytical approach toward challenges.

 Attention to detail in order to produce drawings and designs to exact specifications.

**RESIDENTIAL ARCHITECT** Designs and builds homes and residential properties to be functional and visually appealing. Specialty knowledge of residential building regulations is also important.

**ARCHITECT** Once licensed, an architect can design a variety of different kinds of buildings or choose to specialize.

**COMMERCIAL ARCHITECT** Designs and builds retail, office buildings, and other large commercial structures, cooperating closely with engineers and interior and landscape designers.

**CIVIC ARCHITECT** Designs public buildings, usually working with a local authority, town council, or government agency.

**CONSERVATION ARCHITECT** Specializes in the conservation of old buildings, ranging from ancient monuments to listed residential properties.

# STRUCTURAL ENGINEER

## JOB DESCRIPTION

Structural engineers help to design buildings and infrastructure, such as bridges, railroads, dams, and tunnels. They analyze the forces that a structure may face, such as winds, people loads, and traffic, and work with architects and civil engineers to ensure that it is built to required standards of strength and safety.

### SALARY

Entry level structural engineer ★★★★★
Senior structural engineer ★★★★★

### INDUSTRY PROFILE

Growing industry with opportunities around the globe • Renewable energy projects on the rise • Employers range from governments to a variety of contractors and consulting firms

## AT A GLANCE

**YOUR INTERESTS** Engineering • Mathematics • Physics • Information Technology (IT) • Design • Geography • Drawing and modelmaking

**ENTRY QUALIFICATIONS** A degree in structural or civil engineering from an accredited program is required. Advanced degrees may be needed.

**LIFESTYLE** Regular office hours are the norm, although engineers may need to be on call to deal with emergencies, such as damaged or unstable buildings.

**LOCATION** Most engineers divide their time between an office and construction sites. They may occasionally need to travel around the country for work.

**THE REALITIES** Construction is one of the first sectors to be affected in an economic slump. Sites are often dusty and noisy, and can be dangerous.

## ▼ RELATED CAREERS

▶ **CIVIL ENGINEER** *see pp. 176–177*

▶ **ARCHITECT** *see pp. 194–195*

▶ **BUILDING INSPECTOR** Ensures that building regulations and other laws are followed in the design and construction of houses, offices, and other buildings. Building control officers also make sure that property alterations, such as extensions and conversions, meet all the current regulations.

▶ **COMPUTER-AIDED DESIGN (CAD) TECHNICIAN** Uses computer design software to create plans for buildings and machinery. CAD technicians can work in a range of industries, including construction, manufacturing, and engineering.

Demand for structural engineers is increasing, partly due to growing numbers of aging buildings.

# CAREER PATHS

Qualified structural engineers often specialize in working on one type of building or material—oil platforms or concrete structures, for example. With experience, many move into managing construction projects or become consultants.

## SKILLS GUIDE

Good communication skills—both verbal and written—to deal with clients and prepare reports.

The ability to use mathematical analysis to determine whether a structure can withstand loads.

Problem-solving abilities to spot issues and propose and design solutions throughout project.

Budgeting expertise and commercial awareness of business implications of design decisions.

Excellent organizational skills to schedule and fulfil all stages of the planning and design process.

**INTERN** You can study for an undergraduate engineering degree on the job while working as an intern, or in a co-op program.

**GRADUATE** You will need an accredited degree in a subject such as civil or structural engineering to apply for jobs. Graduate training programs are available.

**STRUCTURAL ENGINEER** After gaining experience in junior roles and passing your professional exams, you can practice as a qualified structural engineer. You can then choose to design a variety of buildings or bridges, or select a specialized area to work in.

**FORENSIC ENGINEER** Investigates the reasons for failure or collapse of a structure in situations such as criminal damage, human error, or natural disaster.

**PROJECT MANAGER** Liaises closely with all of the personnel on a construction project, ensuring that everything happens on time and to brief. A project manager may work independently or as leader of a team.

**CONSERVATION AND RESTORATION ENGINEER** Works on the conservation and restoration of historic buildings and structures, combining old and new construction methods.

**HUMANITARIAN ENGINEER** Contributes to disaster relief work in the reconstruction of infrastructure and buildings damaged by natural disasters.

**SEISMIC ENGINEER** Designs buildings in earthquake-prone areas to ensure that they can cope with seismic movements in the ground in order to minimize building damage and improve safety.

# COST ENGINEER

## JOB DESCRIPTION

Cost engineers, or cost estimators, play a key role in every large construction project. With expertise in building techniques and materials, they calculate, monitor, and control the costs of a construction project to ensure value for money. They also liaise with other experts, such as engineers, to ensure quality standards and analyze risk.

### SALARY

Junior cost engineer ★★☆☆☆
Senior cost engineer ★★★★☆

### INDUSTRY PROFILE

Worldwide opportunities in areas of economic growth • Industry subject to economic downturns • Careers available in both public and private sectors

## CAREER PATHS

Cost engineers can work on a variety of projects at any one time, such as the restoration of historic monuments or the construction of giant skyscrapers. Although most cost engineers work in the construction industry, there are also some jobs to be found in the manufacturing and civil engineering industries.

**INFRASTRUCTURE COST ENGINEER** Specializes in projects involving infrastructure, such as railways, ports, and airports, or energy and water networks.

**INTERN** Employers look for candidates with hands-on experience in the field. One way to earn this experience early on is through industry internships.

**GRADUATE** With a bachelor's degree in a related field, such as industrial and mechanical engineering, you will be able to apply for entry-level positions in the industry.

**COST ENGINEER** You may be asked to obtain additional certification before becoming a cost engineer. With experience, you will be able to specialize in one of several sectors.

# SKILLS GUIDE

Good language skills for producing reports and communicating with many different types of clients.

The ability to work as part of a team, and to persuade and negotiate with other people.

Excellent analytical skills and an organized, logical, and methodical approach to problem-solving.

Strong numerical skills for calculating estimates and costs, and keeping track of budgets.

Extensive knowledge of commercial building methods, materials, and legislation.

**COST DIRECTOR**
Supervises accounts and cost engineers across a variety of projects. This is a more senior and strategic role.

**PROCESS ENGINEER** Helps to manage the processes and facilities in one of many possible energy industries, from oil and gas, to chemical and renewables.

Cost engineers don't only point out inefficiencies—they help fix them.

## ▼ RELATED CAREERS

▶ **CIVIL ENGINEER** *see pp. 176–177*

▶ **BUILDING CONTROL OFFICER** Visits sites to ensure that construction workers follow building regulations, such as fire and safety.

▶ **CONSTRUCTION INSPECTOR** Inspects project sites to ensure that construction professionals meet health, safety, and quality standards in the plans they draw up.

▶ **CONTRACTS MANAGER** Manages all aspects of construction contracts and prepares documents for all project presentations.

▶ **SURVEYOR** Uses a range of techniques to survey land, take measurements, and gather data for companies planning to develop an area. They are also known as geomatic surveyors.

## AT A GLANCE

**YOUR INTERESTS** Construction • Structural engineering • Finance • Mathematics • Economics • Civil engineering • Physics • Geography

**ENTRY QUALIFICATIONS** A degree in an industry-related subject, such as industrial engineering or mechanical engineering, is required.

**LIFESTYLE** Cost engineers typically work regular hours. Overtime may be required to meet deadlines, as well as travel to various sites.

**LOCATION** Traveling to meet clients and view sites is common. Working away from home, even overseas, for several months is also common.

**THE REALITIES** Time constraints can be stressful, and long hours may be necessary to complete projects to strict deadlines.

# TOWN PLANNER

## JOB DESCRIPTION

Shaping the development of towns and cities is a balancing act between the economic and social needs of a community. Environmental concerns, housing, economic development, and cultural and recreational interests are all considered. As a town planner, you must examine and balance these issues, and make a judgment on planning applications proposed by individuals and companies.

### SALARY

Assistant town planner ★★☆☆☆
Chief planning officer ★★★★★

### INDUSTRY PROFILE

Jobs dependent on growing population and their need for houses • Economic fluctuations affect the rise or fall of planning applications • Fierce competition for coveted jobs

## CAREER PATHS

After graduating from college, town planners usually start their careers in local or regional government. With experience, they can progress to more senior planning roles within government agencies, or choose to work with developers and construction firms in the private sector to help them negotiate complex planning regulations.

**SENIOR PLANNING OFFICER** Takes on complex planning projects, such as landscape conservation and large-scale urban developments. This involves supervising junior staff and keeping on top of larger budgets.

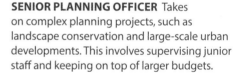

**GRADUATE** You can start with a town planning degree recognized by a professional planning body. Alternatively, you can study for a degree in geography, architecture, statistics, environmental science, or followed by graduate training in town planning.

**TOWN PLANNER** Once qualified as a town planner, you will generally start work as an assistant. After gaining experience, you have a choice between several career routes.

**PLANNING CONSULTANT** Works as a private consultant with property developers, government, charities, and other agencies on a range of major planning projects.

# SKILLS GUIDE

 Good writing skills, and the ability to communicate and negotiate with a wide range of people.

 Time-management skills to meet deadlines on several projects running at once.

 Excellent problem-solving skills for analyzing planning applications from clients.

 Knowledge of new developments in the field, political initiatives, and environmental issues.

 Clear understanding of planning rules and regulations to be able to prepare detailed reports.

**CHIEF PLANNING OFFICER**
Manages a local or regional planning office and works with other branches of government to prepare the designs necessary to shape a town or region.

It is predicted that by 2050 around two-thirds of the global population will live in cities.

## ▼ RELATED CAREERS

▶ **LANDSCAPE ARCHITECT** *see pp. 170–171*

▶ **CIVIL ENGINEER** *see pp. 176–177*

▶ **ARCHITECT** *see pp. 194–195*

▶ **STRUCTURAL ENGINEER** *see pp. 196–197*

▶ **COST ENGINEER** *see pp. 198–199*

▶ **HISTORIC BUILDINGS INSPECTOR** Ensures that a wide variety of historic buildings are preserved and maintained appropriately.

▶ **HOUSING MANAGER** Supports the development of new housing for local authorities and housing associations. Housing managers work with people living in local authority-owned housing schemes.

## AT A GLANCE

 **YOUR INTERESTS** Urban design • Geography • Environmental studies • Mathematics • Landscape design • Computer-aided Design (CAD)

 **ENTRY QUALIFICATIONS** Employers typically look for candidates with a bachelor's degree, a master's degree, and professional accreditation.

 **LIFESTYLE** Work hours are regular, but town planners may have to work overtime to meet clients, view sites, and attend public meetings.

 **LOCATION** Town planners work in an office some of the time, but travel is required to view potential sites and meet with developers and the public.

 **THE REALITIES** Dealing with tight schedules and budgets can be stressful. Local people may also disagree with planning decisions and developments.

# BUILDER

## JOB DESCRIPTION

Builders work on construction sites or existing structures, building anything from houses and office blocks to factories, roads, and bridges. As a builder, you must have a thorough understanding of health and safety requirements and building materials, and often work alongside other construction professionals—like architects—to complete projects on schedule and to design plans.

### SALARY

Junior builder ★☆☆☆☆
Experienced builder ★★★☆☆

### INDUSTRY PROFILE

Huge range of building projects, from highway construction to house renovation • Building work available worldwide • Transferable skills make it easy to switch between industries

## CAREER PATHS

When first entering the construction industry, builders are likely to perform laborious tasks, such as moving materials and assisting other workers. Supervisory roles come as experience is gained. Most builders specialize in a particular area, such as welding or concrete, but it is possible to move into management and remain involved—at a supervisory level—in all stages of construction.

**TRADESPERSON** Works in one or a combination of roles, such as bricklaying, roofing, plumbing, electrical work, drywalling, carpentry, or scaffolding.

**APPRENTICE** You can enter the construction industry out of high school by taking an apprenticeship with a building company. Some groups, including unions, may sponsor you.

**TECHNICAL SCHOOL TRAINING** You will improve your job prospects by taking classes—such as bricklaying, carpentry, or plumbing—at college before finding work as a builder.

**BUILDER** As a builder, you can work on a self-employed basis or join a construction firm, where you could rise through the ranks to become a manager. With experience, you can specialize in roles such as a building technician.

# SKILLS GUIDE

Good numerical skills to take accurate measurements on job site and calculate financial reports.

Strong team-working skills for collaborating with fellow construction staff.

The flexibility to adapt to new projects and to travel to work at different building sites.

Physical fitness and resilience to perform manual work in a range of weather conditions.

Manual dexterity for using hand tools and construction machinery safely and efficiently.

**BUILDING CONTRACTOR**
Oversees a project for a building firm, hiring, managing, and coordinating the required construction workers and equipment to complete the job.

**SITE SUPERVISOR** Manages the day-to-day activities of the bricklayers, electricians, carpenters, and other tradespeople on the building site.

**STONE MASON** Specializes in restoring and creating stonework and decorative features. Masons work on new as well as historic buildings.

**BUILDING TECHNICIAN** Estimates building costs, negotiates the purchase of materials, ensures quality standards are maintained, and supervises contractors on site.

## AT A GLANCE

**YOUR INTERESTS** Construction • Design technology • Technical drawing • Mathematics • Physical education

**ENTRY QUALIFICATIONS** There are no formal entry requirements. Most entrants learn their trade skills at college or as building apprentices.

**LIFESTYLE** Most builders work regular hours. Evening and weekend work may be required to complete a project or to make the most of favorable conditions.

**LOCATION** Builders usually work on construction sites or in buildings. Some travel is required; overnight stays are likely if sites are far from home.

**THE REALITIES** The work is physically demanding and requires strength, agility, and resilience for working in poor weather or challenging conditions.

## ▼ RELATED CAREERS

▶ **CIVIL ENGINEER** *see pp. 176–177*

▶ **STRUCTURAL ENGINEER** *see pp. 196–197*

▶ **CARPENTER** *see pp. 206–207*

▶ **ELECTRICIAN** *see pp. 208–209*

▶ **PLUMBER** *see pp. 210–211*

▶ **SCAFFOLDER** Constructs scaffolding poles, platforms, and ladders to enable builders to access high-level exterior areas of a building. Scaffolders are also trained to use ropes and climbing equipment to reach inaccessible areas.

# CONSTRUCTION MANAGER

## JOB DESCRIPTION

Construction managers plan, coordinate, and oversee construction projects. They ensure that the work is completed according to the client's specifications, and take responsibility for budgets, schedules, health and safety standards, and the hiring of construction staff and subcontractors.

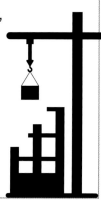

### SALARY

Junior construction manager ★★☆☆☆
Senior construction manager ★★★★★

### INDUSTRY PROFILE

Vast industry, with scope for working for employers of all sizes, in locations around the world • High demand for construction managers • Growth in sustainable ("green") buildings

## AT A GLANCE

**YOUR INTERESTS** Engineering • Design and construction • Project management • Mathematics • Physics • Economics

**ENTRY QUALIFICATIONS** A degree in civil engineering, building studies, or similar is usually required, but work-based routes may be available.

**LIFESTYLE** Construction managers tend to work regular hours, but working evenings and weekends may also be necessary to meet deadlines.

**LOCATION** Work is usually office-based, but construction managers make frequent site visits to oversee projects and check their quality and progress.

**THE REALITIES** It can take up to a decade to gain sufficient industry experience to be considered for construction management jobs.

## CAREER PATHS

There is no defined route to becoming a construction manager, but in-depth industry experience is required. Work opportunities are extensive, from large or small construction companies and specialized building-services contractors to utility firms, government departments, and housing associations.

**ASSISTANT** You can study for work-based qualifications in construction management while working as an assistant. If you have relevant prior experience, such as in surveying, this job can be attained without a degree.

**GRADUATE** You can enter the construction industry if you have a degree in a related subject, and gain the necessary experience to become a construction manager. Alternatively, you can apply for a graduate training program.

## ▼ RELATED CAREERS

▶ **LANDSCAPE ARCHITECT** *see pp. 170–171*

▶ **CIVIL ENGINEER** *see pp. 176–177*

▶ **BUILDER** *see pp. 202–203*

▶ **CONSTRUCTION ARBITRATOR** Investigates and helps to resolve any disputes that arise during building projects. This is a role that requires extensive experience in the construction industry.

▶ **FACILITIES MANAGER** Ensures that business premises and the services required to use and maintain them—such as cleaning, parking, air conditioning, and security—meet the needs of the people who use the facilities.

# SKILLS GUIDE

 Excellent communication skills for working effectively with people at all levels of the industry.

 Good organizational skills for coordinating teams to finish projects on time and to budget.

 Attention to detail to understand complex technical data, and focus to ensure objectives are met.

 Problem solving, leadership, and management skills for motivating and inspiring project personnel.

 Juggling many people with various skills to complete projects on time and budget is important.

**CONTRACTS MANAGER** Identifies potential building contracts for their company to bid for, then manages the bidding process, and may monitor the execution of the subsequent contract.

**CIVIL ENGINEER** Inspects property or land earmarked for construction. Provides the client with a report describing the state of the property and suggests options for repair and maintenance.

**COST ENGINEER/ESTIMATOR** Works on large construction projects, monitoring costs and liaising with experts, such as engineers, to ensure that legal and quality standards are met.

**CONSTRUCTION MANAGER** You will need solid experience in the construction industry to progress. Advanced study or professional accreditation may enhance your career prospects.

**CONSULTANT** Assists on projects and offers expertise and best-practice advice to complete them safely and efficiently. Consultants usually work for a consulting firm or a construction organization.

# CARPENTER

## JOB DESCRIPTION

A carpenter makes and installs the wooden elements of a building. These include its large structural pieces, such as the roof beams, floor supports, and wall partitions, as well as the internal fixtures, such as staircases, kitchen cabinets, doors, and baseboards. Carpenters follow drawings and blueprints, and ensure that their work meets safety and quality standards.

### SALARY

Apprentice carpenter ★☆☆☆☆
Experienced carpenter ★★☆☆☆

### INDUSTRY PROFILE

Self-employment is common • Building of new homes is expected to increase as the population grows • Many experienced carpenters take on contracting roles in construction

## CAREER PATHS

There are many opportunities for carpenters in the construction industry. While working, you can study for further vocational qualifications if you wish to specialize in areas such as cabinet making or building conservation.

**FURNITURE MAKER**
Makes pieces of wooden furniture, such as chairs, tables, and cupboards. Some also carry out restoration work on antique items and properties.

**TRADE SCHOOL STUDENT**
If you have an interest in carpentry, you can study for a certificate in carpentry or joinery in college to help you find employment. You can then study for higher diplomas if you wish to specialize.

**APPRENTICE** Some larger construction or kitchen fitting companies may employ you as an apprentice straight from high school, allowing you to learn on the job.

**CARPENTER** You may focus on one area of construction, such as making the frames of buildings, but most carpenters provide a wide range of services to their clients.

# SKILLS GUIDE

 Ability to work in a team with site manager and coworkers, and strong multitasking skills.

 Creativity to make decorative elements of furniture, unique trims, and fittings.

 Good numerical skills for taking accurate measurements and making calculations.

 Manual dexterity for using a wide range of hand and power tools to cut, shape, and join materials.

 Physical strength for lifting heavy items and holding them in place while fixing them into position.

 **MILL WORKER** Specializes in making wooden items in a workshop. These may include staircases, cupboards, doors, roof beams, and wardrobes.

 **CABINET MAKER/KITCHEN FITTER** Installs and fits kitchen cupboards, worktops, and trims. Fitters follow layouts drawn up by a designer to achieve the look requested by their customers.

 **SITE CARPENTER/FRAMER** Makes the wooden sections of a property on a building site. They also prepare scaffolds or forms (the molds that hold poured concrete).

## ▼ RELATED CAREERS

▶ **PRODUCT DESIGNER** *see pp. 18–19*

▶ **BOAT BUILDER** Builds new boats or carries out repairs on existing vessels using a range of carpentry, engineering, and plumbing skills.

▶ **PAINTER AND DECORATOR** Applies paint, wallpaper, and other coatings to walls and surfaces of a building to improve its appearance.

▶ **ROOFER** Repairs and builds roofs on houses and commercial properties, using materials such as slates, tiles, and wood.

▶ **THEATER SET DESIGNER** Creates the sets that are used for stage shows. They use their artistic skills and knowledge of lighting and costumes to create the right visual setting for the production.

## AT A GLANCE

 **YOUR INTERESTS** Woodwork • Engineering • Design technology • Construction • Mathematics • Art and design • Health and fitness

 **ENTRY QUALIFICATIONS** College courses in carpentry or joinery are not essential, but will help you find work. Apprenticeships are important.

 **LIFESTYLE** Working hours are regular, but early starts are common. Carpenters may need to work overtime on some projects.

 **LOCATION** Some jobs require work on site in harsh weather. Carpenters may need to work away from home for long periods on jobs located far away.

 **THE REALITIES** Carpentry can be physically demanding. Building construction slows down in the colder months, leading to a scarcity of jobs.

# ELECTRICIAN

## JOB DESCRIPTION

Electricians install and repair electrical equipment, such as power circuits, lighting, switches, and other fittings. Most work on site, visiting homes, shops, offices, and factories. Others train in specialized areas, such as street lighting, high-voltage systems used to transmit electricity over long distances, or the electrical wiring that supplies power to heavy industries.

### SALARY

Trainee electrician ★★☆☆☆
Experienced electrician ★★★☆☆

### INDUSTRY PROFILE

Wide variety of employment options • Self-employment is common • Salaries can vary considerably depending on specialty and experience

## AT A GLANCE

**YOUR INTERESTS** Electronics • Mathematics • Physics • Engineering • Information Technology (IT) • Buildings and maintenance

**ENTRY QUALIFICATIONS** There are no set requirements, but employers who offer apprenticeships often look for candidates with a high-school diploma.

**LIFESTYLE** Most electricians have regular hours, but may have to work evenings or weekends, or be on call for emergency repairs.

**LOCATION** Electricians work on site in a variety of settings, such as homes, factories, or shops.

**THE REALITIES** The job can involve working in cramped or dirty spaces. Keeping track of changing building regulations can be challenging.

## ▼ RELATED CAREERS

▶ **ELECTRICAL ENGINEER** *see pp. 186–187*

▶ **HEATING, AIR CONDITIONING, AND REFRIGERATION MECHANIC** Works on heating, ventilation, cooling, and refrigeration systems.

▶ **HOME APPLIANCE TECHNICIAN** Installs and repairs appliances, such as washing machines.

▶ **KITCHEN INSTALLER** Installs kitchen interiors, including countertops, cabinets, and trims.

▶ **ELEVATOR INSTALLER AND REPAIRER** Installs, fixes, and maintains elevators and other lifts.

▶ **WIND TURBINE TECHNICIAN** Tests and maintains wind turbines to ensure they are working smoothly and efficiently.

The demand for electricians will increase as the renewable energy industry grows.

## CAREER PATHS

The industry is tightly regulated, so you will need to complete approved training, finish an apprenticeship, and, in most states, obtain a license. Many electricians are self-employed or work as contractors for construction companies. Others are employed by manufacturers, engineering companies, or government bodies.

**TRAINEE** Apprenticeships are available and a vital part of becoming an electrician. These combine college study through community colleges or technical schools with on-the-job training for a complete overview of the electrician's role.

**ELECTRICIAN** Once qualified and licensed, you can take more vocational training courses to expand your range of skills or specialize in a specific area, to earn a better salary.

**ENGINEERING TECHNICIAN** Works on industrial equipment, such as generators, production lines, and control systems. This job requires further training.

**INSTALLATION ELECTRICIAN** Fits lighting, sockets, network cables, and other electrical equipment in commercial and domestic properties.

**MAINTENANCE ELECTRICIAN** Repairs, tests, and certifies equipment used by businesses to ensure they meet safety standards.

**HIGHWAY ELECTRICIAN** Specializes in installing and maintaining street lighting, traffic controls, and other electrical equipment used by the transportation system.

**SITE MANAGER** Oversees the entire electrical installation at a business or residential construction site, or manages the electrical systems in a factory.

### SKILLS GUIDE

 The ability to communicate effectively with customers, verbally and in writing.

 Analytical skills for diagnosing faults and finding cost-effective solutions to electrical problems.

 Good numerical skills for calculating electrical loads and taking accurate measurements.

 Manual dexterity to perform complex wiring tasks and handle power tools and other devices.

 The physical ability to work in confined spaces. Normal color vision is required.

# PLUMBER

## JOB DESCRIPTION

Plumbers install and repair heating systems, boilers, water pipes, drainage systems, air-conditioning units, and domestic equipment such as washing machines. They work in homes, offices, or at industrial locations, and may be self-employed or an employee of a larger firm or business. The work involves using a wide range of equipment, from power tools to welding gear, often in wet and cramped conditions.

### SALARY

Trainee plumber ★☆☆☆☆
Experienced plumber ★★★★☆

### INDUSTRY PROFILE

Numerous employment opportunities, including growth in renewable energy systems • Skilled plumbers in demand in many countries worldwide

## ▼ RELATED CAREERS

▶ **BUILDING-SERVICES ENGINEER** Designs and builds a wide range of systems within buildings, from lighting, heating, fire protection, and power to internal features such as elevators and escalators. Works on large- and small-scale construction projects, and may have a college degree.

▶ **DOMESTIC APPLIANCE ENGINEER** Installs and repairs appliances, such as washing machines and refrigerators, in people's homes.

▶ **ENERGY ENGINEER** Develops new ways of producing energy, such as electricity, from a range of technologies, such as wind turbines.

▶ **KITCHEN FITTER** Installs and fits kitchen worktops, cupboards, and decorative trims. Kitchen fitters follow detailed plans to achieve the layout and look required by the customer.

▶ **HEATING, AIR CONDITIONING, AND REFRIGERATION MECHANIC** Works on heating, ventilation, cooling, and refrigeration systems. The mechanics are often called HVACR Technicians.

## AT A GLANCE

 **YOUR INTERESTS** Engineering • Mathematics • Physics • Design technology • Information Technology (IT)

 **ENTRY QUALIFICATIONS** There are no formal entry requirements. To work with oil and gas appliances, plumbers need to be certified.

 **LIFESTYLE** Working hours are fairly regular although plumbers may need to work evenings or weekends, or remain on call in case of emergency repairs.

 **LOCATION** Travel between customers is required—plumbers work in a variety of locations, such as customers' offices, homes, factories, and stores.

 **THE REALITIES** Being self-employed requires hard work and determination. Some work is carried out at late or early hours, or in wet or cold conditions.

## CAREER PATHS

Gaining qualifications and membership of a professional body are useful for working as a plumber, and are essential for gas installation. Domestic plumbing is the most common area of work, but there are several options for specialization.

### SKILLS GUIDE

The ability to communicate effectively with both customers and colleagues.

Good interpretative and analytical skills for following technical drawings and building plans.

Confidence in using hand-held tools, including power tools and monitoring devices.

Physical stamina and the ability to work in confined spaces, such as attics and ventilation shafts.

Attention to detail, especially when working with gas and oil due to fire risks.

### APPRENTICE
You can enter plumbing straight from high school as an apprentice, training on the job and learning from colleagues.

### GRADUATE
Although a degree isn't required, finishing technical school or college programs may make it easier for you to secure an apprenticeship.

**PLUMBER** As a plumber, you will stay up to date with safety standards and technological advances throughout your career. Once you have built a good reputation, you can set up and run your own business for domestic customers.

### HEATING ENGINEER
Specializes in the design, installation, and commissioning of a wide variety of heating systems, such as oil, gas, or electrical systems.

### GAS SERVICE
**TECHNICIAN** Installs, repairs, and services gas appliances and systems such as stoves, water-heaters, and gas fireplaces.

**INDUSTRIAL PLUMBER**
Works on major plumbing projects at factories, hospitals, and offices to ensure heating, water, and drainage systems are running efficiently.

**PLUMBING ESTIMATOR**
Assesses the scope of new plumbing projects and estimates the cost of labor and fittings. This is usually a senior role within a large plumbing firm.

**RENEWABLE ENERGY
ENGINEER** Designs, installs, and maintains eco-friendly domestic and industrial systems, such as solar panels or biomass heating systems, which use organic fuels rather than gas, oil, or electricity.

# TRANSPORTATION

With international travel and trade on the rise, the transportation industry is a growing sector around the world. Opportunities are increasingly available transporting passengers or goods by air, road, rail, and water, in both planning roles and as a crew member, driver, pilot, or captain.

## AIRLINE PILOT
*Page 214*

Responsible for passenger well-being and the safe control of an aircraft, airline pilots use their flying skills and experience to transport travelers in comfort.

## AIR TRAFFIC CONTROLLER
*Page 216*

The ever-increasing volume of traffic using the world's airspace requires planning to ensure safety in the skies. Air traffic controllers perform a key role in this process.

## TRANSPORTATION PLANNER
*Page 218*

Making policies encouraging better travel, transportation planners advise on how to keep transportation networks, and the modern economies they serve, moving.

## SHIP'S CAPTAIN
*Page 220*

Commanding vast container boats, cruise liners, and a range of other sea-faring vessels, captains are responsible for the safe operation of their ship at sea.

## RAILROAD ENGINEER
*Page 222*

Whether driving high-speed trains or powerful freight engines, railroad engineers are the skilled personnel who transport passengers or goods safely on rail networks.

## TRUCK DRIVER
*Page 224*

Delivering a range of cargo—such as food products, shipping containers, furniture, or chemicals—truck drivers are the mainstay of the road haulage network.

## LOGISTICS MANAGER
*Page 226*

Coordinating the work of truck drivers, warehouse staff, and suppliers, logistics managers ensure goods arrive at the right destination, in excellent condition, and on time.

# AIRLINE PILOT

## JOB DESCRIPTION

Piloting an aircraft is an exciting job that offers the chance to see the world. It is also a role that carries heavy responsibilities, as pilots are in charge of an expensive aircraft and must ensure the safety and comfort of the passengers. They also must adhere to rigid schedules and standards. Before they qualify, pilots must undergo strict background and security checks, and a period of intense training.

### SALARY

Newly qualified pilot ★★☆☆☆
Experienced captain ★★★★☆

### INDUSTRY PROFILE

Industry run by a few large companies • Male-dominated profession • Global pilot shortage, with more than 1.2 million pilots and technicians needed by 2036 to staff the aviation industry

## AT A GLANCE

**YOUR INTERESTS** Aviation • Mathematics • Physics • Engineering • Travel and tourism • Computers • Meteorology

**ENTRY QUALIFICATIONS** A pilot's license is required. Pilots may train at colleges, private flying schools, or through the armed forces.

**LIFESTYLE** Unusual working hours go with the job, and pilots usually work in shifts. They will often spend long periods away from home.

**LOCATION** Travel is unavoidable. Pilots on long-haul flights typically spend a rest day at their destination before flying home.

**THE REALITIES** Private training for a pilot's license is costly, and there is a lot of competition for good jobs. Pilots spend most of their time in the cockpit.

## CAREER PATHS

Earning a pilot's license is the first step toward a career as a pilot. With sufficient experience and flying hours, you can work toward becoming a captain. Pilots can work for passenger airlines, charter airlines, freight carriers, or private jet operators.

**PRIVATE PILOT** You can train for a pilot's license with a private flying school. It may take 18 months to earn the required flying hours.

**ARMED FORCES PILOT** If you serve for a given period of time as a pilot in the armed forces, you may be able to take a conversion course to qualify as a commercial pilot.

**GRADUATE** A degree in aviation studies or a similar subject will help your chances of finding a role with an airline company.

## ▼ RELATED CAREERS

▶ **AEROSPACE ENGINEER** *see pp. 190–191*

▶ **AIR TRAFFIC CONTROLLER** *see pp. 216–217*

▶ **AIR FORCE PILOT** *see pp. 232–233*

▶ **AIRLINE CABIN CREW** *see pp. 308–309*

▶ **HELICOPTER PILOT** Usually flies as the sole pilot, servicing oil platforms, police forces, and rescue teams, and carrying out other survey work.

Pilots train on flight simulators once every year to renew their flying license.

## SKILLS GUIDE

 An ability to understand and remember technical and procedural information.

 Excellent skills in spoken and written English, the international language of the aviation industry.

 An ability to remain focused under pressure and to think quickly to resolve problems.

 Manual dexterity, sharp eyesight, a good level of physical fitness, and excellent coordination.

 Confidence and communication skills to interact with the crew in a calm and efficient manner.

**AIRLINE PILOT** Major airline pilots fly larger planes on long and short routes. Regional pilots fly smaller planes on shorter routes.

**CORPORATE JET PILOT** Flies smaller planes, often to smaller airports for private customers.

**CARGO PILOT** Flies cargo planes, often overnight when airports carry fewer passengers. Shifts are usually fairly predictable, allowing for greater stability in home life.

**AIRLINE MANAGER** Works as a manager for an airline or for an airport. The job does not involve much time spent in the cockpit.

**FIRST OFFICER** Shares duties with the captain in flying the plane. After five to ten year's experience, you can progress to captain.

**CAPTAIN** Following rigorous training and selection, you can become captain, taking overall control of commanding the aircraft.

**INSTRUCTOR** Trains new pilots on simulators, and works on airline company guidelines.

# AIR TRAFFIC CONTROLLER

## SALARY

Trainee controller ★☆☆☆☆
Senior controller ★★★★★

## INDUSTRY PROFILE

Highly competitive industry • Aviation sector growing as global air traffic increases • Concerns for job security due to privatization of airlines and airport authorities

## JOB DESCRIPTION

Air traffic controllers are responsible for managing aircraft traffic, ensuring that flights are completed safely and that airport runways and parking stands are used efficiently. In this role, you must be calm under pressure while tracking aircraft in flight and directing them at takeoff, landing, and also on the ground.

## CAREER PATHS

Most controllers train with their country's aviation authority to gain the license required to work. Training takes several years to complete and involves specializing in one area of air traffic control. Progression comes in the form of increased seniority and responsibility; changing to a different specialty is rare, due to the high cost of retraining.

**AREA CONTROLLER**
Tracks and monitors aircraft as they fly across one of a number of defined areas of air space. The job is usually based at a large regional control center.

**GRADUATE** You must have a bachelor's degree or three years of work experience to apply. A rigorous application process tests your skills, aptitude, and general health. You must also pass a background check to get security clearance.

**ASSISTANT** In some regions, you can apply directly to airport operators to work as an air traffic control assistant, training on the job to qualify as a controller.

**AIR TRAFFIC CONTROLLER** As an air traffic controller, you will be trained to specialize in one of three distinct roles: area controller, approach and departure controller, or tower/aerodrome controller. With experience, you can take on management responsibility.

# SKILLS GUIDE

 Good speaking and listening skills for communicating with pilots and other personnel.

 Excellent organizational skills to coordinate the arrival and departure of simultaneous flights.

 Good numerical skills to ensure accurate calculation of the speed of aircraft and distance traveled.

 The ability to solve complex and urgent problems with rapid, safe, and innovative solutions.

 Concentration, accuracy, and attention to detail for ensuring that aircraft safety is maintained.

**APPROACH AND DEPARTURE CONTROLLER** Maintains contact with aircraft pilots as flights arrive or depart from an airport, arranging the sequence of landing and takeoff, and keeping pilots updated on weather conditions and other vital information.

**TOWER/AERODROME CONTROLLER** Works in an airport control tower to guide pilots in to land. Tower controllers also direct planes on the ground to ensure they reach the correct parking stand. They also coordinate the movement of service vehicles, such as baggage carts.

## ▼ RELATED CAREERS

▶ **AIRLINE PILOT** see pp. 214–215

▶ **AIRLINE CABIN CREW** see pp. 308–309

▶ **POLICE, FIRE, AND AMBULANCE DISPATCHERS** Answer emergency and nonemergency calls. They are also called public safety telecommunicators.

▶ **FLIGHT OPERATIONS MANAGER** Coordinates the daily operation of an airline, monitors flights, and negotiates with ground services.

In the United States alone, air traffic controllers coordinate the movements of up to 50,000 planes a day.

## AT A GLANCE

 **YOUR INTERESTS** Aviation • Mathematics • Physics • Engineering • Information Technology (IT) • Electronics • Transportation

 **ENTRY QUALIFICATIONS** A high school education, including English and mathematics, is needed to start training. A relevant college degree is useful.

 **LIFESTYLE** Working hours are regular, but controllers work in shifts to cover nights, weekends, and holidays in order to track flights over a 24-hour period.

 **LOCATION** Controllers usually work on computers and radar tracking equipment in an office, or within an airport control tower or center.

 **THE REALITIES** Responsibility for the safety of aircraft and passengers requires intense concentration, and can be stressful and exhausting.

# TRANSPORTATION PLANNER

## JOB DESCRIPTION

Transportation planners study and advise on the growth and management of road, rail, and aviation transportation networks, and the impact they have both locally as well as nationally. They also examine transportation patterns, such as walking or cycling, and recommend improvements to systems to meet government targets.

### SALARY

Graduate trainee ★★☆☆☆
Consultancy director ★★★★★

### INDUSTRY PROFILE

Wide range of employers • Growth in areas such as sustainable transport, automated driving, and environmental conservation • Increasing demand for experienced transportation planners

## ▼ RELATED CAREERS

▶ **CIVIL ENGINEER** *see pp. 176–177*

▶ **TOWN PLANNER** *see pp. 200–201*

▶ **LOGISTICS MANAGER** *see pp. 226–227*

▶ **CAR FLEET MANAGER** Manages a fleet of vehicles belonging to a company. Duties include overseeing servicing, maintaining, and replacing vehicles.

▶ **HIGHWAY MAINTENANCE MANAGER** Plans and manages highway maintenance, and coordinates repairs with utility providers.

Around 14 million people in the US work in transportation and related industries.

## AT A GLANCE

**YOUR INTERESTS** Transportation • Town planning • Geography • Engineering • Mathematics • Economics • Environmental science

**ENTRY QUALIFICATIONS** Most entrants have a college degree in a relevant subject. Nongraduates can train and study for a degree on the job.

**LIFESTYLE** Regular office hours are the norm, but evening and weekend work may be necessary to meet deadlines or to attend public consultations.

**LOCATION** Work is primarily office-based, but travel to visit projects, survey sites, and to meet clients is a common feature of the job.

**THE REALITIES** Advising on a project and seeing it through to completion may take a long time. A shortage of staff with experience means salaries are rising.

## CAREER PATHS

Transportation planners are employed by public-sector bodies, private-sector consultancies, rail and bus providers, and logistics companies. Most study for professional accreditation or a qualification in transportation planning in order to improve their career prospects.

**ASSISTANT** With a good high school education or vocational training, you may find employment as an assistant, and then study for a degree on the job.

**GRADUATE** You can apply for a job in transportation planning with a college degree in any discipline, but employers prefer subjects such as town planning, civil engineering, and geography.

**TRANSPORTATION PLANNER** Work as a planner is varied, ranging from improving road safety to reducing traffic pollution in an urban area. You can advance your career by moving between the public and private sectors.

### SKILLS GUIDE

 Good written and verbal skills for delivering reports and making recommendations.

 The ability to work well with different personnel, from company directors to construction workers.

 Strong analytical skills for studying data and devising new transportation strategies.

 Excellent numerical skills to gather, analyze, and interpret data and provide statistics.

 Expertise in transportation-modeling programs for creating reports and presentations.

 Good commercial and political awareness in order to gather support for proposals.

**TRAFFIC ENGINEER** Conducts research into traffic flow and safety, and designs new roads or reconfigures existing ones to achieve the most efficient movement of vehicles and pedestrians.

**TRANSPORTATION MODELER** Uses computerized software to create models that simulate different scenarios, then analyzes them in order to identify what action to take.

**SUSTAINABLE TRANSPORTATION PLANNER** Specializes in policy and planning for sustainable forms of transportation, such as low-emission vehicles.

**TRANSPORTATION PLANNING CONSULTANT** Provides advice to a wide range of clients, such as local and national authorities, hospitals, and construction firms. Also develops plans, conducts assessments, and writes proposals.

# SHIP'S CAPTAIN

## JOB DESCRIPTION

A ship's captain takes overall command of a vessel, its cargo or passengers, and crew. In this role, you oversee the navigation and handling of the ship, manage the crew, and ensure the safe and timely passage of cargo or passengers. Each class of vessel—from cruise ships and ferries to tankers and cargo ships—requires specialized skills, and every captain has a legal duty to keep an accurate log of voyages.

### SALARY

Newly qualified officer ★★☆☆☆
Experienced captain ★★★★☆

### INDUSTRY PROFILE

Wide range of opportunities across various sectors • Reduced demand for travel and goods during economic downturn can affect job prospects

## AT A GLANCE

**YOUR INTERESTS** Seas and oceans • Ships and sailing • Geography • Mathematics • Engineering • Physics • Information Technology (IT)

**ENTRY QUALIFICATIONS** A high school education is required to train as a ship's officer. A degree in maritime science or similar is desirable.

**LIFESTYLE** Captains work in shifts and may also be on call. Leave periods vary in length, but are often one-for-one—the same length as your previous voyage.

**LOCATION** The captain is stationed on the ship's bridge, but also has an office onboard for paperwork. Captains spend long periods of time away from home.

**THE REALITIES** Responsibility for crew and passenger safety, and valuable cargo, makes this a high-pressure job. Overtime and reimbursed living costs boost pay.

## CAREER PATHS

To become the captain of a ship, it is necessary to become licensed, either through an accredited training program or by passing a series of exams after spending many hours at sea. As you gain experience as a deck (navigation) or technical officer, you move through the ranks, taking more responsibility for other officers and crew.

**TRAINEE** With good school grades in English, science, and mathematics, you can apply to train as an officer. Training allows you to study while gaining onboard experience in junior positions.

**GRADUATE** You can apply for accelerated officer-training posts, or a range of junior officer positions, with a specialized industry-accredited degree.

## ▼ RELATED CAREERS

▶ **NAVY SAILOR** *see pp. 234–235*

▶ **COAST GUARDSMAN** *see pp. 238–239*

▶ **DOCK WORKER** Works at a port, loading and unloading cargo using cranes and forklifts.

▶ **FISHING VESSEL SKIPPER** Manages the running of a commercial fishing vessel. Roles include piloting, navigation, using fish-locating sonar, and bringing in, storing, and arranging the sale of the catch.

▶ **MARINA MANAGER** Coordinates staff and services in a marina, from allocating moorings to ensuring that maintenance and refueling facilities are available.

## SKILLS GUIDE

Excellent communication skills for making clear radio transmissions, often in international waters.

The ability to form and motivate a team of crew members with varying levels of experience.

Strong leadership skills and the ability to motivate, instruct, and inspire confidence in your crew.

Effective problem-solving skills for dealing with issues or emergencies in a calm, controlled manner.

Excellent numerical skills in order to perform accurate navigational calculations.

**CRUISE LINER CAPTAIN**
Commands all onboard staff, from engineers to entertainers, oversees operational functions, such as planning routes and docking at port, and socializes with passengers at the captain's table.

**CONTAINER SHIP CAPTAIN**
Has responsibility for loading and unloading containers safely, and for navigating and course-setting this class of exceptionally large vessel.

**SUPPORT VESSEL CAPTAIN**
Commands a range of specialized vessels, such as survey ships, anchor-handling ships for oil rigs, and transportation vessels for positioning new offshore wind farms.

**SHIP'S CAPTAIN** To become the captain of a ship, you will spend several years working in different officer roles. After reaching the rank of captain, you can choose to command a vessel at sea or work onshore for a maritime agency or port authority.

**TANKER OR BULK VESSEL CAPTAIN**
Oversees the transportation of liquids, such as oil, or gases, and bulk cargos, such as grain, ore, and coal. Tanker captains have specialized training in transporting hazardous materials safely.

# RAILROAD ENGINEER

## JOB DESCRIPTION

This skilled profession involves operating passenger or freight trains on local or national rail networks, stopping at stations or depots to collect and deliver passengers or cargo. The role requires acute concentration over long periods of time, and the ability to react quickly and calmly to unexpected situations. Engineers may specialize in a particular type of train, such as high-speed trains.

### SALARY

Trainee railroad engineer ★★★★★
Experienced railroad engineer ★★★★★

### INDUSTRY PROFILE

Large industry • Passenger transportation is the largest employer, followed by freight services • Competitive field, with many more applicants than jobs

## AT A GLANCE

**YOUR INTERESTS** Trains and railroad equipment • Travel and transportation • Vehicle mechanics • Mathematics • Physics • Engineering • Geography

**ENTRY QUALIFICATIONS** Typically, a high school education is required, but some rail companies may ask for higher-level qualifications.

**LIFESTYLE** Railroad engineers work in shifts at any time of the day or night, during the working week, and on weekends and holidays.

**LOCATION** When working on long-distance routes, overnight stays may be required. Most engineers must live within an hour's travel from their home station.

**THE REALITIES** As they have to work alone for long periods, engineers must be self-motivated. Experienced staff are well-paid and receive free rail travel.

## ▼ RELATED CAREERS

▶ **TRUCK DRIVER** *see pp. 224–225*

▶ **BUS DRIVER** Drives a bus on a particular route, picking up and dropping off passengers at marked bus stops. Bus drivers ensure the safety of passengers, sell tickets, and check bus passes.

▶ **COACH DRIVER** Drives a coach—either hired by a private group, or a public service that makes scheduled stops—to destinations such as airports, tourist attractions, or major cities. Coach drivers load and unload luggage, take fares, and check passenger lists.

▶ **RAIL ENGINEERING TECHNICIAN** Builds, maintains, and repairs train engines, cars, and wagons. Servicing a train's mechanical and electrical systems is an important part of the job.

▶ **RAIL YARD ENGINEER** Moves locomotives between tracks to keep trains organized and on schedule.

▶ **STREETCAR DRIVER** Operates streetcars or trams on a fixed rail route in a town or city, taking on and dropping off passengers at stations.

## CAREER PATHS

Prospective railroad engineers must first pass a series of aptitude tests and medical examinations. Once they have qualified, engineers undergo further training specific to the route and class of train on which they will be operating.

**RAIL TECHNICIAN** While most firms require drivers to be 21, you can join a rail technician apprenticeship out of high school. This can lead to a trainee engineer job.

**TRAINEE** You can apply for a place as a trainee engineer with a national or regional rail company, then undergo practical and theoretical training to qualify as an engineer.

### SKILLS GUIDE

 Attention to detail in order to interpret line-side signals and follow rules and procedures.

 Good communication skills for answering customer inquiries when not in the driver's cab.

 Strong problem-solving skills to resolve issues, such as service delays or a lack of trains or staff.

 Physical and mental resilience to concentrate for long periods of time while driving at high speed.

 A willingness to work flexibly when colleagues are absent or services are disrupted.

**RAILROAD ENGINEER** As well as controlling the train, you must check the engine and the train's systems before setting off and follow line-side signals. With experience, you can move into training, safety, or management roles.

**TOURIST TRAIN DRIVER** Operates trains on themed or heritage railroads, including vintage or steam-powered engines, which require specialized skills to operate.

**ENGINEER TRAINER** Instructs new recruits to become engineers, training them in railroad regulations, signals, the principles of train movement and handling, and route awareness.

**TRAIN SAFETY INSPECTOR** Assesses other train engineers to ensure they are working efficiently and safely by accompanying them on train trips and simulations to ensure that safety standards are met.

**LIGHT-RAIL TRAIN ENGINEER** Operates passenger trains or trams on urban underground and light-rail services. This specialized role involves rapid passenger transfers and frequent stops.

**TRAIN OPERATIONS MANAGER** Works in a management position for a train operating company, overseeing engineer routes, schedule changes, and the maintenance and deployment of trains.

# TRUCK DRIVER

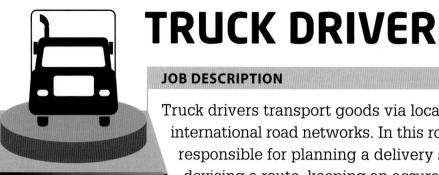

## JOB DESCRIPTION

Truck drivers transport goods via local, national, or international road networks. In this role, you may be responsible for planning a delivery schedule and devising a route, keeping an accurate record of trips, checking and maintaining your vehicle, and loading and unloading items. With additional licenses you can drive specialized trucks, such as tankers and hazardous-substance vehicles.

### SALARY

Novice truck driver ★☆☆☆☆
Experienced truck driver ★★★☆☆

### INDUSTRY PROFILE

Employers range from small haulage companies to multinational logistics firms • High demand for truck drivers • Union jobs command highest pay levels

## AT A GLANCE

**YOUR INTERESTS** Driving • Transportation • Travel and distribution • Motor vehicle engineering • Vehicle mechanics • Health and safety

**ENTRY QUALIFICATIONS** While there are no formal educational requirements, a full driving license is required to start training as a truck driver.

**LIFESTYLE** Driving hours are regulated, with rest breaks required for safety. Most drivers work 42 hours a week, driving by day or night as required.

**LOCATION** Truck drivers spend the majority of their driving time inside the truck's cab. Long periods away from home are common.

**THE REALITIES** Driving long-distance is physically exhausting, and overtime pay can be limited. Long periods of time may be spent away from home.

## CAREER PATHS

A full car driving license is required before taking the specialized theory and practical examinations required to gain a truck driver's license. After qualifying, it is common for drivers to move between employers in different sectors.

**HIGH SCHOOL GRADUATE** You can become a truck driver from the age of 18. Studying mechanics or transportation at high school or college may improve your prospects.

**CAREER CHANGER** You can take the various truck driver's tests while working in another job, then switch careers once you have the necessary qualifications.

## ▼ RELATED CAREERS

▶ **RAILROAD ENGINEER** *see pp. 222–223*

▶ **CAR FLEET MANAGER** Manages a fleet of company cars for a business, overseeing servicing and maintenance of the vehicles, their safe and secure storage when not in use, and replacing them after they have reached a set mileage.

▶ **DISPATCH DRIVER** Transports and delivers items that require urgent, secure, or confidential delivery by motorcycle, car, van, or bicycle.

▶ **FORKLIFT TRUCK DRIVER** Uses a forklift truck to move heavy goods around warehouses, factories, and industrial premises, or to load and unload goods onto trucks, container units, or into industrial storage.

## SKILLS GUIDE

 Good writing skills for maintaining accurate records of trips, cargo, and maintenance.

 Flexibility to deal with route changes, bad weather, traffic conditions, and breakdowns.

 Good organizational skills for planning routes and delivery schedules efficiently.

 Manual dexterity for loading, securing, and handling unusual goods safely.

Physical and mental resilience to concentrate for long periods while driving, often on the same routes.

Attention to detail for following route and delivery instructions and possibly border checks.

**HAZARDOUS LOAD DRIVER**
Transports potentially dangerous chemicals, fuels, and hazardous waste. Hazardous load drivers need specialized training and must also hold an appropriate license.

**TRANSPORTATION MANAGER**
Manages the work of drivers by planning routes and schedules, liaising with customers, and organizing contracts with staff and clients.

**CONSTRUCTION/ MINING PLANT OPERATOR**
Specializes in driving industrial vehicles— such as dump trucks, diggers, and earth-movers—in various sectors, from mining and construction to waste management.

**TRUCK DRIVER** As a truck driver, you will need to retake a driving test every four years in order to keep your license. You can drive different types of truck, such as hazardous-load tankers, by obtaining specialized licenses.

In the US, there are about 200,000 women long-haul truck drivers—and growing.

# LOGISTICS MANAGER

## JOB DESCRIPTION

Logistics managers coordinate the transportation and storage of products and raw materials, liaising with suppliers, manufacturers, and retailers to ensure customers receive the goods they order. The rise of e-commerce—the sale of goods via electronic systems, such as the Internet—has increased demand for stock control and delivery services, making logistics managers crucial to today's economy.

### SALARY

Logistics manager ★☆☆☆☆
Senior logistics manager ★★★★☆

### INDUSTRY PROFILE

Increasing demand for logistics managers due to rapid expansion of the sector • Supply chain, from manufacturing to delivery, is changing due to drones and driverless vehicles

## CAREER PATHS

Careers in logistics have been transformed by new technologies, such as online ordering and real-time tracking of goods. Entry-level roles may involve managing distribution, warehousing, Information Technology (IT) systems, or individual contracts with customers. These lead to senior positions in management and in planning distribution networks.

**BUSINESS DEVELOPMENT MANAGER** Works on the commercial development of a logistics company, negotiating new contracts, seeking new business opportunities, and increasing orders from existing customers.

**APPRENTICE** You can gain work experience by participating in internships or apprenticeships, which are offered by many employers. You can supplement this with a combination of college-level courses and private study.

**GRADUATE** You can apply for entry-level positions with a degree in any discipline. However, subjects such as logistics, business, transportation, or geography can boost your chances of landing a job.

**LOGISTICS MANAGER** To ensure your company's business is run efficiently, you must use IT systems to monitor stock levels, fuel costs, and estimated supply times continually. With experience, you can work in a range of industries, such as mining and oil.

## SKILLS GUIDE

 Excellent communication skills to keep suppliers and customers fully informed.

 Effective team-working for coordinating the work of every member of the supply chain.

 Strong leadership abilities to motivate a range of people—from truck drivers to managers.

 Sharp analytical skills and a logical approach for effective scheduling and stock control.

 The ability to use computerized systems efficiently for tracking goods, supply levels, and costs.

 **LOGISTICS CONSULTANT** Provides specialized services, often on a freelance basis, helping firms to plan and set up supply chains and advises on global transportation networks.

 **QUALITY MANAGER** Focuses on minimizing shipment errors, delays, and goods damaged in transit. Quality managers also review the supply chain to identify areas that can be improved.

Globally, 46 billion tons of goods are transported each year by air—four times more than by boat.

## ▼ RELATED CAREERS

▶ **TRANSPORTATION PLANNER** see pp. 218–219

▶ **CRANE OPERATOR** Uses a crane to load containers and items of cargo on and off ships, trucks, and trains, to be transported locally or around the globe.

▶ **HUMANITARIAN AID WORKER** Manages the collection, transportation, and delivery of food, clothing, medicines, and other vital supplies to people following natural disasters or during conflicts.

▶ **PURCHASING MANAGER** Buys in any product or service required for a business to help it to carry out its core activities.

## AT A GLANCE

 **YOUR INTERESTS** Mathematics • IT • Planning • Business studies and efficiency • Management • Geography • Languages

 **ENTRY QUALIFICATIONS** Most logistics manager positions require a degree, but it is possible to start as an assistant and work your way up.

 **LIFESTYLE** Large logistics firms operate around the clock, so logistics managers may be required to work full-time hours in shifts.

 **LOCATION** Mostly office-based, but logistics managers may also need to visit warehouses and suppliers during the working week.

 **THE REALITIES** Travel, sometimes to international destinations, is common. Long hours are often required, but the rewards can be generous.

# SECURITY AND EMERGENCY SERVICES

If you want to take an active role in helping people and society, a career in the security and emergency services may be for you. Some jobs in this sector involve national and international travel, but all of them require an active approach and a willingness to engage with people.

## ARMY SOLDIER
*Page 230*

With a primary goal of defending the nation, Army soldiers embrace loyalty, duty, respect, selfless service, honor, integrity, and personal courage above all else.

## AIR FORCE PILOT
*Page 232*

Air Force pilots protect their nation's airspace, using technical know-how and specialized skills to carry out important—and potentially dangerous—missions.

## NAVY SAILOR
*Page 234*

Navy sailors value honor, courage, and commitment as they work at sea, in the air, and on land to ensure the freedom of their nation's seas and waterways.

## UNITED STATES MARINE
*Page 236*

Ready to jump into action at a moment's notice, Marines are highly trained and skilled members of the armed forces, often serving on the front lines.

## COAST GUARDSMAN
*Page 238*

Coast guardsmen, trained to be ready in all different types of situations, ensure maritime safety and carry out often intricate water-rescue missions.

## POLICE OFFICER
*Page 240*

Serving the public with honesty, integrity, and diligence, police officers work to deter criminal activity, solve crimes, and help to improve society at large.

## CORRECTIONS OFFICER
*Page 242*

Supervising the activities of inmates in jail, corrections officers maintain order and ensure that the prisoners are secure and supported while serving their sentences.

## PROBATION OFFICER
*Page 244*

Probation officers work with prisoners released from jail or on community sentences to ensure that they complete their sentences and reintegrate after release.

## INTELLIGENCE OFFICER
*Page 246*

Specialists in investigating matters of national security, intelligence officers use a variety of means—from covert surveillance to data monitoring—to protect citizens.

## FIREFIGHTER
*Page 248*

Protecting the public and property from fires, natural disasters, and accidents, firefighters risk their own safety to assist people in hazardous situations.

## PARAMEDIC
*Page 250*

Responding quickly to emergency calls, paramedics use their medical training to provide emergency care to people with different types of injuries and illnesses.

# ARMY SOLDIER

## JOB DESCRIPTION

Army soldiers work to protect their country around the world using land-based military operations. They perform missions assigned by the President and the Secretary of Defense, as well as combatant commanders. Soldiers also aid in disaster relief and humanitarian missions. With more than 150 US Army jobs, there are many specializations for recruits to choose from.

### SALARY

Private ★★★★★
Four-star general ★★★★★

### INDUSTRY PROFILE

Hiring for various job opportunities happens on a continuous cycle • May hire fewer new recruits at certain times depending on the state of the economy and/or funding

## AT A GLANCE

**YOUR INTERESTS** Serving your country • Combat • Security • Science • Technology • Engineering • Mechanics • Mathematics • Aviation

**ENTRY QUALIFICATIONS** Age, education, and residency requirements must be met in order to join the military. Physical and written exams are required.

**LIFESTYLE** Working hours are around the clock, and soldiers can be deployed at any time, anywhere in the world. Army soldiers must wear a uniform.

**LOCATION** Most US Army soldiers work on or near military bases, facilities, or war zones in the US and elsewhere. They may need to travel on short notice.

**THE REALITIES** Soldiers may move often and be away from their families for long periods of time when deployed. Work is high-risk and physically demanding.

## ▼ RELATED CAREERS

▶ **MOTOR VEHICLE TECHNICIAN** *see pp. 184–185*

▶ **TELECOM ENGINEER** *see pp. 188–189*

▶ **AIR FORCE PILOT** *see pp. 232–233*

▶ **POLICE OFFICER** *see pp. 240–241*

▶ **CUSTOMS OFFICER** Monitors, investigates, and prevents illegal trade across international borders. Activities include intelligence gathering and inspecting suspicious cargo at ports.

▶ **STORE DETECTIVE** Monitors and protects items on sale in stores.

In 2019, around 480,000 men and women were serving in the US Army.

## CAREER PATHS

To enlist in the US Army, entrants must be at least 17 years old, have a high-school diploma or General Educational Development (GED), and be a citizen or permanent resident of the US. They also need to pass a physical and written exam, background check, and drug test. Specialized positions may need additional qualifications.

**HIGH SCHOOL GRADUATE** You need a high-school diploma, a GED, or 15 or more college credits to enlist in the Army.

**COLLEGE GRADUATE** A four-year college degree is required for some roles, such as officer. For certain specialized careers, such as in the medical field, you need a master's degree.

### SKILLS GUIDE

 Good communication skills with unit members, officers, and civilians at home and abroad.

 The ability to work as a member of a close-knit team, follow rules, and have respect for authority.

 Flexibility to adapt to frequently changing work environments and locations anywhere in the world.

 Strong physical and mental fitness for taking part in land-force missions.

 The perseverance to solve problems efficiently, sometimes in stressful and dangerous situations.

**ARMY SOLDIER** Once recruited, you begin with Basic Combat Training (BCT), which teaches skills needed to perform essential Army duties. After BCT, you must complete Advanced Individual Training (AIT) to learn specialized skills for specific Army jobs.

**INTELLIGENCE ANALYST** Seeks out and analyzes information about the enemy to help inform battle strategy and assist troops serving on the battle front.

**AVIONIC COMMUNICATIONS EQUIPMENT REPAIRER/ MECHANIC** Member of the Army communications maintenance team. Responsible for performing repairs and maintenance on aircraft communications equipment.

**NURSE CORPS OFFICER** Leads a team of Army Nurse Corps nurses who provide care and special services for soldiers and their families. Requires a bachelor's degree in nursing from an accredited school.

**AIR DEFENSE ARTILLERY OFFICER** Leads the air defense artillery branch, which shields the Army and its forces from aerial strikes and defends against missile attacks and enemy surveillance. Expert in air defense systems with special training in leadership, tactics, and weapons.

# AIR FORCE PILOT

## JOB DESCRIPTION

Air Force pilots fly some of the most advanced aircraft in the world. They provide defense and safety for national airspace, serving at home and abroad. Pilots operate weapons and perform defense tactics for air and ground targets. From conducting search and rescue missions to giving humanitarian aid, pilots serve one of the most powerful military operations in the world.

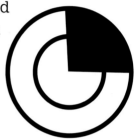

### SALARY

Enlisted pilot ★☆☆☆☆
Chief of staff ★★★★★

### INDUSTRY PROFILE

Highly competitive entry • Recruitment to US Air Force expected to increase in the next few years • Growing opportunities as a drone operator for surveillance and reconnaissance

## ▼ RELATED CAREERS

▶ **AIRLINE PILOT** *see pp. 214–215*

▶ **AIR TRAFFIC CONTROLLER** *see pp. 216–217*

▶ **ARMY SOLDIER** *see pp. 230–231*

▶ **HELICOPTER PILOT** Flies helicopters and can choose from a variety of work such as cargo delivery, law enforcement, firefighting, search and rescue, emergency medical services, and aerial photography. Training is expensive and working hours can be irregular. Fewer companies operate helicopters than planes; opportunities are scarce.

The first female fighter pilot in the US Air Force, Jeannie Leavitt, entered training in 1993.

## AT A GLANCE

**YOUR INTERESTS** Aviation • Serving your country • Mathematics • Engineering • Technology • Firefighting

**ENTRY QUALIFICATIONS** Age, education, and residency requirements must be met in order to join the military. Physical and written exams are required.

**LIFESTYLE** The job is highly varied, with a range of intellectual and physical demands. Working hours are long when on operations.

**LOCATION** Pilots live, work, and train on or near military bases and facilities around the globe. They can expect to travel anywhere in the world.

**THE REALITIES** Navigating top-secret missions is stressful and high-risk. Pilots work long hours and are away from home and family often.

## CAREER PATHS

Some specialized positions require additional training and qualifications. Pilots can advance to senior roles that might include commanding an air base, making tactical decisions, or liaising with government officials. After leaving the armed forces, pilots may choose to retrain as commercial pilots or instructors.

**HIGH SCHOOL GRADUATE**
You must have a high school diploma or a GED with 15 or more college credits to enlist in the US Air Force. Strong math and reading and writing skills are necessary for passing the military's entrance exam.

**COLLEGE GRADUATE**
With a college degree, you are able to enter the Air Force as an officer. Some specialties may require a master's degree.

**AIR FORCE PILOT** You begin your training with Basic Combat Training (BCT); piloting skills are taught along with conditioning to become physically fit. After BCT, pilots become experts in their fields of choice by attending Air Force Technical Training.

**FUELS SPECIALIST**
Receives, stores, and tracks all fuel for vehicles and aircraft on a daily basis. Maintains the facility where the fuel is stored; ensures planes and helicopters are properly fueled before they head out on a mission.

**SPACE SYSTEMS OPERATIONS SPECIALIST** Detects sea-launched ballistic missiles, and tracks satellites to assist in rocket launches and space flight operations.

**COMBAT RESCUE OFFICER**
Organizes and strategizes recovery missions. Conducts rescue and recovery operations to evacuate injured servicemen from the front lines.

**AIRCRAFT LOADMASTER**
Loads aircraft and ensures passengers or cargo arrive safely at their destination. May participate in air deliveries using parachutes.

# NAVY SAILOR

## JOB DESCRIPTION

In the air, on land, and at sea, Navy sailors are an essential part of the armed forces. They engage in combat, provide warfare support, and keep waterways safe and open. Their job is to maintain freedom of seas and waterways. Sailors also provide humanitarian assistance as well as disaster relief nationally and abroad.

### SALARY

Seaman ★☆☆☆☆
Chief of Navy Operations ★★★★★

### INDUSTRY PROFILE

Higher test scores required for new enlistees than other branches of the military • Opportunities vary depending on the economy and any recent conflicts

## AT A GLANCE

**YOUR INTERESTS** Boats • Swimming • Technology • Science • Engineering • Oceanography • Meteorology • Aviation • Serving your country

**ENTRY QUALIFICATIONS** Enlisted sailors must have a high school diploma or GED. Officers must have a 4-year bachelor's degree and strong grades.

**LIFESTYLE** The job requires long periods of time spent at sea far from home and exposure to a variety of work environments.

**LOCATION** Sailors will spend time serving on a base and at sea aboard surface ships or submarines at the far corners of the world.

**THE REALITIES** Schedules for sailors are very regimented. Working aboard a submarine can be isolating. Secretive work is not for everyone.

## CAREER PATHS

Experience earned in the Navy can lead to qualifications in specialized fields, from flying to weapons maintenance, logistics, and engineering. Once your period of service is over, these qualifications can be used in a civilian career.

### HIGH SCHOOL GRADUATE

You must have a high school diploma or a GED with 15 or more college credits to enlist as a sailor in the US Navy. No additional schooling is needed for many of the jobs open to sailors.

### COLLEGE GRADUATE

You will need a degree to train as a naval officer in a specialized area, such as logistics, medicine, engineering, or flying.

## SKILLS GUIDE

 The ability to work as an effective member of a large, diverse crew on complex missions.

 The skill to adapt to various work environments around the globe, on sea and on land.

 Good organizational and communication skills for ensuring successful missions.

 Determination to face challenges and solve problems, especially in the face of danger.

 High levels of strength, fitness, and agility to work in all conditions for extended periods of time.

## ▼ RELATED CAREERS

▶ **TELECOM ENGINEER** *see pp. 188–189*

▶ **SHIP'S CAPTAIN** *see pp. 220–221*

▶ **COAST GUARDSMAN** *see pp. 238–239*

▶ **NAVY INFORMATION SYSTEMS TECHNICIAN** Uses radio and satellite systems to send and receive vital communications, to and from ship and shore.

▶ **OCEANOGRAPHER** Studies the physical and biological aspects of the ocean. There are several different kinds of oceanographers, including those who study oceanic plants and animals.

▶ **MARINA MANAGER** Coordinates staff and services in a marina, from allocating moorings to ensuring maintenance and refueling.

**NAVY SEAL** Conducts raids and extractions of hostages, most-wanted enemies and terrorists, and sneaks behind enemy lines to collect information and intelligence.

**NAVAL AVIATOR** Flies sophisticated aircraft and helicopters. Participates in missions that include collecting intelligence and combat operations.

**SUBMARINE OFFICER** Drives, arms, and operates nuclear-powered submarines. Maintains weapons systems and operates communication and intelligence equipment onboard.

**AVIATION RESCUE SWIMMER** Uses search-and-rescue and swimming skills to jump from helicopters into the water to save downed pilots, stranded boaters, and hikers on land.

**SONAR TECHNICIAN** Conducts underwater surveillance, collects scientific data, and tracks enemy targets using sonar and oceanographic equipment and the latest underwater technologies.

**SAILOR** As an enlistee, you attend Recruit Training Command (RTC), or bootcamp, for both classroom and field training. After graduating, you can train further for specific careers.

**MEDICAL OFFICER** Provides medical care for servicemembers and their families and assists in humanitarian relief efforts.

# UNITED STATES MARINE

## JOB DESCRIPTION

Marines operate simultaneously on the sea, on shore, and in the air. They are often called upon first for their rapid and efficient response to conflicts or humanitarian efforts anywhere in the world. Marines also deal with unexpected threats, stopping them from becoming more dangerous.

### SALARY

Enlisted Marine ★★★★★
Commandant ★★★★★

### INDUSTRY PROFILE

Training is ongoing throughout the year and entry is easier than other areas of service for those who are physically and mentally fit • Women have been part of the US Marines for more than 100 years

## AT A GLANCE

**YOUR INTERESTS** Serving your country • Mathematics • Engineering • Technology • Firefighting • Boats • Security • Aviation

**ENTRY QUALIFICATIONS** Age, education, and residency requirements must be met in order to join the military. Physical and written exams are required.

**LIFESTYLE** Marines must be ready to move into action on extremely short notice. As with other military careers, a uniform is required.

**LOCATION** Marines live, serve, and train primarily on the East and West coasts. Missions can take them to extreme locations all over the world.

**THE REALITIES** An intense recruit training process and high levels of risk in extreme conditions make this a physically and mentally strenuous job.

## ▼ RELATED CAREERS

▶ **AIRLINE PILOT** see pp. 214–215

▶ **ARMY SOLDIER** see pp. 230–231

▶ **POLICE OFFICER** see pp. 240–241

▶ **FIREFIGHTER** see pp. 248–249

▶ **HELICOPTER PILOT** Flies helicopters and can choose from a variety of work such as law enforcement, firefighting, emergency medical services, search and rescue, aerial photography, and cargo delivery. Training can be expensive and working hours can be irregular.

Many Marines find the reserves a great way to serve part-time while balancing military and civilian life.

## CAREER PATHS

Initial training to be a US Marine begins with Recruit Training followed by the second stage of training, Infantry Training Battalion for infantry or Marine Combat Training Battalion for noninfantry. Officers are evaluated at Officer Candidate School.

**HIGH SCHOOL GRADUATE** You must have a high school diploma or a GED with 15 or more college credits to enlist in the US Marines.

**COLLEGE GRADUATE** A bachelor's degree is required for those who are considering becoming a Marine Officer. Some specialties may require a master's degree.

### SKILLS GUIDE

 Extremely high levels of fitness, courage, resilience, energy, stamina, and determination.

 The ability to work effectively as part of a disciplined team and respond quickly to orders.

 Excellent spatial awareness and coordination for using weapons accurately in all conditions.

 Good communication skills to interact, live, and work with people, often in confined spaces.

 Perseverance and self-discipline for withstanding rigorous training and challenging conditions.

**UNITED STATES MARINE** Specialized training school is available for those Marines who wish to sharpen skills in a specific area of expertise.

**COMBAT ENGINEER** Knowledgeable in a variety of engineering and construction tasks, combat engineers repair, construct, and alter various structures and buildings. They also help to rebuild infrastructures and facilities, such as hospitals.

**INFANTRY MACHINE GUNNER** Works as part of a fire team defending against enemy forces operating and maintaining a variety of weapons and weapon systems in close combat. This is a direct combat position.

**MILITARY POLICE OFFICER** Performs police duties to maintain law and order. They perform police intelligence and security operations, and maintain security at police posts. May also participate in imprisonment and mobile operations.

**MILITARY FIREFIGHTER** Responsible for saving human lives and property from fires on base or aboard ships when in active duty. May also assist in controlling wildfires. An expert in fire protection and fire prevention, military firefighters maintain and repair equipment used to fight fires, and drive rescue vehicles and fire trucks.

# COAST GUARDSMAN

## JOB DESCRIPTION

Coast Guardsmen undertake search-and-rescue missions in coastal areas, providing emergency support to ships and people in difficulty at sea. They also monitor shipping movements, recommend safety procedures, and are responsible for checking and maintaining safety equipment, as well as reporting any pollution incidents and illegal shipping activities in a specific area.

### SALARY

Seaman recruit ★★★★★
Chief Master Petty Officer ★★★★★

### INDUSTRY PROFILE

Smallest branch of the military • Approximately 42,000 coast guardsmen on active duty

## CAREER PATHS

Initial training to be a US Coast Guardsman begins with Basic Training. Around the fourth week of training, you can request a location for your first assignment and the type of unit you wish to serve. You can also request to serve ashore or afloat.

**HIGH SCHOOL GRADUATE** You must have a high school diploma or a GED with 15 or more college credits to enlist in the US Coast Guard.

**COLLEGE GRADUATE** A bachelor's degree is required for those who wish to apply to Officer Candidate School. Some specialties may require a master's degree.

### ▼ RELATED CAREERS

▶ **SHIP'S CAPTAIN** see pp. 220–221

▶ **NAVY SAILOR** see pp. 234–235

▶ **CUSTOMS OFFICER** Monitors and prevents illegal trade across international borders.

▶ **FISHING VESSEL SKIPPER** Takes overall responsibility for a commercial fishing boat, planning routes, ensuring that the crew is safe, and arranging sale of the catch once in port.

**COAST GUARDSMAN** Once you become a Coast Guardsman, you may choose to specialize. Advanced courses and secret security may be required for some specializations.

## SKILLS GUIDE

 Excellent communication skills for giving clear instructions over radio and in person during rescues.

 The ability to work effectively as part of a team in dangerous and high-pressure conditions.

 Good leadership skills for directing rescues, which may involve multiple air- and sea-rescue teams.

 The ability to solve complex, high-risk problems in dangerous conditions while protecting lives.

 Excellent numerical skills for keeping accurate logs and using navigational equipment.

## AT A GLANCE

 **YOUR INTERESTS** Serving your country • Security • Law Enforcement • Mathematics • Environmental Science • Geography • Boats • Navigation

 **ENTRY QUALIFICATIONS** Age, education, and residency requirements must be met in order to join the military. Physical and written exams are required.

 **LIFESTYLE** Deployment is generally for a few days to a few weeks at a time, although some deployments can be up to three months or longer.

 **LOCATION** Guardsmen can request a location, but final determination is made by an assignment officer based on need. Locations can be ashore or afloat.

 **THE REALITIES** The US Coast Guard has one of the oldest fleets afloat. The vessels are not built for comfort, and work can often be dangerous.

 **MARINE SCIENCE TECHNICIAN**
Keeps waters clean and mariners safe, from ports to shorelines. Responds to oil and hazardous waste spills in national waters, inspects vessels for safety, protects wildlife and natural resources, and keeps waters free from international violators.

 **MARITIME ENFORCEMENT SPECIALIST**
Protect national ports and waterways by providing security and law enforcement. Maritime enforcement specialists also guard against terrorism and ensure force protection and port security and safety.

 **BOATSWAIN'S MATE** Responsible for deck maintenance, small boat operations, and navigation. Supervises all personnel assigned to a ship's deck force or shore unit. Also conducts search and rescue missions and assists navigation teams.

 **INTELLIGENCE SPECIALIST** Collects and analyzes communication signals using computer technology, then produces and identifies intelligence from information collected. Intelligence specialists also maintain intelligence databases, libraries, and related files.

# POLICE OFFICER

## JOB DESCRIPTION

Police officers maintain law and order on a local and national level. In this role, you may conduct patrols to reassure the public and deter criminal activity, work with community groups to promote lawful behavior, respond to calls from the public for assistance, catch and testify against offenders, and investigate crimes by gathering evidence and questioning suspects and witnesses.

## SALARY

Trainee police officer ★★☆☆☆
Senior police officer ★★★☆☆

## INDUSTRY PROFILE

A varied, diverse, and expanding profession • Strong competition for entry-level jobs • Opportunities for promotion and career development are good

## ▼ RELATED CAREERS

▶ **PROBATION OFFICER** *see pp. 244–245*

▶ **BODYGUARD** Accompanies individuals or groups of people and takes any necessary action to protect them from harmful or violent situations.

▶ **CRIMINAL INTELLIGENCE ANALYST** Protects national security, detecting and preventing serious organized crime.

▶ **CUSTOMS OFFICER** Monitors, investigates, and prevents illegal trade across international borders. Activities include intelligence gathering and inspecting suspicious cargo at ports.

▶ **STORE DETECTIVE** Uses closed-circuit television and in-store observation of shoppers and staff to prevent shoplifting or damage to property in retail stores and shopping malls.

There are more than 700,000 sworn law-enforcement officers in the United States.

## AT A GLANCE

**YOUR INTERESTS** Law enforcement • Criminal law • Psychology • Sociology • Physical Education (PE) • Mathematics • Information Technology (IT)

**ENTRY QUALIFICATIONS** Entry requirements vary, but potential officers must pass stringent aptitude and fitness tests as well as background checks.

**LIFESTYLE** Official working hours are regular, but shiftwork to cover evenings, weekends, and public holidays may be required. Overtime is available.

**LOCATION** Work is in a wide range of settings, from investigating crime scenes to desk work at a police station or testifying in a court of law.

**THE REALITIES** Police officers get excellent benefits, but they encounter high-risk situations and work long hours. Serving a community is rewarding.

## CAREER PATHS

Although competition for entry-level jobs is high, police work offers good prospects for career progression. After initial training and a probationary period, police officers become eligible for promotion to more senior and specialized roles. Officers are also encouraged to take ongoing training throughout their career.

### SKILLS GUIDE

 The ability to communicate clearly and confidently in potentially dangerous situations.

 Good team-working skills for collaborating on cases with colleagues and specialty officers.

 The capacity to behave with tact, diplomacy, and respect when dealing with the public.

 Solid problem-solving skills to respond quickly, effectively, and appropriately to crisis situations.

 Physical strength to pursue and apprehend criminals, and mental stamina to stay calm at all times.

**GRADUATE** The exact requirements vary between regional police forces, but a bachelor's degree along with experience of community work, volunteering alongside police officers in your local area, or working as a police community support officer will improve your prospects.

**POLICE OFFICER** After a probationary period involving extensive training in investigative methods, policing skills, laws, and understanding new technologies, you can progress by choosing from a range of specialties.

**SPECIALTY OFFICER** Prevents crime or apprehends criminals using specialized training or techniques. Officers can work in areas such as child protection, vice, fraud, or narcotics (drugs), or undergo training in the use of firearms and special tactics, such as anti-terrorism.

**MARINE POLICE** Performs river or coastal patrols on specialty police vessels, investigating illegal activity and arresting criminals. River police train in areas including advanced boat handling or diving.

**DETECTIVE** Investigates serious crimes, including murder, assault, theft, sexual offenses, and fraud. A detective's duties include gathering information, collecting evidence, and interviewing suspects.

**TRAFFIC OFFICER/ PATROLMAN** Specializes in road safety, dealing with traffic offenses, responding to accidents, and checking vehicles to ensure they are insured and taxed.

# CORRECTIONS OFFICER

## JOB DESCRIPTION

Corrections, or correctional, officers supervise the activities of convicted offenders in a prison. They monitor inmates at all times, enforce regulations, and maintain order. Officers also watch out for those at risk of harm and supervise the movement of prisoners in the vicinity. With experience, they may train new recruits or oversee a part of the institution.

### SALARY

Entry-level officer ★★★★★
Senior officer ★★★★★

### INDUSTRY PROFILE

Increasing job opportunities due to rising prison populations • Work mainly in the public sector but private prisons operate in some countries alongside government facilities

## CAREER PATHS

Prisons are usually run by national or state authorities. Once trained, and with experience, you can apply for more senior roles within the service, or use your skills in other related areas, such as counseling and rehabilitation.

**SPECIAL OFFICER** Trains in various areas, such as drug and alcohol counseling, suicide prevention, health care, or physical education, with the aim of helping prisoners overcome their problems and adjust to life after prison.

**TRAINEE** To be accepted as a trainee, you will need to be at least 18 years of age and pass a number of physical and mental assessments. Basic training usually lasts for several weeks.

### ▼ RELATED CAREERS

▶ **POLICE OFFICER** *see pp. 240–241*

▶ **PROBATION OFFICER** *see pp. 244–245*

▶ **PSYCHOLOGIST** *see pp. 254–255*

**CORRECTIONS OFFICER** As well as running the prison community, you help rehabilitate prisoners and work toward providing them with new skills that will be useful in the future.

## AT A GLANCE

 **YOUR INTERESTS** Law and the legal system • Psychology • Sociology • Languages • Physical education • Counseling and helping people

 **ENTRY QUALIFICATIONS** A high school diploma or GED is usually required; some prisons may require a degree or relevant experience.

 **LIFESTYLE** Corrections officers are usually expected to work shifts, including nights, weekends, and public holidays.

 **LOCATION** Corrections officers are based in the prison, supervising inmates indoors, during outdoor activities in prison yards, and on outings and transfers.

 **THE REALITIES** Work conditions can be stressful. You may have to deal with inmates who may be prone to aggression, and may need to resolve inmates' disputes.

## SKILLS GUIDE

 Good communication and mediation skills to help defuse potentially volatile situations.

 Strong team-working skills to work alongside other personnel to control and safeguard inmates.

 The ability to stay calm and remain patient despite stressful and challenging circumstances.

 Strength and endurance for dealing quickly and efficiently with displays of aggression from inmates.

 Strong powers of observation to detect any unusual activities and behaviors in the prison.

 **SERGEANT** Supervises a small team of other officers or takes responsibility for one wing (area) of the prison. As well as making sure corrections officers carry out their duties, senior officers must undertake administrative work in the prison office. This role is a promotion, following several years' experience and some further training.

 **PRISON WARDEN** Manages a prison and takes responsibility for controlling budgets and other resources, supervising junior officers, and liaising with social workers and other agencies involved in the rehabilitation and welfare of inmates.

In 2016, more than 468,000 people worked as correctional officers in the US.

# PROBATION OFFICER

## JOB DESCRIPTION

Probation officers work with criminal offenders before, during, and after they are sentenced by the courts. In this job, you ensure that offenders carry out their sentences and help them return to the community, monitoring them carefully, and working toward their rehabilitation. You may work with courts, prison and police services, and social and community organizations on initiatives to prevent reoffending.

### SALARY

Probation services officer ★★★★★
Senior probation officer ★★★★★

### INDUSTRY PROFILE

Political factors determine the resources available to probation services • Intense scrutiny of the profession by media and government

## CAREER PATHS

Probation officers work for a regional or national probation service, or for a private company that specializes in the rehabilitation of offenders. Routes into the career vary greatly country by country, but a relevant degree and vocational qualifications are expected. Once qualified, you can choose to move into managing the work of other officers, or specialize in one area of offender rehabilitation.

**REHABILITATION OFFICER** Helps people addicted to drugs, alcohol, or other substances, or those with behavioral issues, to lead active, independent lives.

**TRAINEE** You can join a state or federal government training program once you have completed vocational requirements. Experience working with prisoners or providing support to victims of crime is helpful. Many permanent positions require you to be a trainee for one year first.

**GRADUATE** A degree in areas related to criminal justice, criminology, police studies, or behavioral science is beneficial. However, graduates of any discipline may also be accepted into training for this profession.

**PROBATION OFFICER** You supervise offenders on parole or assess the risks they may pose to the community, and write reports for the courts and prison authorities. You may specialize in areas including high-risk offenders, people with addiction problems, or hostel management.

# SKILLS GUIDE

 The ability to work with people from all walks of life, and to understand their individual needs.

 Good team-working skills for collaborating with the agencies involved in offender care.

 The ability to listen, negotiate, and remain calm when dealing with challenging behavior.

 An organized approach and the ability to prioritize work for handling several cases at once.

 The ability to make objective and analytical assessments of behavior and circumstances.

 **TREATMENT PROGRAM DIRECTOR** Oversees the running of a program and/or facility that provides treatment for offenders who have recently left prison, or inmates who are undergoing treatment for addiction.

 **PROFESSIONAL DEVELOPMENT OFFICER** Advises and guides ex-offenders through the options available to them regarding education, training, and work, and helps them integrate into society following a prison term.

## ▼ RELATED CAREERS

▶ **POLICE OFFICER** *see pp. 240–241*

▶ **CORRECTIONS OFFICER** *see pp. 242–243*

▶ **COUNSELOR** *see pp. 256–257*

▶ **SOCIAL WORKER** *see pp. 258–259*

▶ **FORENSIC PSYCHOLOGIST** Works with offenders in prisons and in the community to devise and deliver treatment programs that will counter antisocial behavior. They also carry out research to profile and understand criminal behavior, and may give expert testimony in court and advise parole boards and police forces.

## AT A GLANCE

 **YOUR INTERESTS** Sociology and social work • Law • Psychology • Politics • Counseling • Mathematics • Information Technology (IT)

 **ENTRY QUALIFICATIONS** Entry requirements vary, but a degree (or equivalent) and vocational training in probation work are usually needed.

 **LIFESTYLE** Office hours are regular, but probation officers may need to work late or on weekends to deal with heavy caseloads or when on call.

 **LOCATION** The work of a probation officer is mainly office-based, but they may need to travel frequently to courts, police stations, and prisons.

 **THE REALITIES** Making positive changes to people's lives is satisfying, but dealing with offenders and victims of crime can be distressing.

# INTELLIGENCE OFFICER

## SALARY

Trainee ★★★★★
Senior officers ★★★★★

## INDUSTRY PROFILE

Growing job sector due to heightened global security concerns • Cyber crime is a major area of growth • Option for working freelance

## JOB DESCRIPTION

Intelligence officers protect their country from security threats and serious and organized crime, such as terrorism or human trafficking. They may use data-analysis skills to interpret intelligence from "sources"—people with access to sensitive information—about organizations or individuals who pose a risk to national security.

## CAREER PATHS

To become a government intelligence officer, applicants must hold appropriate citizenship and pass a series of physical, psychological, and background checks. Your career path will depend on the skills for which you were recruited, but there is scope for specializing in particular areas—such as military intelligence—and progressing to senior roles in an agency.

**GRADUATE** You can apply to enter the intelligence service after earning your bachelor's degree in nearly any subject. Some nongraduates with significant relevant experience may also be considered.

### ▼ RELATED CAREERS

▶ **CYBERSECURITY ANALYST** *see pp.132–133*

▶ **FORENSIC SCIENTIST** *see pp.146–147*

▶ **CRIMINAL INTELLIGENCE ANALYST** Examines crime data to investigate patterns in criminal activity, target individual offenders or gangs, and plan future crime-reduction initiatives.

▶ **CRYPTOLOGIST** Deciphers and creates coded messages for organizations, including the military, who need to encrypt essential information. Cryptologists are usually trained in mathematics or linguistics, or both.

**INTELLIGENCE OFFICER** After a period of on-the-job training, you can serve in your first post for 18 months to three years. You can specialize in certain areas, or take a job rotation to another department or agency.

## AT A GLANCE

**YOUR INTERESTS** Psychology • Current affairs • Languages • Mathematics • Science • Information Technology (IT) • History • Economics

**ENTRY QUALIFICATIONS** Intelligence officers usually have a degree, or higher, qualification in a subject related to their specialization, such as forensics.

**LIFESTYLE** Intelligence officers typically work regular office hours, but overtime is often required during investigations.

**LOCATION** Most intelligence officers are mainly office-based, but may need to travel to the scene of a crime or to a location that is under surveillance.

**THE REALITIES** Intelligence work can be intensive and must be kept secret. During selection, candidates are subject to intrusive vetting procedures.

# SKILLS GUIDE

Excellent written and verbal skills for writing and presenting intelligence reports.

The ability to work with fellow colleagues and specialists from other agencies.

Excellent observational, analytical, and research skills, and an aptitude for creative problem-solving.

Proficiency in computer software for identifying significant data, and analyzing and recording it.

An organized approach to tasks, which may last many years, and the ability to prioritize.

**HUMAN OPERATIONS OFFICER**
Gathers intelligence by making contact with sources, ranging from covert conversations with unsuspecting targets to the interrogation of suspects. Also plans and executes cover missions and briefs government officials.

**IMAGERY INTELLIGENCE OFFICER**
Collects vital information via satellite and aerial photography. The information received will form the basis of many military operations.

**SIGNALS INTELLIGENCE OFFICER** Specializes in gathering intelligence by analyzing intercepted communications, both personal (such as telephone calls) and electronic (such as encrypted emails).

The United States' intelligence agency, the CIA, monitors millions of tweets every day.

# FIREFIGHTER

## JOB DESCRIPTION

Firefighters are emergency personnel who rescue and protect people, animals, and property in a range of accidents or emergencies, from fires, traffic incidents, and floods, to bomb threats and environmental hazards. They educate the public on fire prevention and safety, and respond to emergency call-outs in order to extinguish fires, bring trapped people or animals to safety, and administer first aid before medical services arrive.

### SALARY

Newly qualified firefighter ★★★★★
Station officer ★★★★★

### INDUSTRY PROFILE

Competitive industry in which applicants often outnumber vacancies • Challenging profession with a tough selection process • Good opportunities for promotion and career development

## AT A GLANCE

**YOUR INTERESTS** Health and safety • Community welfare and service • Physical Education (PE) • Mathematics • Science

**ENTRY QUALIFICATIONS** A high school diploma and postsecondary certificate are required. Firefighters must pass a series of physical, psychological, and written tests.

**LIFESTYLE** Firefighters work on call or in shifts to provide 24-hour cover, including weekends and holidays. They typically work 48 hours a week.

**LOCATION** Firefighters are based at a fire station that houses firefighting equipment, and travel to locations to respond to emergencies as they occur.

**THE REALITIES** The job can be stressful and physically demanding. Firefighters are exposed to dangerous situations, such as unstable, smoke-filled buildings.

## ▼ RELATED CAREERS

▶ **ARMY SOLDIER** *see pp. 230–231*

▶ **POLICE OFFICER** *see pp. 240–241*

▶ **PARAMEDIC** *see pp. 250–251*

▶ **DOG HANDLER** Works with trained dogs to detect and prevent crime, protect property, or find missing people. Dog handlers may work for the police force, the fire and rescue services, the armed services, the security industry, or customs and border control.

In the US, 33 percent of firefighters have made it their career; 67 percent are volunteers.

## CAREER PATHS

Probationary firefighters usually start their careers working at a local fire department, each of which recruits on a local basis. Other employers include airports and the military services. Progressing to senior roles depends on gaining qualifications in areas such as advanced firefighting techniques, emergency medical technology, and disaster management (coordinating the response to disasters).

# SKILLS GUIDE

 Physical strength and endurance to carry heavy equipment and injured or unconscious victims.

 Good verbal and written skills to communicate clearly and write accurate incident reports.

 Strong team-working skills for collaborating effectively and quickly with emergency staff.

 Good interpersonal skills for responding sensitively and reassuring people in distress.

 Excellent problem-solving skills for effective decisionmaking in life-or-death emergencies.

**TRAINEE** Your personal and physical attributes are more important than academic results, but a high school education is essential. To gain experience before applying, you can volunteer in support roles with a local fire station.

**FIREFIGHTER** Once you have gained front-line experience, you will have good prospects for advancing to senior and management roles. You can also specialize in a particular area, such as hazardous materials, fire investigation, or fire inspection.

**FIRE PREVENTION OFFICER** Visits homes and business premises to check that they are free from fire hazards and meet fire and safety regulations, such as having working fire alarms and extinguishers.

**FIRE INVESTIGATOR** Examines evidence at the scene of an incident to determine the causes of a fire, explosion, or other accident. Fire investigators are usually experienced former firefighters.

**AIRPORT FIREFIGHTER** Responds to aviation emergencies using specialty equipment, including suppressant foam for fighting aviation-fuel fires.

**STATION OFFICER** Manages the crew on shift—or watch—at a fire station, and ensures that crew are fully trained and firefighting equipment and vehicles are in a good condition. With experience, and after passing further exams, station officers can move up in rank, gaining additional responsibilities.

# PARAMEDIC

## JOB DESCRIPTION

Paramedics are health care experts who usually work as part of an ambulance crew. When called to the scene of an accident or emergency, a paramedic assesses the patient's condition and provides essential, sometimes life-saving care. They are trained to deal with minor injuries, such as cuts and fractures, as well as critical health conditions, such as heart attacks or strokes.

### SALARY

Newly qualified paramedic ★★☆☆☆
Senior paramedic ★★★☆☆

### INDUSTRY PROFILE

Number of jobs set to grow by as much as 15 percent in 2026 • Most employment with ambulance and health service providers • Some opportunities in the armed forces

## CAREER PATHS

You must start out as an emergency medical technician (EMT) before training for the role of paramedic. Once licensed as a paramedic, there are opportunities for further training in clinical practice or in rapid-response units.

**EMERGENCY CARE PARAMEDIC** Works alongside other medical staff in hospitals, prisons, or other institutions, providing emergency treatments on site. Further training is required to gain additional clinical skills.

**EMT** After earning your high school degree, you can enroll in an EMT training program. This training is likely to include hands-on experience in the field.

**GRADUATE** Paramedic training programs can last up to two years and result in an associate's degree. After completing the training program and passing state exams, you can apply for work as a paramedic.

**PARAMEDIC** With experience, you can specialize in heading up an emergency response team, which involves making quick decisions about surgical procedures and using advanced life support techniques.

# SKILLS GUIDE

 Team-working skills for cooperating with other health personnel in emergency situations.

 Strong leadership and organizational skills to direct team members during medical crises.

 Compassion and empathy when giving emotional support to patients and their families.

 Quick-thinking and decision-making skills for responding effectively to emergency situations.

 The confidence to carry out emergency procedures quickly in often tough conditions.

 High levels of physical fitness to use patient lifting devices and other equipment safely.

## AT A GLANCE

 **YOUR INTERESTS** Health and Medicine • Biology • Chemistry • Physics • Mathematics • Helping and caring for others

 **ENTRY QUALIFICATIONS** You must have a CPR certification and complete a training program. All states require paramedics to be licensed.

 **LIFESTYLE** Working hours are regular but usually involve shifts, covering nights, weekends, and public holidays.

 **LOCATION** Based at a hospital or an ambulance station, paramedics travel to emergencies and spend a lot of time on the road.

 **THE REALITIES** The work is physically tough and can be emotionally draining. Accident sites are often harrowing, so you need to keep calm and focused.

 **CRITICAL CARE PARAMEDIC** Provides advanced care for patients being transported between medical facilities: this may include managing airways, administering drugs, and monitoring signs of life.

 **RAPID RESPONSE PARAMEDIC** Works as part of a specialized rapid-response team, providing emergency care via a motorcycle, car, or air ambulance (helicopter) unit.

## ▼ RELATED CAREERS

▶ **FIREFIGHTER** see pp. 248–249

▶ **MEDICAL DOCTOR** see pp. 276–277

▶ **NURSE** see pp. 278–279

▶ **MIDWIFE** see pp. 280–281

▶ **AMBULANCE CARE ASSISTANT** Moves disabled, elderly, or vulnerable people to and from health clinics, and for routine hospital admissions.

# SOCIAL SERVICE AND TEACHING

Careers in this sector focus on improving the lives of individuals, families, groups, and wider society by caring for, training, developing, and supporting people. If you enjoy working with others and have good interpersonal skills, this may be the field for you.

## PSYCHOLOGIST
*Page 254*

Applying scientific methods to analyze human behavior, emotions, and thought processes, psychologists also deliver therapies to treat psychological conditions.

## COUNSELOR
*Page 256*

Using a range of behavioral and talking therapies, counselors help their clients explore, understand, and overcome their personal issues and problems.

## SOCIAL WORKER
*Page 258*

Working closely with hospitals, schools, and prisons, social workers aim to improve people's lives by providing help, support, and advice during difficult times.

## YOUTH WORKER
*Page 260*

Helping young people to reach their potential, youth workers provide a range of activities for children and teenagers, and offer them advice and support.

## CARE HOME MANAGER
*Page 262*

Working in a residential care home, care home managers ensure that elderly or ill residents are looked after in a supportive and stimulating environment.

## DAY CARE WORKER
*Page 264*

Encouraging the young children in their care to learn through play, day care workers organize activities, read stories, and play games to help them develop key skills.

## ELEMENTARY SCHOOL TEACHER
*Page 266*

In order to give children the best start to their education and encourage social development, elementary school teachers work to make learning fun and engaging.

## SECONDARY SCHOOL TEACHER
*Page 268*

With excellent communication skills, understanding, and a good sense of humor, secondary school teachers use their subject knowledge to educate and inspire students.

## COLLEGE PROFESSOR
*Page 270*

Working in a college or university, professors combine teaching undergraduate or graduate students with academic research in their chosen area of expertise.

## LIBRARIAN
*Page 272*

With a passion for knowledge, librarians catalog, store, and retrieve information in public, college, and university libraries—and, increasingly, in collections held online.

# PSYCHOLOGIST

## JOB DESCRIPTION

Psychologists apply scientific methods to analyze and explain human behavior. They use this understanding to help people overcome mental health problems, or to shape the way we organize many areas of society—for example, the way we are taught, and how people are treated and rehabilitated in hospitals and prisons. Specialty branches of psychology require special training.

### SALARY

Bachelor's graduate ★★☆☆☆
Doctoral graduate ★★★★☆

### INDUSTRY PROFILE

Large sector • Growing demand for psychologists as new areas of expertise develop • Most jobs in educational services, health care, and social service

## AT A GLANCE

**YOUR INTERESTS** Psychology • Biology • Mathematics (especially statistics) • Helping and caring for people

**ENTRY QUALIFICATIONS** Graduate-level qualifications are required; you will usually need to be licensed in order to practice.

**LIFESTYLE** Depending on their specialty, psychologists usually work normal office hours. If employed in a hospital, they may work shifts.

**LOCATION** Most psychologists see clients in person, but some are adopting a hybrid working space between home, offices, clinics, and institutions.

**THE REALITIES** The job can be emotionally stressful. In some branches of the profession, a psychologist can be on call for long periods of time.

## CAREER PATHS

You will need a minimum of a bachelor's degree to enter the profession. With relevant work experience, you can then study for a higher degree that will enable you to specialize in an area, from clinical to organizational psychology.

**BACHELOR'S GRADUATE**
With a degree in psychology and internship experience, you can work in many educational, rehabilitation, or health care settings.

**GRADUATE** To qualify as a psychologist, you generally need a doctoral degree in psychology and a license to practice. Master's degrees holders can be licensed in many of the same fields, but they are not called psychologists.

## SKILLS GUIDE

 Excellent verbal and written communication, and the ability to listen carefully to clients.

 The ability to work with other health care professionals to ensure the welfare of patients.

 An interest in science and a strong commitment to keep learning new skills.

 An ability to relate to people and remain calm with clients who may be distressed.

 Good problem-solving and decision-making skills, and the discipline to follow set guidelines.

## ▼ RELATED CAREERS

▶ **COUNSELOR** *see pp. 256–257*

▶ **SOCIAL WORKER** *see pp. 258–259*

▶ **SPEECH PATHOLOGIST** *see pp. 290–291*

▶ **TRAINING AND DEVELOPMENT SPECIALIST**
Plans and administers programs that improve the skills and knowledge of their employees.

There is growing demand for online therapy using video conferencing, apps, email, and messaging.

 **ORGANIZATIONAL PSYCHOLOGIST** Analyzes the working environment of an organization and suggests ways to improve staff welfare and productivity in the workplace.

 **FORENSIC PSYCHOLOGIST** Works with prison and probation services to develop effective programs that aim to prevent people from reoffending.

 **COUNSELING PSYCHOLOGIST** Helps people to manage difficult life events and circumstances, such as dealing with grief, anxiety, or depression.

 **SPORTS PSYCHOLOGIST** Helps athletes and sports teams overcome psychological barriers to their performance and training on the field of play.

 **SCHOOL PSYCHOLOGIST** Liaises with families and schools to address behavioral and learning difficulties in children and young people.

 **PSYCHOLOGIST** Once qualified, you will need to complete a graduate-level degree in a chosen area, which can lead to a range of different jobs.

 **CLINICAL PSYCHOLOGIST** Deals with the assessment and treatment of mental, emotional, and behavioral disorders in clients.

# COUNSELOR

## JOB DESCRIPTION

People seek a counselor's assistance to guide them through issues they encounter throughout various stages of their lives. Using talking therapies to build trust, counselors create a safe place for their clients to help them make choices that lead to positive changes or a new way of thinking. A counselor needs to have a high regard for confidentiality and professional ethics, and may use different counseling styles according to their client's needs.

### SALARY

Newly qualified counselor ★★★★★
Experienced counselor ★★★★★

### INDUSTRY PROFILE

Job opportunities in a variety of settings, from offices to schools • Growing demand for counseling drug and other substance addicts • Strong competition for jobs

## CAREER PATHS

Counselors require maturity and experience; many take up the job as a new career later in life for this reason. A bachelor's degree in social work or psychology is useful, and a master's degree in counseling is required. There are many forms of counseling and a variety of career paths.

**SCHOOL/COLLEGE COUNSELOR** Works with adolescents to help guide them through academic, personal, emotional, and social concerns.

**CASE MANAGER**
A good first step into the counseling profession, case managers support counselors' clients. These paraprofessionals do not require master's degrees.

**GRADUATE** To become a counselor, you must study counseling at a master's degree level.

**COUNSELOR** Once qualified and certified, most counselors choose to specialize in one of a number of areas. Further training and certification may be required for some of these paths.

# SKILLS GUIDE

 Excellent verbal, written, and listening skills for effective communication with clients.

 An ability to work with people in health care and refer clients to further sources of help.

 An interest in working with diverse organizations and with different kinds of people.

 High levels of empathy, patience, and a nonjudgemental attitude toward people in general.

 Good organizational skills for managing a large number of clients in a given period.

 The ability to help clients resolve their issues and find ways to improve their lives.

## AT A GLANCE

 **YOUR INTERESTS** Psychology • Sociology • Biology • Health care • Helping and supporting people

 **ENTRY QUALIFICATIONS** An appropriate degree and extensive therapy training are essential, as is accreditation by a professional body.

 **LIFESTYLE** Hours can vary due to clients' schedules. The majority of the work is one-on-one, but it may involve group therapy.

 **LOCATION** Most counselors are office-based but may need to visit clients in the community. Increasingly, they are working with clients online.

 **THE REALITIES** Counselors may hear about distressing situations, so the job can be emotionally demanding. Pay rates vary according to experience.

**MARRIAGE & FAMILY COUNSELOR** Helps couples and families to evaluate relationships with each other, or to resolve specific issues by encouraging communication and reflection.

**REHABILITATION COUNSELOR** Helps people with physical or intellectual disabilities overcome obstacles and achieve personal, career, and independent living goals.

**ADDICTION COUNSELOR** Supports people with drug, alcohol, or gambling dependence to help them to deal with the issues underlying their addiction.

## ▼ RELATED CAREERS

▶ **PROBATION OFFICER** see pp. 244–245

▶ **PSYCHOLOGIST** see pp. 254–255

▶ **SOCIAL WORKER** see pp. 258–259

▶ **CAREER ADVISOR** Works with adults or children to help them make choices about their future careers.

▶ **LIFE COACH** Helps people to achieve success in their lives by figuring out their goals and discussing ways to achieve desired outcomes.

▶ **PSYCHIATRIC NURSE** Uses a variety of treatments to support people with mental health conditions.

# SOCIAL WORKER

## JOB DESCRIPTION

For those committed to creating positive changes in people's lives, social work can be a rewarding career. Social workers provide help, support, and advice to vulnerable people in the community. They work closely with agencies, such as schools, hospitals, and probation services, to recommend ways in which struggling members of society can improve their lives.

### SALARY

Bachelor's level social worker ★★☆☆☆
Experienced social worker ★★★☆☆

### INDUSTRY PROFILE

Growing demand for social workers, especially to help aging population adjust to new treatments, medications, and lifestyles • Majority of work in the public sector

## AT A GLANCE

**YOUR INTERESTS** Sociology • Health and social service • Psychology • Child care and development • Helping and caring for people

**ENTRY QUALIFICATIONS** A degree in social work or a related field is required. Some jobs require a master's degree and accreditation by a professional body.

**LIFESTYLE** Many full-time social workers have normal office hours, but others can have nontraditional schedules. Part-time jobs are available.

**LOCATION** Although social workers work mostly from one location, they regularly visit clients at home or in schools and other community settings.

**THE REALITIES** Working with disadvantaged groups and making decisions that will affect a person's future can be emotionally challenging.

## ▼ RELATED CAREERS

▶ **PSYCHOLOGIST** *see pp. 254–255*

▶ **COUNSELOR** *see pp. 256–257*

▶ **YOUTH WORKER** *see pp. 260–261*

▶ **OCCUPATIONAL THERAPIST** *see pp. 292–293*

▶ **FAMILY SUPPORT WORKER** A type of social worker who offers practical and emotional support to people who are experiencing problems in their personal lives, such as families going through divorce, people with disabilities, and children whose parents are incarcerated.

▶ **SUBSTANCE ABUSE COUNSELOR** Helps people overcome their dependence on alcohol and over-the-counter or illegal drugs, providing them with practical advice and referrals to specialty organizations to plan recovery and treatment programs.

# CAREER PATHS

Social workers choose to specialize in one of many areas, such as homelessness or education, or move into management and training. Some social workers research, develop, and implement programs to address social issues.

**ASSISTANT SOCIAL WORKER** A bachelor's degree and an internship lets you work as a residential counselor, mental health assistant, or program coordinator.

**GRADUATE** To become a licensed clinical social worker, a master's or doctorate degree in social work is required. Licensure is required for independent practice.

## SKILLS GUIDE

 The ability to listen to, understand, and talk to clients in order to provide them with practical solutions.

 Good team-working skills, and the ability to work with organizations such as the police and schools.

 Empathy to understand a client's challenges in life and develop a good relationship with them.

 Excellent organizational skills to maintain accurate records for multiple cases and clients.

 The ability to solve problems efficiently to help people lead better and more fulfilling lives.

 Tact and perseverance with clients who are reluctant to accept help.

**SOCIAL WORKER** Once hired by an agency or company, you will be assigned a caseload while continuing your development. Later on you may choose an area to specialize in.

**MENTAL HEALTH SOCIAL WORKER** Works alongside health professionals and social service agencies to provide therapy and community-based services for people with mental illness.

**HEALTH CARE SOCIAL WORKER** Helps patients adjust to long periods of time in a hospital. Also helps those who have been discharged after a long-term illness or who are coping with a disability.

**SCHOOL SOCIAL WORKER** Supports families to ensure that children are attending school and reaching their full potential.

**CHILDREN'S SERVICES SOCIAL WORKER** Specializes in supporting children and families who are at risk or in trouble with the law. May work with adoptions or foster care.

# YOUTH WORKER

## JOB DESCRIPTION

Youth workers support and empower young people—often from disadvantaged or at-risk backgrounds—to improve their personal and social development. They may act as a mentor or counselor, organize activities, or run a drop-in center. Youth workers may specialize in working with young people in a local area or with specific needs, and may be employed by a nonprofit, faith-based group, or government body.

### SALARY

Newly qualified youth worker ★★☆☆☆
Youth service manager ★★★★☆

### INDUSTRY PROFILE

Increasing employment opportunities • Most youth workers employed in the public sector, but jobs also exist in nonprofit and voluntary sectors

## AT A GLANCE

**YOUR INTERESTS** Social work • Sociology • Psychology • Physical Education (PE) • Languages • Team sports • Performing arts • Music

**ENTRY QUALIFICATIONS** A good secondary education and a degree or postgraduate qualification in youth work or community services are useful.

**LIFESTYLE** Working hours vary, with evening and weekend duties often required. Part-time and self-employed work is available.

**LOCATION** Most of the work is office-based, but many youth workers visit clients in their homes, at school, in the community, or in prison.

**THE REALITIES** Working with disadvantaged young people requires resilience, and may occasionally involve conflict or threats to personal safety.

## CAREER PATHS

Most youth workers are graduates, with many courses including both academic study and practical work to allow students to gain hands-on experience while studying. You can specialize in a number of areas and will be able to apply for more managerial and senior roles after around five years of experience in the job.

**ASSISTANT YOUTH WORKER**
There may be opportunities for high school graduates to train on the job as a youth support worker. You can then study for a degree.

**GRADUATE** You will need an undergraduate degree in a relevant subject—or a graduate conversion course—and professional accreditation to apply for a job as a youth worker.

## ▼ RELATED CAREERS

▶ **SOCIAL WORKER** *see pp. 258–259*

▶ **FAMILY SUPPORT WORKER** Works with at-risk families to provide practical and emotional support, such as caring for children whose parents are divorcing or apart due to incarceration.

▶ **HOUSING OFFICER/MANAGER** Works for social housing associations and rehabilitative housing projects, providing on-site advice and support to residents and specific vulnerable groups, such as the homeless, refugees, ex-offenders, or disabled people.

▶ **LIFE COACH** Helps people achieve goals in their lives by figuring out their goals and discussing ways to achieve desired outcomes.

## SKILLS GUIDE

 Excellent interpersonal skills and emotional maturity for relating to young people and their problems.

 The ability to work closely with other professionals, such as police, teachers, and probation officers.

 Creative skills for organizing activities that build young people's self-esteem and personal skills.

 Good written and verbal skills for producing reports for funding, regulatory, or community groups.

 Strong self-management skills for handling a number of different cases at the same time.

**SUBSTANCE ABUSE WORKER**
Supports individuals seeking to overcome a dependency on illegal, prescription, or over-the-counter drugs and alcohol. Also provides referrals to other professionals, such as social workers, to plan a recovery and treatment program.

 **STUDENT COUNSELOR** Provides support and structured therapy to help young people overcome emotional and social problems that may affect their studies. Counselors usually work in a student-services department at a school, college, or university.

 **YOUTH/COMMUNITY CENTER LEADER** Organizes sports, arts, drama, and other activities at a local youth club, community center, or faith center. Leaders also develop and run projects that help young people deal with issues such as bullying or drug abuse.

**YOUTH WORKER** You may work with teenagers and young adults in areas that suffer from high unemployment and limited opportunities. With experience, you can move into management roles.

# CARE HOME MANAGER

## JOB DESCRIPTION

A care home manager oversees the day-to-day running of a residential care home and ensures that its residents receive a high standard of care. In this role, you manage the home's staff, ensure that it runs as a successful business, and plan activities, coordinate medical care, and provide support for residents.

### SALARY

Newly qualified manager ★★★★★
Experienced manager ★★★★★

### INDUSTRY PROFILE

Qualified managers in demand • Growing sector in many countries due to aging population and increasing need for care • Jobs in public, private, nonprofit, and voluntary sectors

## ▼ RELATED CAREERS

▶ **SOCIAL WORKER** *see pp. 258–259*

▶ **NURSE** *see pp. 278–279*

▶ **CARE ASSISTANT** Supports health care professionals in hospitals, care homes, sheltered housing, and other care environments.

▶ **HOME HEALTH NURSE** Visits the homes of patients who require care such as intermittent health monitoring, medication administration, and postsurgical wound care.

▶ **RETIREMENT COMMUNITY MANAGER** Manages the running of a retirement community, including overseeing the care and upkeep of the buildings, executing community events, and assisting the people who live there.

Of the 76 million baby boomers, 70 percent will need long-term care.

## AT A GLANCE

**YOUR INTERESTS** Health care • Sociology • Psychology • Mathematics • Biology • Physics • Chemistry • Business studies • Finance

**ENTRY QUALIFICATIONS** Experience in a social or health care role is essential. A degree in nursing or social work helps, but apprenticeships are also available.

**LIFESTYLE** Work is normally done in shifts to provide continual care. Managers may need to be on call to deal with emergencies at the home.

**LOCATION** The work may be based at a care home, sheltered accommodation, nursing home, or hospice. Some travel may be required for meetings or outings.

**THE REALITIES** This is an emotionally and physically demanding job, especially if living on-site. Regular inspections by regulatory bodies can be stressful.

## CAREER PATHS

Prospects for advancement in the residential care industry are good. As well as specializing in a particular client group, experienced managers may move into freelance consultancy or regional management, or become care home inspectors.

### SKILLS GUIDE

 Empathy, patience, and sensitivity for working with patients who have a range of medical needs.

 Physical and mental stamina in order to manage demanding and distressing situations.

 Effective leadership skills to manage and motivate a team of care workers and domestic staff.

 Strong organizational skills for supervising and coordinating the varied activities of a care home.

 Good business-management skills for recruitment, budgeting, marketing, and fundraising duties.

**ASSISTANT** You can gain experience by working on either a paid or voluntary basis after high school, and then study for qualifications in social service.

**QUALIFIED CARER** You need a degree-level qualification in social work, nursing, or a similar subject, as well as professional registration and management experience to apply for managerial jobs.

**CARE HOME MANAGER** In this role you care for residents of a home, meeting their physical, emotional, and medical needs. You can choose to specialize in a particular type of care home, or move into senior management roles.

**CHILDREN'S HOME MANAGER** Delivers care to children who have been placed under the protection of a local authority. A qualification in the social care of children is required to work in this field.

**NURSING HOME MANAGER** Specializes in the management of residential care for elderly people, who may have mental and physical health problems and complex medical needs.

**HOME CARE MANAGER** Works for a registered care agency, managing a team of health care professionals who administer care in a patient's own home.

**HOSPICE CARE MANAGER** Coordinates care, counseling, and support for patients in a hospice, an institution for seriously or terminally ill patients. A nursing qualification is required for this specialized role.

# DAY CARE WORKER

## JOB DESCRIPTION

Day care workers care for, educate, and supervise babies and young children at play, helping them to develop and learn. In this role, you are responsible for safeguarding the children and will encourage them to develop their numeracy, language, and social skills through games, activities, and excursions. Much of the work is with children under the age of five, but some nurseries offer after-school and care for older children.

### SALARY

Day care assistant ★★★★★
Day care manager ★★★★★

### INDUSTRY PROFILE

Growing sector in most parts of the world due to rapidly expanding population • Wide variety of employment options, including part-time and self-employed work

## CAREER PATHS

Day care workers are employed in many settings—from public- and private-sector day care centers to playgroups and children's centers—so job prospects in this sector are good. Specialized areas, such as caring for children with disabilities or learning difficulties, require more training and certification.

**HOSPITAL DAY CARE WORKER** Works with hospitalized children up to the age of five, caring for the needs of newborn babies or using play as a means of helping older children to cope with illness or hospital treatments.

**DAY CARE ASSISTANT** You can volunteer or work as a supervised day care assistant after high school, combining on-the-job experience with studying for a degree or certificate in childcare.

**GRADUATE** In some states, you will be required to earn an early childhood education certification before you can begin working in a day care center.

**DAY CARE WORKER** Most employers encourage you to continue your professional development, with courses in areas such as child welfare and preparing young children for school. With experience, you can specialize in different types of childcare.

# SKILLS GUIDE

Perseverance and patience for motivating young children to engage in play activities.

Excellent communication skills for interacting with children, parents, other carers, and day care staff.

Creativity and imagination for planning activities to stimulate the children to learn and play.

Attentiveness, empathy, and intuition to understand children's social and emotional needs.

Good observational skills to assess children and keep written reports on their development.

Good organizational skills for following health and safety rules and ensuring each child stays safe.

**DAY CAMP DIRECTOR** Runs summer vacation programs for day cares and other organizations, organizing activities such as sports, drama, and outings for children of all ages.

**NANNY** Looks after young children in a domestic setting. Nannies typically work in the home of the client family, caring for one or more children while their parents are at work.

**DAY CARE MANAGER** Oversees the day-to-day running and business operation of a day care center. Managers recruit staff and plan all the childcare and educational activities at the center.

## ▼ RELATED CAREERS

▶ **YOUTH WORKER** *see pp. 260–261*

▶ **CARE ASSISTANT** Supports health care professionals in hospitals, care homes, sheltered housing, and other care environments.

▶ **PEDIATRIC NURSE** Provides care and treatment for children under the age of 18, working with doctors, social workers, and health care assistants.

▶ **PRESCHOOL TEACHER** Teaches young children between the ages of three and five, covering subjects in the school curriculum. Jobs can be found in state or private schools.

▶ **TEACHING ASSISTANT** Helps out with school classroom activities and programs for learning.

## AT A GLANCE

**YOUR INTERESTS** Education • Caring for children • Psychology • Sociology • Arts and crafts • Storytelling • Physical Education (PE)

**ENTRY QUALIFICATIONS** A certificate or diploma in childcare is required. A degree in early childhood education may hasten promotion in the industry.

**LIFESTYLE** Day care workers usually work 40 hours a week. Many centers are open from 8am to 6pm, or longer, to fit in with parents' work routines.

**LOCATION** In addition to day care centers, playgroups, and children's centers, day care workers can work in households as nannies.

**THE REALITIES** Working with children requires patience and stamina. Starting salaries are usually low, and working hours may be longer than average.

# ELEMENTARY SCHOOL TEACHER

## SALARY

Newly qualified teacher ★★★★★
Elementary school principal ★★★★★

## INDUSTRY PROFILE

Elementary schools may be public or privately run • Many jobs available worldwide • Pay levels generally low to begin with but increase with experience

## JOB DESCRIPTION

Teaching at the elementary level is ideal for those who enjoy working with young children and are interested in education. Elementary school teachers need creativity and enthusiasm to design lessons to help children learn new skills and develop their interests. It is rewarding to help shape a child's emotional, educational, and social growth.

## AT A GLANCE

 **YOUR INTERESTS** Working with children • Mathematics • Science • Arts and crafts • Computers • Reading • Writing

 **ENTRY QUALIFICATIONS** Employers look for a degree in early childhood or elementary education. In most states, teachers must pass the PRAXIS I exam.

 **LIFESTYLE** Though they have summers off, hours are long. Teachers use time outside the classroom to plan lessons, talk to parents, and do further training.

 **LOCATION** Most jobs are found in elementary schools, but you may need to work flexibly delivering lessons online. Some teachers offer private tutoring.

 **THE REALITIES** Class sizes can be very large. Teachers can expect to have to instruct children of varying skill levels and backgrounds.

## CAREER PATHS

Once qualified, and with several years of experience, elementary school teachers can choose to coordinate school-wide efforts in key areas, such as numeracy, literacy, or special needs, or take up senior positions, such as a assistant principal or principal.

**ASSISTANT** Working as a paid or volunteer teaching assistant supporting teachers is an excellent way for you to gain relevant experience.

**GRADUATE** To become an elementary school teacher, you must be proficient in reading, writing, mathematics, and science. Most teachers hold a bachelor's degree, and some hold graduate-level teaching qualifications. Courses typically include a student-teaching program.

a

## ▼ RELATED CAREERS

▶ **COUNSELOR** *see pp. 256–257*

▶ **SOCIAL WORKER** *see pp. 258–259*

▶ **DAY CARE WORKER** *see pp. 264–265*

▶ **SECONDARY SCHOOL TEACHER** *see pp. 268–269*

▶ **THERAPEUTIC SUPPORT STAFF** Provides one-on-one behavioral interventions to children, while also supporting their families.

> Research has found that effective teachers in a child's early years can make a huge difference to their success in life.

## SKILLS GUIDE

 Good communication skills for giving instructions and relaying information clearly and simply.

 Creativity and innovation when designing activities to inspire and educate young children.

 Flexibility and adaptability to respond to different needs and situations.

 Good team-working and people skills for daily interaction with colleagues and parents.

 The ability to solve a wide range of problems, both academic and social.

 A good sense of humor and patience with young children in day-to-day classroom situations.

**PRINCIPAL** Runs the school, from leading and managing teachers to deploying the school's resources effectively.

**ELEMENTARY SCHOOL TEACHER** In charge of the class assigned to them. As a teacher, you may also specialize in a specific subject and oversee its running throughout the school.

**SPECIAL NEEDS TEACHER** Works with children who have a range of special educational needs. Extra training is required for this job.

**ESL TEACHER** English as a Second Language (ESL) teachers instruct students whose first language is a language other than English. They must undergo special training in order to teach these classes.

**PRIVATE TUTOR** Works privately with students to improve their performance in a particular subject or to prepare them for an examination.

# SECONDARY SCHOOL TEACHER

## JOB DESCRIPTION

A secondary school teacher prepares and teaches young people, and helps shape their interests and develop their future career options. They teach students in middle schools and high schools, and often specialize in one or two subjects from the curriculum. Many also mentor and provide learning support to students.

$$E = mc^2$$

### SALARY

Newly qualified teacher ★★★★★
High school principal ★★★★★

### INDUSTRY PROFILE

Increased demand as a large number of older teachers are expected to retire • Higher salary for teachers in leadership roles • Part-time work is available • High demand for private tutors

## CAREER PATHS

Secondary school teachers use curriculum-based teaching to prepare pupils of different abilities for postsecondary education, entry into the workforce, and standardized testing. They also liaise with parents and school administrators. With experience and training, they can move into a variety of senior roles at a school, or branch into policy and administration or curriculum development.

**DEPARTMENT SUPERVISOR** Assumes responsibility for the department in their subject area. This role usually requires years of teaching and may require additional coursework.

**STUDENT TEACHER** While studying for their teaching degree, student teachers gain valuable classroom experience under the guidance and supervision of a certified teacher.

**GRADUATE** You will need a good standard of education followed by a degree in a subject in the school curriculum. A graduate-level teaching qualification may be required.

**SECONDARY SCHOOL TEACHER** As a qualified teacher, you can teach pupils aged between 11 and 18, in one or two subjects. Teachers equip students with a range of life skills and prepare them for examinations.

## SKILLS GUIDE

 Excellent communication skills, and thorough mastery of material in subject(s) taught.

 Creativity for planning stimulating lessons, and to inspire and motivate students.

 The ability to handle and defuse any potentially distracting behavior.

 Highly developed organizational and time-management skills to prepare and deliver lessons.

 Flexibility in teaching style and the ability to adapt to the individual needs of students.

 **PRINCIPAL** Oversees the leadership and management of a school. Principals manage staff and make strategic decisions about the needs of the school and budget constraints.

 **SUPERINTENDANT** Acts in an advisory capacity for local authorities and government bodies, making decisions on education policy and strategy.

 **PRIVATE TUTOR** Offers private tutoring to pupils who need extra support beyond school lessons, or to prepare them for standardized tests. This role offers flexible hours.

## AT A GLANCE

 **YOUR INTERESTS** Teaching • Working with children • Problem-solving • Strong interest in at least one subject taught at school

 **ENTRY QUALIFICATIONS** Secondary school teachers require a bachelor's degree or higher. Some states require other licensure.

 **LIFESTYLE** Work runs through the academic year. Outside school hours, teachers plan lessons, grade exams, and take development courses.

 **LOCATION** Most jobs are found in secondary schools, but you may need to work flexibly delivering lessons online. Some teachers offer private tutoring.

 **THE REALITIES** The role may involve long hours, challenging situations between students, dealing with parents, and evening work.

## ▼ RELATED CAREERS

► **ELEMENTARY SCHOOL TEACHER** *see pp. 266–267*

► **COLLEGE PROFESSOR** *see pp. 270–271*

► **ADULT EDUCATION TEACHER** Works with people aged 19 and over to provide tutoring, training, and assessment in the workplace and in classrooms.

► **CAREER ADVISOR** Helps children and adults to make choices about their careers.

► **EDUCATION COORDINATOR** Escorts parties of schoolchildren around a museum or art gallery, and provides information on exhibits.

► **LEARNING MENTOR** Supports students who need extra help to address barriers to their learning.

# COLLEGE PROFESSOR

## JOB DESCRIPTION

If you are knowledgeable in and passionate about a particular subject and are interested in teaching, you could be a successful professor. College professors teach courses that lead to undergraduate or graduate degrees. They may combine teaching with carrying out research in their area of specialization.

### SALARY

Assistant professor ★★☆☆☆
Dean ★★★★★

### INDUSTRY PROFILE

Number of permanent, or tenured, positions is declining • Growth in opportunities in online education • Employment mostly on short-term contract basis

## AT A GLANCE

**YOUR INTERESTS** Teaching • Writing scholarly articles • Planning and problem-solving • Reading and research within a chosen field.

**ENTRY QUALIFICATIONS** A PhD is usually required, although a master's degree may suffice for more junior positions at some colleges.

**LIFESTYLE** Hours are long but flexible. You may work longer hours if doing research alongside giving lectures. Part-time positions may be available.

**LOCATION** Professors work in colleges and universities. Field work in an area of research may take them abroad or allow for a yearlong sabbatical.

**THE REALITIES** Administrative tasks can take up a lot of time. Competition for senior academic posts is intense. There is pressure to continually publish.

## ▼ RELATED CAREERS

▶ **SECONDARY SCHOOL TEACHER** *see pp. 268–269*

▶ **LIBRARIAN** *see pp. 272–273*

▶ **DISTANCE-LEARNING TEACHER** Supports and teaches distance-learning students remotely (very occasionally conducting seminars at university study centers and summer schools). Provides feedback on assignments, helps students understand material, and prepares them for examinations and end-of-module assessments.

▶ **INDEPENDENT RESEARCHER** Holds a research post or fellowship at a national or international research council, nonprofit, or commercial organization. This position usually follows many years' experience in academic research.

> The best professors have strong public speaking skills, in-depth subject knowledge, and the desire to motivate students.

## CAREER PATHS

College professors must be experts in their field. They need not have any formal teaching qualifications; however, some colleges do prefer candidates who have some teaching experience. Progress is related to your academic profile—which is formed in part by the quality of your published research—and your networking skills.

### SKILLS GUIDE

 In-depth knowledge and proficiency in a chosen area of expertise.

 Excellent communication skills for delivering lectures both in person and online.

 Well-developed leadership and management skills to direct a research team.

 Good organization skills to juggle teaching responsibilities, administrative tasks, and research.

High level of perseverance and dedication to complete research projects to a publishable standard.

**GRADUATE** One route is to obtain a graduate degree in a subject for which you have a passion. You will likely obtain some teaching experience along the way.

**INDUSTRY PROFESSIONAL** A good academic background plus work experience in a particular industry will help you find posts in subject areas such as finance or business studies.

**DOCTORAL CANDIDATE** PhD programs can take up to six years to complete, and include writing a dissertation, or a paper that details your research. You may be paid to teach undergraduates while working toward your PhD.

**ASSISTANT PROFESSOR** Delivers lectures and seminars while doing original research and publishing papers to raise their profile. May take on departmental tasks.

**ASSOCIATE PROFESSOR** Commonly a tenured position. Teaches classes and does scholarly work for publication in academic journals. Has an expanded role in the department.

**PROFESSOR** Leads the research culture of their department's faculty and focuses primarily on their scholarly activities.

**DEAN** Directs an institution's teaching and research, funding, and administration. The dean is the head of the college or university, with the position equivalent to being the director of a company.

# LIBRARIAN

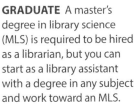

## JOB DESCRIPTION

Librarians organize and manage collections of books, journals, magazines, electronic documents, and more. Some of these collections are available to the public, while others are owned by colleges, museums, or professional bodies, like hospitals or law firms. Librarians select and buy books and other documents, catalog them so they can be located, and help the public find information.

### SALARY

Library assistant ★★★★★
Senior librarian ★★★★★

### INDUSTRY PROFILE

Rising employment opportunities • Growing use of electronic resources is expected to increase demand for roles in research libraries, where patrons need help sorting through digital data

## CAREER PATHS

A master's degree in library science (MLS) or a higher qualification in information management is usually required to become a librarian. Libraries range from small, local collections for children, to vast archives of medical, technical, or historical documents. Your career path will depend on your academic background and the area in which you choose to specialize.

**LIBRARY ASSISTANT** You can gain experience as an assistant. Duties include checking out materials to patrons, reshelving and organizing books, and responding to inquiries. A degree is needed to progress.

**GRADUATE** A master's degree in library science (MLS) is required to be hired as a librarian, but you can start as a library assistant with a degree in any subject and work toward an MLS.

**PUBLIC LIBRARIAN**
Helps users with research into printed and online information, and organizes collections that serve the needs of the local community and often acts as a hub for local events and cultural activities.

**LIBRARIAN** Experienced librarians develop a deep knowledge of the collections they manage and are skilled researchers. You can work in local or regional libraries and schools, but at the highest levels, you may manage large university libraries or national collections.

## SKILLS GUIDE

 Interpersonal skills to interpret the needs of users and direct them to the desired resources.

 Excellent organizational ability for maintaining extensive catalogs and managing staff.

 Patience to deal with requests from library users and track down elusive resources.

 Analytical thinking skills to develop new or revised systems, procedures, and work flows.

 Good computer skills for helping with online research and keeping abreast of new technologies.

 Strong team-working skills for interacting with staff, volunteers, and community agencies.

 **ACADEMIC LIBRARIAN** Works in higher education and research institutes, providing specialized and subject-specific support to students, teachers, and researchers.

 **MUSIC LIBRARIAN** Manages a collection of musical scores, books, and recordings. Music libraries are held at colleges and universities, national archives, and by record companies.

 **MEDICAL LIBRARIAN** Serves doctors, nurses, and families in health-care settings, managing medical documents on clinical trials, treatments, and procedures.

## ▼ RELATED CAREERS

▶ **EDITOR** *see pp. 56–57*

▶ **SECONDARY SCHOOL TEACHER** *see pp. 268–269*

▶ **ARCHIVIST** Stores and maintains materials that record the culture, history, and achievements of individuals or groups of people. These may include letters, photographs, maps, books, and objects.

▶ **BOOKSELLER** Buys books from publishers or wholesale suppliers and sells them to customers. Helps customers track down hard-to-find books.

▶ **INFORMATION SCIENTIST** Collects, stores, catalogs, and distributes printed and digital information within an organization. Most information scientists work in scientific, research, or technical companies.

## AT A GLANCE

 **YOUR INTERESTS** Writing • Literature • Reading • Research • Public service • Sciences • History • Information Technology (IT)

 **ENTRY QUALIFICATIONS** To be considered a full librarian, a master's degree in library and information science is required.

 **LIFESTYLE** Some libraries stay open late and over weekends, or host programs, so librarians may need to work beyond regular office hours.

 **LOCATION** Most of the working day is spent within the library building at a school, college, hospital, or academic institution.

 **THE REALITIES** Library users can be difficult, but helping people to find elusive information that they need can be rewarding.

# HEALTH AND MEDICINE

The health-care sector is a large industry with a variety of roles based in hospitals or in the community. If you have an interest in promoting health and well-being and an aptitude for science and technology, health and medicine could be for you.

## MEDICAL DOCTOR
*Page 276*

The medical profession is built upon the expertise and skill of doctors, who diagnose illness and injuries, and prescribe treatments to protect our health.

## NURSE
*Page 278*

Supporting doctors and other skilled medical personnel, nurses provide hands-on care and treatment to patients in a range of settings, from hospitals to health centers.

## MIDWIFE
*Page 280*

Caring for expectant mothers and unborn children during pregnancy and throughout labor, midwives play the vital role of delivering new life into the world.

## DENTIST
*Page 282*

From promoting good dental hygiene to performing reconstructive oral surgery, dentists apply a range of treatments to teeth and gums to promote dental health.

## PHARMACIST
*Page 284*

Ensuring that the appropriate medications are given to patients, pharmacists sell prescription and over-the-counter drugs to customers and advise on their safe use.

## RADIOGRAPHER
*Page 286*

Using X-ray equipment, radiographers create detailed internal images of the body for diagnostic purposes, or deliver radioactive treatment for tumors or tissue defects.

## PHYSICAL THERAPIST
*Page 288*

Experts in massage techniques, exercise programs, and complementary therapies, physical therapists work to encourage physical rehabilitation after injury or illness.

## SPEECH PATHOLOGIST
*Page 290*

Speech difficulties can be caused by trauma or may have been present from birth. Speech pathologists work with their patients to overcome or manage these problems.

## OCCUPATIONAL THERAPIST
*Page 292*

Based in hospitals or clinics, occupational therapists offer advice and practical help with everyday tasks to people in need due to illness, injury, aging, or disability.

## OPTOMETRIST
*Page 294*

Working on the front line of eye health, optometrists use specialized equipment to test patients' eyesight, prescribing glasses or contact lenses where required.

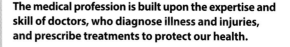

# MEDICAL DOCTOR

## JOB DESCRIPTION

Medical doctors examine patients to diagnose illnesses, injury, and medical conditions, and prescribe an appropriate course of treatment. They may also advise patients on how to lead a healthy lifestyle or refer them to specialists for further care. Doctors work in a wide variety of settings, including hospitals, community health centers, and the armed forces.

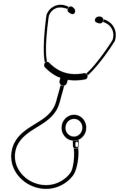

### SALARY

Medical resident ★★☆☆☆
Attending physician ★★★★★

### INDUSTRY PROFILE

Many unfilled vacancies, so future demand is high • Medical training is lengthy, but can lead to exciting job prospects worldwide • Can specialize in a certain type of care and work flexibly

## AT A GLANCE

**YOUR INTERESTS** Medicine • Caring for people • Physics • Chemistry • Biology • Mathematics • Psychology • Anatomy and physiology • Ethics

**ENTRY QUALIFICATIONS** A recognized medical degree is required, followed by training in a chosen area and passing required licensing exams.

**LIFESTYLE** Doctors work long hours and in shifts, especially during the earlier years of their career. Medical practitioners are never fully off duty.

**LOCATION** Doctors may work in hospitals, general practitioners' offices, or in the community. Some doctors choose to work in the armed forces.

**THE REALITIES** The medical profession is competitive, and training is long and demanding. Responsibility for patients brings intense scrutiny.

## CAREER PATHS

After earning their bachelor's degree, aspiring doctors must take the Medical College Admission Test (MCAT) and enroll in medical school, where they will combine internships and hands-on clinical experience with academic study. One or more residencies, which can last up to seven years depending on a person's chosen specialty, follows medical school.

**GRADUATE** You will need to complete a medical-school degree—entry to which is fiercely competitive—typically lasting four years.

**MEDICAL RESIDENT** You work and continue study in a residency program, treating patients under an experienced doctor's supervision.

## SKILLS GUIDE

 Empathy to understand people's problems, a caring approach, and the ability to put people at ease.

 Excellent communication skills for explaining diagnoses and treatments to patients with clarity.

 Analytical skills for diagnosing the best course of treatment after assessing illness and injury.

 Precision and dexterity to carry out both common medical procedures and complex surgery.

 Good technical and computer skills to keep records and operate sophisticated medical hardware.

## ▼ RELATED CAREERS

▶ **NURSE** *see pp. 278–279*

▶ **PHYSICAL THERAPIST** *see pp. 288–289*

▶ **CHIROPRACTOR** Cares for patients with health problems of the neuromusculoskeletal system, which includes nerves, bones, muscles, ligaments, and tendons.

▶ **DIETICIAN/NUTRITIONIST** Works with patients who struggle with maintaining healthy eating habits or who have food allergies, creating appropriate treatment programs for them.

▶ **PHYSICIAN'S ASSISTANT** Helps doctors diagnose and treat patients, recording medical histories, reporting test results, and compiling plans to manage a patient's treatment.

**HOSPITAL PHYSICIAN** Practices general medicine in a hospital, diagnosing and treating medical problems, usually in adults.

**PRIMARY CARE DOCTOR** Based in a practice within a community, they are usually the first point of contact for patients experiencing health problems.

**SURGEON** Works with other medical specialists (and may use robotic equipment) to treat injuries and diseases. There are numerous specialist areas within surgery.

**PSYCHIATRIST** Works with patients suffering from mental illnesses, diagnosing problems and determining treatment programs that may include medication and counseling.

**MEDICAL DOCTOR** Once qualified and licensed, you will use your specialized training to enter one of more than 60 different areas, such as pediatrics, radiology, anesthetics, surgery, general practice, or psychiatry.

**CLINICAL SPECIALIST** Practices one area of medicine, such as obstetrics and gynecology, or emergency medicine.

**NONCLINICAL SPECIALIST** Specializes in an area of medicine that has little contact with patients, such as radiology, pathology, or epidemiology (the study of how disease spreads).

# NURSE

## JOB DESCRIPTION

Nurses provide care and assistance for people who are ill, injured, or suffering from health problems. They administer treatments and therapies, plan patient care, and provide advice and practical support. There are opportunities to specialize and work at different locations, including hospitals, health centers, schools, and hospices, as well as in private practices.

## SALARY

Licensed practical nurse ★★☆☆☆
Nurse practitioner ★★★★☆

## INDUSTRY PROFILE

Great demand for nurses across the world • Numbers expected to rise along with the aging population and advances in medical science • Pay levels very structured

## ▼ RELATED CAREERS

▶ **MEDICAL DOCTOR** *see pp. 276–277*

▶ **MIDWIFE** *see pp. 280–281*

▶ **HOME HEALTH NURSE** Visits the homes of patients who require care such as intermittent health monitoring, medication administration, and postsurgical wound care.

▶ **PHYSICIAN'S ASSISTANT** Helps doctors diagnose and treat patients, recording medical histories, reporting test results, and compiling plans to manage a patient's treatment.

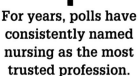

For years, polls have consistently named nursing as the most trusted profession.

## AT A GLANCE

**YOUR INTERESTS** Biology • Health and social service • Caring for people • Science • Psychology • Sociology • Medicine and pharmaceuticals

**ENTRY QUALIFICATIONS** A nursing degree, or degree-level apprenticeship, and membership of a professional body are required to practice.

**LIFESTYLE** Nurses usually work a standard work week overall. However, this includes shifts in the evenings, overnight, and on weekends.

**LOCATION** Nurses work out of hospitals, day care centers, schools, or hospices. They may also see patients for home visits or talk to children in schools.

**THE REALITIES** Nursing can be physically and emotionally demanding. Financial rewards improve with further qualifications and increased responsibility.

## CAREER PATHS

Depending on where you study, you may need to choose a specialty during your degree, although you can usually change direction later. Experienced nurses are valued in hospital management and public health roles, and some become nursing consultants.

**ASSISTANT (CNA)** Working as a Certified Nursing Assistant is useful experience. You can study part-time for a nursing degree.

**GRADUATE** You must have a nursing degree to register as a nurse. The course can take four years to complete and includes supervised clinical rotations.

## SKILLS GUIDE

 Good communication skills to help when working with people from different backgrounds.

 The ability to work successfully as part of a team in this busy, demanding profession.

 Natural compassion and empathy when providing support to patients and their families.

 A sense of humor to help motivate patients suffering from challenging conditions.

 Physical strength and good stamina when moving patients and equipment.

**LICENSED PRACTICAL NURSE**
Takes samples, removes or replaces dressings, and performs other health checks. Doctors rely heavily on the help of practical nurses to support them.

**PEDIATRIC NURSE**
Works with children of all ages to provide health care in children's homes and hospitals.

**REGISTERED NURSE**
Most nurses begin work with the general adult population, where there are the largest number of job vacancies. They can then specialize.

**HOSPICE NURSE**
Provides supportive care to people who are terminally ill and works with their families to plan end-of-life responsibilities.

**PSYCHIATRIC NURSE**
Helps patients in their recovery from mental health conditions. They administer appropriate medication and work with patients to help them lead fuller, more independent lives.

**NURSE PRACTITIONER**
Very experienced nurse, with advanced education and clinical training. Many focus in a certain area, like neonatal or psychiatric health.

# MIDWIFE

## JOB DESCRIPTION

A midwife specializes in supporting and protecting the health of a mother-to-be and her baby during pregnancy, childbirth, and the baby's first weeks of life. They may also offer other health care services for women, such as exams and prescriptions counseling. In this role, you will advise and assist women and their families with the emotional and practical issues associated with pregnancy, labor, and newborn care.

### SALARY

Midwifery assistant ★★★★★
Certified nurse-midwife ★★★★★

### INDUSTRY PROFILE

Many vacancies across the world · Demand for midwives growing as birth rates rise · Regulated profession with positions available in hospitals and in the community

## AT A GLANCE

**YOUR INTERESTS** Women's health and welfare · Health and social service · Biology · Science · Mathematics · Social sciences

**ENTRY QUALIFICATIONS** Professional midwives must have degrees in nursing, midwifery, or both. Requirements vary based on the type of certification.

**LIFESTYLE** Due to the unpredictable nature of childbirth, midwives work in shifts. Community-based midwives must be on call in case of emergency.

**LOCATION** Midwives work in hospital wards, community health centers, or birthing units. Community-based midwives may visit parents at home.

**THE REALITIES** Pregnancy and labor can involve medical complications and emergencies, which can be emotionally stressful. Shift work can be tiring.

## ▼ RELATED CAREERS

▶ **COUNSELOR** *see pp. 256–257*

▶ **HEALTH VISITOR** Visits patients in their homes to provide care following surgery, after childbirth, or for a range of other health issues.

▶ **NEONATAL NURSE** Provides nursing care for newborn babies who are premature or sick. Neonatal nurses work in special units in hospitals.

▶ **PEDIATRIC NURSE** Provides health care to children of all ages in hospitals, care homes, and schools. Pediatric nurses have to work closely with parents.

▶ **SONOGRAPHER** Uses ultrasound to examine unborn babies, checking their development and screening them for medical conditions.

There are more than 12,000 practicing midwives in the United States.

## CAREER PATHS

Midwifery offers opportunities for working in a range of settings around the world. Midwives may be based in hospitals, maternity clinics, midwife units, and birth centers, or even make home visits.

**NURSE** You can earn a nursing degree, then specialize in midwifery by undertaking training after you have qualified as a nurse.

**GRADUATE** A college education and work experience will help you when applying for a midwifery degree, which is the usual route of entry into the job.

### SKILLS GUIDE

 Good communication skills for interacting with patients from different backgrounds.

 The ability to work with other health care professionals, such as doctors and health visitors.

 Compassion and empathy for delivering care with sensitivity to expectant parents.

 Persistence, a good sense of humor, and the ability to motivate patients and staff.

 Physical strength to lift patients and equipment, and stamina to endure long hours and stress.

**MIDWIFE** As a qualified midwife, you can work in a variety of settings or follow a number of specialized career paths. You can also choose to alternate between prenatal, delivery, and postnatal jobs.

**HOSPITAL MIDWIFE** Works in the prenatal, labor, and postnatal wards of hospitals to provide care to expectant and new mothers.

**COMMUNITY-BASED MIDWIFE** Runs clinics, refers cases to doctors when required, and cares for women in labor, especially those having home births.

**CLINICAL RESEARCHER** Conducts clinical studies with the aim of improving the care of expectant mothers, procedures used in childbirth, and the treatment of children in their early months.

**CONSULTANT MIDWIFE** Provides specialized care in complicated deliveries, such as Caesarian sections, as well as helping to train new midwives. May also participate in research programs to assess and improve midwifery methods.

**MIDWIFERY TEAM MANAGER** Manages a team of midwives on a hospital maternity ward, combining hands-on duties with overseeing the work of other midwives.

# DENTIST

## JOB DESCRIPTION

Dentists diagnose and treat damage, disease, and decay to the teeth, gums, and mouth, and provide cosmetic treatments to improve their appearance. They also educate and advise patients on effective cleaning techniques, mouth hygiene, and diet to maintain oral and dental health. Dentists might work in a hospital to carry out reconstructive surgery for patients with facial injuries, or perform routine dental care in a clinic.

### SALARY

Newly qualified dentist ★★★☆☆
Senior dental practitioner ★★★★★

### INDUSTRY PROFILE

Good job prospects and opportunities for career advancement • High salaries • Continued growth in demand for dental services • Strong competition for training programs and residencies

## AT A GLANCE

**YOUR INTERESTS** Medicine • Biology • Chemistry • Physics • Biochemistry • Anatomy • Information Technology (IT) • Public health

**ENTRY QUALIFICATIONS** A degree in dentistry is required. Work experience, such as shadowing a dentist, will help when applying for courses.

**LIFESTYLE** Work hours vary by practice, and may include evening or weekend duties, and periods on call over public holidays.

**LOCATION** Most dentists work in a consulting room within a private dental practice, a hospital, or a clinic. Some dentists work for the armed forces.

**THE REALITIES** Dentists might have to work with patients who are unhygienic or who have oral diseases. Some patients might become stressed during treatment.

## CAREER PATHS

Many aspiring dentists complete a bachelor's degree before entering four-year dental school, where they can choose a specialization. Most dentists work on a self-employed basis as general practice dentists, owning or being a partner in a clinic. Switching between general practice and hospital dentistry is less common.

**UNDERGRADUATE** If your grades do not meet the minimum level required for entry into dental school, you may find it helpful to take a year-long foundation course before applying again.

**DENTAL SCHOOL GRADUATE** You have to take the Dental Admissions Test to enter dental school and complete a doctorate in dentistry in order to practice as a dentist. Some students can pursue a combined bachelor's and doctorate degree.

## ▼ RELATED CAREERS

▶ **MEDICAL DOCTOR** *see pp. 276–277*

▶ **NURSE** *see pp. 278–277*

▶ **PHARMACIST** *see pp. 284–285*

▶ **OPTOMETRIST** *see pp. 294–295*

▶ **DENTAL HYGIENIST** Advises patients on how to care for their teeth and gums to help prevent tooth decay and gum disease. Dental hygienists use dental instruments to clean patients' teeth and remove dental plaque.

▶ **DENTAL TECHNICIAN** Designs and constructs a range of dental devices to repair decaying teeth, replace lost teeth, and improve the general appearance of teeth.

# SKILLS GUIDE

 Excellent communication skills to interact with patients and explain treatments to them.

 Strong leadership abilities for recruiting, training, and managing a dental practice team.

 Good interpersonal skills to understand patients' problems and to put them at ease.

 Excellent manual dexterity for carrying out intricate dental work using medical instruments.

 Attention to detail and precision to ensure that treatments are administered accurately.

**ORTHODONTIST** Corrects the abnormal alignment of the teeth and jaws by fitting dental appliances, such as dental braces and space retainers.

**MAXILLOFACIAL SURGEON** Offers reconstructive surgery to patients who have defects or injuries—such as cleft palates, accident injury, or cancers—to the mouth, teeth, jaws, and face.

**HOSPITAL DENTIST** Treats patients in a hospital setting, carrying out complex dental and surgical procedures. Hospital dentists may specialize in restorative surgery, or in pediatric dentistry—treating children—for example.

**DENTIST** The requirements for becoming a licensed dentist vary by state. To specialize, you will need to undergo up to six years of further training in your chosen specialization.

**PUBLIC HEALTH DENTIST** Assesses the dental needs of a region, rather than of an individual patient. Also gives advice on preventing dental disease, and ensures that dental services meet public needs.

**COMMUNITY DENTIST** Works at health centers, mobile clinics, or care homes to offer dental care to children, people with specialized needs, and the elderly.

# PHARMACIST

## SALARY

Trainee pharmacist ★☆☆☆☆
Senior pharmacist ★★★★★

## INDUSTRY PROFILE

Good employment opportunities • Expanding sector due to development of new medical products and increasing life expectancy, leading to rising demand for pharmaceuticals

## JOB DESCRIPTION

Pharmacists are responsible for the safe supply of medicines to hospital patients and the general public. They prepare medicines for use, checking the dosage, ensuring compatibility with other drugs a patient may be taking, and labeling the medicine clearly. They also counsel and give advice to customers on prescription drugs, over-the-counter products, and the treatment of minor ailments.

## CAREER PATHS

After a relatively lengthy training period and passing state and national exams, pharmacists can choose from a wide range of career options. Moving between the branches of pharmacy—such as clinical, hospital, or retail work—is common. Experience brings opportunities in management, sales, consultancy, research, or training.

**CLINICAL PHARMACIST** Works in a hospital, clinic, or doctor's surgery with other medical specialists, ensuring that patients receive the correct medication and that regulations on prescriptions are followed.

**PHARMACY ASSISTANT** You can apply for jobs as a pharmacy assistant after a period of foundation-level study, but you will need a degree to become a pharmacist.

**GRADUATE** To obtain a license as a registered pharmacist, you need to obtain your doctor of pharmacy (PharmD) degree and complete internships for hands-on experience.

**PHARMACIST** As a pharmacist, you can study for postgraduate qualifications or take professional training to enhance your skills. You could choose to specialize in a particular area, such as complementary medicine, or move into research.

# SKILLS GUIDE

Good communication skills to listen to patients' needs and give instructions on taking medicines.

Strong mathematical skills for using scientific formulae and making complex calculations.

The ability to interact clearly and sympathetically with customers and health care professionals.

Good analytical skills and scientific understanding for diagnosing a patient's medication needs.

An eye for detail and a systematic approach to ensure medications are dispensed accurately.

**COMMUNITY PHARMACIST** Provides health care advice and dispenses or sells medications in a retail pharmacy. May also deliver medication to home-bound patients, visit care homes, and give immunizations.

**INDUSTRIAL PHARMACIST** Conducts research into the properties of new drugs, testing and developing products in order to bring them to market. Industrial pharmacists also perform checks to ensure that existing drugs meet safety and quality standards.

**NUCLEAR PHARMACIST** Specializes in preparing and dispensing radioactive drugs, which are used in hospitals and clinics to treat cancer, and to diagnose disorders.

## ▼ RELATED CAREERS

▶ **PHARMACOLOGIST** *see pp. 140–141*

▶ **BIOCHEMIST** Studies chemical reactions in living organisms, proteins, cells, and DNA to understand the effects of drugs, foods, allergies, and diseases.

▶ **BIOMEDICAL RESEARCH SCIENTIST** Performs clinical trials and laboratory tests to research new methods for treating diseases, ailments, and health conditions.

▶ **HOMEOPATH** Treats physical, psychological, and emotional conditions by using natural substances to stimulate the body's natural healing processes.

▶ **TOXICOLOGIST** Conducts experiments to research the impact of toxic and radioactive materials on people, animals, and the environment.

## AT A GLANCE

**YOUR INTERESTS** Medicine • Health care • Chemistry • Biology • Physics • Mathematics • Anatomy • Social welfare

**ENTRY QUALIFICATIONS** A degree in pharmacy is required, followed by study for professional qualifications needed by regulatory bodies.

**LIFESTYLE** Work can either be full-time or part-time. Some weekend work may be required for pharmacists who work in hospitals or in retail.

**LOCATION** The work is community-based, in a pharmacy or retail store, or in a hospital or clinic, either on the ward or in a dispensary.

**THE REALITIES** Mistakes in dispensing medication can endanger patients' health. Preparing and dispensing medicines can be repetitive in nature.

# RADIOGRAPHER

## JOB DESCRIPTION

A vital part of a hospital team, radiographers use X-rays and sound waves to specialize in either diagnosing disorders and injuries, such as broken bones, or in treating illnesses, including some types of cancer. They combine knowledge of human biology with the technical skills needed to operate sophisticated equipment, including (in some locations) artificial intelligence that can assist with accurate diagnoses.

### SALARY

Newly qualified radiographer ★★☆☆☆
Experienced radiographer ★★★★☆

### INDUSTRY PROFILE

Growing profession within the health care industry • Opportunities in government-run and private settings • Rapidly changing technologies and techniques require regular training

## AT A GLANCE

**YOUR INTERESTS** Biology • Human anatomy • Physics • Technology • Medicine • Helping people • Problem-solving

**ENTRY QUALIFICATIONS** Most radiographers earn an associate's degree in radiation science. You must also pass a board exam before practicing.

**LIFESTYLE** Diagnostic radiographers work in shifts, while those working in the therapeutic branches of radiography have more regular hours.

**LOCATION** Radiographers mainly work in a hospital or clinic, within a specialized radiography unit or in an operating theater.

**THE REALITIES** Shift-work does not suit everyone, and financial rewards can be modest. The hospital environment is physically and emotionally stressful.

## CAREER PATHS

The radiography profession is split into two distinct strands. Diagnostic radiographers use imaging technologies, such as X-rays, Computed Tomography (CT), and ultrasound to diagnose illness and injury. Therapeutic radiographers use targeted doses of radiation to treat patients with conditions such as cancer.

**ASSISTANT** You may be able to help radiographers in day-to-day work as an assistant while studying to qualify as a radiographer.

**GRADUATE** When opting for a degree in radiography, you will study topics such as biology and anatomy and complete clinical rotations.

## ▼ RELATED CAREERS

▶ **MEDICAL DOCTOR** *see pp. 276–277*

▶ **CLINICAL SCIENTIST** Specializes in the research, development, and testing of medical equipment and advances in diagnostic techniques.

▶ **MEDICAL PHYSICIST** Develops new methods and technologies to investigate and treat illness, and also assists medical staff with the use and maintenance of complex medical equipment.

▶ **RADIATION THERAPIST** Treats cancer and other diseases in patients by administering radiation treatments.

▶ **RADIOLOGIST** Diagnoses illnesses based on the interpretation of radiographic tests. Radiologists are qualified hospital doctors.

# SKILLS GUIDE

Clear and effective communication skills for dealing with patients of all ages and from all backgrounds.

Care and consideration for others for dealing sympathetically with patients who are ill.

Being a team player in coordinating patient treatments with other health care staff.

A natural flair for working with complex technology and sophisticated scanning equipment.

An eye for detail when interpreting scans to maintain high standards of patient care.

**DIAGNOSTIC RADIOGRAPHER**
In this role, you use high-tech scanning equipment to diagnose illness and injury.

**THERAPEUTIC RADIOGRAPHER**
This type of radiography involves you planning and delivering doses of radiation to treat patients suffering from cancer.

**SPECIALIST RADIOGRAPHER**
Uses advanced types of diagnosis radiography, such as ultrasound or Magnetic Resonance Imaging (MRI), and becomes involved in research into new imaging techniques.

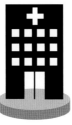

**CONSULTANT RADIOGRAPHER**
Works in a range of settings, including hospitals, to develop and promote new and exciting research.

# PHYSICAL THERAPIST

## JOB DESCRIPTION

Physical therapists play a vital part in treating people with physical difficulties resulting from injury, illness, disability, or aging. A physical therapist uses treatments including massage, hydrotherapy, and exercise to help patients recover or manage their condition. They may work in private practices, or in hospitals alongside other health care experts, such as doctors, nurses, occupational therapists, and social workers.

### SALARY

Physical therapy assistant ★★★★★
Physical therapist ★★★★★

### INDUSTRY PROFILE

Strong competition for jobs • Most opportunities in hospitals and private clinics • Growing demand for physical therapists as aging population wants to stay active

## AT A GLANCE

**YOUR INTERESTS** Physical therapy • Massage • Exercise • Health and social service • Sports • Biology • Anatomy • Health science • Psychology

**ENTRY QUALIFICATIONS** Undergraduate, postgraduate, or apprenticeship degree is necessary, along with ongoing training.

**LIFESTYLE** Physical therapists typically have a normal work week, although some clinics are open in the evening and on weekends.

**LOCATION** Most therapists work in hospitals, nursing homes, schools, and outpatient practices. Home visits are also possible.

**THE REALITIES** Treating patients over several weeks or months can be physically and mentally demanding, but rewarding when patients show improvement.

## CAREER PATHS

Physical therapists have several career options. They could work in a hospital or choose one of the specialty areas within the profession. Clinical experience in physical therapy may open up a career in hospital or health service management, or in teaching. Many physical therapists also move into private practice once they have gained extensive experience.

**ASSISTANT** You can start by assisting a qualified physical therapist while studying for your bachelor's degree.

**GRADUATE** Before practicing, you must graduate from an accredited doctoral program, pass the national physical therapy exam, and apply for a license in the state in which you want to work.

## ▼ RELATED CAREERS

▶ **OCCUPATIONAL THERAPIST** *see pp. 292–293*

▶ **PERSONAL TRAINER** *see pp. 300–301*

▶ **ATHLETIC TRAINER** Works alongside athletes to ensure they are training in a safe and smart way, allowing them to achieve their potential.

▶ **MASSAGE THERAPIST** Uses massage to ease the aches and pains of patients and clients, treat specific muscular problems, such as spasms and sprains, or enhance their general well-being.

▶ **SPORTS SCIENTIST** Applies a science-based knowledge of sports and human biology to work with athletes, doctors, and other health care professionals. Helps athletes to improve their performance and take better care of their bodies.

## SKILLS GUIDE

 Effective communication with a wide range of patients and health care workers.

 The ability to work in teams alongside a range of other health care professionals.

 Empathy and sensitivity in understanding patients' problems to provide the right treatment.

 Problem-solving skills to diagnose and treat conditions, which may require technical equipment.

 Physical strength and stamina to carry out massage treatments on patients.

**ORTHOPEDIC PHYSICAL THERAPIST** Assesses and treats patients recovering from surgery, accidents, or other injuries.

**GERIATRIC PHYSICAL THERAPIST** Specializes in helping elderly patients improve their mobility, adjust to living at home after surgery, or manage pain from medical conditions such as arthritis.

**PEDIATRIC PHYSICAL THERAPIST** Works with children to address physical problems and in rehabilitation after surgery or accidents.

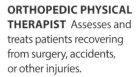

**PHYSICAL THERAPIST**
Once working as a qualified physical therapist, you can take specific courses to expand your skills and knowledge.

**SPORTS PHYSICAL THERAPIST**
Treats a range of sports-related injuries. They also offer guidance on prevention of injury, fitness programs, and nutrition.

**NEUROSCIENCE PHYSICAL THERAPIST** Assesses and treats patients after stroke, spinal cord injury, or traumatic brain injury. Helps to retrain the brain.

# SPEECH PATHOLOGIST

## SALARY

Newly qualified pathologist ★★☆☆☆
Team leader ★★★★☆

## INDUSTRY PROFILE

Job opportunities available worldwide • Most speech and language therapists work for educational or public sector health organizations • Increasing number of freelance therapists

## JOB DESCRIPTION

A speech pathologist assesses, diagnoses, and supports people with speech and communication problems. They also help people who are experiencing difficulties in eating, drinking, and swallowing. They may treat patients, both children and adults, with neurological disorders or developmental delays.

## CAREER PATHS

A newly qualified speech pathologist or therapist usually joins an expert care team, which includes teachers, nurses, doctors, and psychologists. Once licensed, you can gain clinical experience on a broad level or specialize in one area of therapy before looking to progress into a managerial role.

**CHILD SPEECH AND LANGUAGE THERAPIST** Works alongside hearing specialists (audiologists), and Ear, Nose, and Throat (ENT) doctors, to assess and treat children. In schools, they work with teachers and parents to provide support in classroom activities.

**ASSISTANT** After graduating college, you can gain valuable experience assisting a qualified speech pathologist while you study for your master's degree.

**GRADUATE** You must have a master's degree in speech pathology in order to enter the profession. Requirements to become a speech pathologist can vary by state.

**SPEECH PATHOLOGIST** In this job, you assess a client's needs to deliver a course of treatment in consultation with other health professionals and the client's family or teachers.

## SKILLS GUIDE

 The ability to listen carefully and communicate clearly with both children and adults.

 Good team-working skills to cooperate with teachers, social workers, and health professionals.

 The ability to be sensitive and compassionate toward vulnerable and anxious patients.

 Attention to detail for interpreting measurements to make a correct diagnosis.

 Persistence, a good sense of humor, and the ability to motivate patients.

**ADULT SPEECH PATHOLOGIST** Works with adults suffering from speech and communication problems that may have resulted from injury, stroke, cancer, or age-related disorders.

**TEAM LEADER** Takes charge of the work and staffing of a unit, or joins a hospital's management team. This job requires work experience because it is a leadership role.

**CLINICAL RESEARCHER** Conducts clinical trials on patients with the goal of improving medical procedures and clinical practices.

## ▼ RELATED CAREERS

▶ **PSYCHOLOGIST** *see p. 254–255*

▶ **PHYSICAL THERAPIST** *see pp. 288–289*

▶ **OCCUPATIONAL THERAPIST** *see pp. 292–293*

▶ **HEARING THERAPIST** Works with adults and children who experience disruptions to their hearing or loss of hearing, and balance problems.

▶ **NUTRITIONIST** Offers advice and information about healthy diets and lifestyles. Nutritionists can also conduct research and make recommendations to food companies and health care authorities.

▶ **RECREATIONAL THERAPIST** Devises health treatment programs based on the arts, music, or sports.

## AT A GLANCE

 **YOUR INTERESTS** Medicine • Biology • Psychology • Science • Health and social service • Social sciences • Languages • Linguistics

 **ENTRY QUALIFICATIONS** A master's degree and professional license are required to be able to practice as a speech pathologist.

 **LIFESTYLE** Working hours are usually regular. Part-time work and freelance positions are also available, offering more flexibility.

 **LOCATION** Pathologists work in hospitals, community health or assessment centers or schools. They may travel to work at different locations.

 **THE REALITIES** Although patient expectations can be high and the work itself can be relentless and tiring, it is also extremely rewarding.

# OCCUPATIONAL THERAPIST

## JOB DESCRIPTION

Occupational therapists use individual treatment programs, exercise, and psychological therapies to help people overcome problems caused by disability, illness, injury, or aging. The therapist trains patients to carry out daily tasks so they can lead full, independent lives.

### SALARY

Occupational therapy assistant ★★★★★
Occupational therapy manager ★★★★★

### INDUSTRY PROFILE

Rising demand for occupational therapists • Majority of work in government-sector areas, such as health and social service • Job opportunities worldwide

## AT A GLANCE

**YOUR INTERESTS** Biology • Health and social service • Psychology • Social sciences • Supporting people with mobility problems

**ENTRY QUALIFICATIONS** A graduate degree in occupational therapy is required. You must also pass the national exam and apply for state licensure.

**LIFESTYLE** Most therapists work regular hours, but some work shift patterns. Part-time and flexible work options are also available.

**LOCATION** Occupational therapists work in hospitals, prisons, at social service offices, and in private practices. They may travel to visit their patients.

**THE REALITIES** Some patients can be challenging. Occupational therapists need physical strength and agility, as well as patience and a sense of humor.

## ▼ RELATED CAREERS

▶ **PSYCHOLOGIST** *see pp. 254–255*

▶ **SOCIAL WORKER** *see pp. 258–259*

▶ **PHYSICAL THERAPIST** *see pp. 288–289*

▶ **SPEECH PATHOLOGIST** *see pp. 290–291*

▶ **HEARING THERAPIST** Works with adults and children who are experiencing hearing loss, hearing disturbances, and balance problems. Hearing therapists mainly work in hospitals and health centers where they assess patients and develop treatment plans.

▶ **MASSAGE THERAPIST** Provides massages to patients and clients to relieve any physical discomforts, enhance general well-being, and treat specific muscular problems, such as spasms and strains.

▶ **OCCUPATIONAL HEALTH NURSE** Promotes better health and well-being in the workplace, usually as part of a health and safety team.

## CAREER PATHS

A master's degree and professional license is necessary to practice as an occupational therapist. The work is highly varied with opportunities to specialize in different areas or to progress into management, research, or teaching. Some experienced therapists choose to take up roles in industry or to establish themselves in private practice.

### SKILLS GUIDE

 Excellent communication skills in order to interact with patients and other people in medical care.

 The willingness to work in a team with other medical and social service staff.

 The ability to be sensitive and empathize with people who have physical and emotional problems.

 Good decision-making and organizational skills to prioritize and manage case loads.

 Patience and perseverance in assisting patients unwilling to accept help.

 Physical strength and stamina to lift heavy equipment and help maneuver patients.

**ASSISTANT** After graduating high school, you can support a qualified therapist while studying for a degree.

**GRADUATE** You must earn a bachelor's degree in occupational therapy and pass the national exam before you can practice.

**OCCUPATIONAL THERAPIST** Assesses their clients and draws up suitable treatment plans, then works with them to achieve their targets.

**ORTHOPEDIC OCCUPATIONAL THERAPIST** Works as part of a health care team, helping patients recover after surgery on, or injury to, bones and muscles.

**PEDIATRIC OCCUPATIONAL THERAPIST** Works with children with developmental challenges including autism. Travels to schools to assess children and consult with teachers on appropriate activities.

**MENTAL HEALTH OCCUPATIONAL THERAPIST** Helps people, including children in schools, adjust to living with mental health issues.

**GERIATRIC OCCUPATIONAL THERAPIST** Assists elderly clients with age-related problems and medical conditions, such as dementia, impaired vision or hearing, and poor mobility.

# OPTOMETRIST

## JOB DESCRIPTION

An optometrist is a specialized doctor who examines a patient's eyes to test their sight and check for injury, disease, or other eye-related conditions. They use specialty eye-testing equipment to diagnose eyesight problems, prescribe glasses or contact lenses to correct defects in vision, and prescribe medications to treat and manage eye diseases.

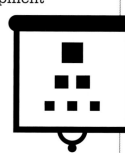

## AT A GLANCE

**YOUR INTERESTS** Eye care • Health care • Biology • Physics • Chemistry • Mathematics • Science • English • Information Technology (IT)

**ENTRY QUALIFICATIONS** A degree in optometry and professional license are required before practicing as an optometrist.

**LIFESTYLE** Optometrists work regular office hours, but evening and weekend work may be required. Part-time consultancy work is also available.

**LOCATION** Optometrists spend most of their time working in a private consulting or treatment room in an optician's practice, a clinic, or a hospital.

**THE REALITIES** Most of the work is spent conducting eye examinations inside a small room with no natural light, in close proximity to patients.

## CAREER PATHS

After qualifying, most optometrists find work in independent practices or with larger companies that provide eye care to the public. Some work in hospitals, supporting other doctors and surgeons to deal with more complex eye problems; others work for manufacturers of spectacles and contact lenses, developing new products.

**OPTICIAN** If you have worked as an optician or optometric technician, your experience will help you when applying to medical school.

**GRADUATE** You need a bachelor's degree and doctorate of optometry degree, and to pass a series of exams, before becoming an optometrist.

## ▼ RELATED CAREERS

▶ **MEDICAL DOCTOR** *see pp. 276–277*

▶ **DENTIST** *see pp. 282–283*

▶ **OPHTHALMOLOGIST** Diagnoses, treats, and prevents eye diseases. Ophthalmologists are medical doctors who carry out eye surgery in hospital eye departments, as well as in outpatient units and private laser-eye-surgery clinics.

▶ **OPTICIAN** Fits and supplies glasses and contact lenses according to prescriptions written by optometrists.

▶ **VISION THERAPIST** Investigates, diagnoses, and treats any abnormalities in eye movement and eye function.

## SKILLS GUIDE

 Excellent communication skills for explaining treatments to patients and answering their queries.

 Flexibility to adapt to advances in optometric practice, such as improved scientific techniques.

 Strong interpersonal skills to liaise with and put patients at ease, and interact with colleagues.

 The ability to analyze scientific and mathematical data, and to diagnose patients accurately.

 Good manual dexterity for using sophisticated optometric equipment correctly.

 Concentration, precision, and attention to detail for examining patients' eyesight accurately.

**PRIVATE PRACTICE OWNER** Oversees the running of an optometry practice, managing the business, recruiting staff, and ordering stock, often in addition to seeing patients.

**CONSULTANT (HOSPITAL) OPTOMETRIST** Assesses, treats, and monitors patients suffering from sight loss or complex or serious eye conditions. The role also involves helping patients in their rehabilitation following surgery or disease.

**OPTICAL DESIGN CONSULTANT** Works with technologists in the optical manufacturing industry, helping to shape the design of glasses, contact lenses, and optical products for other purposes, such as telescopes or scanning systems.

**OPTOMETRIST** You will need to undertake continued training in order to have your professional license renewed each year. You can specialize in a particular area (such as children or partially sighted patients), work in a shop or hospital, or open your own clinic.

# SPORTS, LEISURE, AND TOURISM

As the world economy expands, the global demand for recreational pursuits increases every year. Enthusiasm, excellent communication skills, and the ability to help people enjoy their leisure time are prerequisites for working in this growing sector.

## PROFESSIONAL ATHLETE
*Page 298*

With exceptional athletic ability, professional athletes are the lucky few who are paid to compete with the best as they try to reach the top of their chosen game.

## PERSONAL TRAINER
*Page 300*

Health and well-being is a booming sector, with massive demand for personal trainers who can develop training plans and coach their clients to reach peak fitness.

## COSMETOLOGIST
*Page 302*

From massages and nail art to facials and spray tanning, cosmetologists use the latest techniques and products to make their customers look and feel good.

## HOTEL MANAGER
*Page 304*

In this competitive sector where hotels vie with one another for customers, hotel managers strive to make their guests' stays as relaxing and enjoyable as possible.

## TRAVEL AGENT
*Page 306*

Liaising with vacation companies, airlines, and resorts on behalf of customers, travel agents aim to turn their clients' travel dreams into reality within a specified budget.

## AIRLINE CABIN CREW
*Page 308*

Working on board aircraft, cabin crew attend to the needs of passengers to ensure they have a safe, comfortable, and enjoyable flight.

## CHEF
*Page 310*

Taking a creative approach to ingredients and cooking techniques, chefs combine artistry with a taste for flavors and textures to bring each plate of food to life.

## MUSEUM CURATOR
*Page 312*

Using their knowledge of history, archaeology, or the arts, museum curators display the exhibits and artifacts in their collection to engage and inspire visitors.

# PROFESSIONAL ATHLETE

## JOB DESCRIPTION

With the talent to be paid to practice their sport, professional athletes compete to achieve individual and team success and to entertain fans. They work hard at training to stay in peak physical condition and perfect their skills. As well as their athletic duties, many professionals perform educational or charity work.

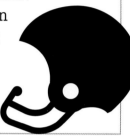

### SALARY

Low-earning professional ★☆☆☆☆
Top-earning professional ★★★★★

### INDUSTRY PROFILE

Extremely competitive, varied industry • Limited opportunities to reach highest level • Work may be part-time • Lucrative profession with international fame and wealth for successful athletes

## AT A GLANCE

**YOUR INTERESTS** Competitive sport • Physical Education (PE) • Fitness • Health and nutrition • Business and marketing • Anatomy • Biology

**ENTRY QUALIFICATIONS** There are no minimum entry requirements to be a sportsperson, other than talent and dedication to a sport.

**LIFESTYLE** Hours of work may be long and irregular, with some form of training taking place most days. Competitions may occur on weekends and evenings.

**LOCATION** Sports professionals train and compete indoors and outdoors. Competitive events sometimes require national and international travel.

**THE REALITIES** Success can make this a highly rewarding and satisfying career, but many professional athletes have to supplement their income with other jobs.

## ▼ RELATED CAREERS

▶ **PERSONAL TRAINER** see pp. 300–301

▶ **COMMUNITY SPORTS LEADER** Encourages public participation and access to sports and physical activity. Community sports leaders may work with specific groups, such as young people, elderly people, or those with physical challenges.

▶ **E-SPORTS PROFESSIONAL** Competes in pro gamer tournaments for prize money.

▶ **PHYSICAL EDUCATION TEACHER** Teaches a range of sports to young people at a school or college, promoting the benefits of physical activity and encouraging and developing sporting potential.

▶ **SPORTS PHYSICAL THERAPIST** Works with people with sports- or exercise-related injuries, improving their physical capabilities, providing advice on how to avoid further injury, and administering treatment to aid recovery. Sports physical therapists also diagnose injuries and may recommend nontraditional treatments, such as massage and hydrotherapy.

# CAREER PATHS

There is no defined career path for professional athletes, but most naturally talented individuals achieve some success as children, before working with coaches at college or amateur level. Early retirement is common due to the physical demands of professional sports, and many ex-athletes move into media or management.

**AMATEUR** You can hone your sporting talent by competing at amateur or college level. Participating in national and international events will increase your chances of being spotted by a talent scout.

**PROFESSIONAL ATHLETE** As a professional athlete, your competitive career is likely to be short in duration. Many professionals diversify into areas such as business ownership or commentary in the later years of their careers, or study for qualifications in coaching.

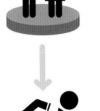

## SKILLS GUIDE

 Absolute dedication to improve and maintain individual athletic skill and physical fitness.

 The ability to employ competitive tactics and strategies for gaining an advantage over competitors.

 Strong team-working skills to be part of a competitive or coaching set-up, especially in team sports.

 Physical strength, endurance, and fitness to maintain performance throughout a sports event.

 Good hand-eye coordination and rapid reflexes to excel in competitive sports.

**SPORTS JOURNALIST** Specializes in a particular sport, using their insight and industry contacts to conduct interviews, attend sporting events, and compile reports for television, radio, Internet, or print media.

**COACH** Trains promising competitors or sports teams. This specialized area requires additional qualifications, which athletes can study for during their playing careers.

**MANAGER** Works with professional, school, or college athletes to manage teams, resources, and training. Managers may also direct an organization's athletics program or manage sports facilities.

**SPORTS AGENT** Represents a professional athlete in the negotiation of contracts and sponsorships, and often handles their public relations and finances.

**SPORTS COMMENTATOR** Provides live commentary and analysis for sports events that are broadcast on television, radio, or the Internet. This job is open to sports personalities with media presentation skills.

# PERSONAL TRAINER

## JOB DESCRIPTION

Personal trainers coach people to achieve their health and fitness goals, and they help create fitness programs to suit the individual. Personal trainers may also provide guidance on health, diet, and lifestyle changes. Excellent knowledge of the human body enables trainers to set realistic targets for clients, while motivating them to stay on track so they reach their goals.

### SALARY

Fitness instructor ★★★★★
Personal trainer ★★★★★

### INDUSTRY PROFILE

Many freelance personal trainer roles available • Increasing opportunities due to rise in health awareness • Growing number of companies opening up their own exercise facilities

## AT A GLANCE

**YOUR INTERESTS** Sports • Human biology and physiology • Food and nutrition • Sports psychology • Teaching • First aid • Business and management

**ENTRY QUALIFICATIONS** Certification in fitness and personal training or a degree in sports science or a health-related discipline is required.

**LIFESTYLE** Personal trainers may stick to regular working hours or adjust according to their client's availability. Self-employed trainers usually travel on demand.

**LOCATION** Trainers work in a gym or similar facility; those self-employed may also work in resorts, country clubs, and other indoor and/or outdoor client sites.

**THE REALITIES** Competition is fierce. Self-employed trainers often have to work long hours and stay focused, which can be tiring both physically and mentally.

## CAREER PATHS

A certification in sports and fitness is necessary to enter this career. You may work at health studios, rec centers, or hospitals, or for sports clubs or other professionals, and with experience, you can choose to provide customized training to individual clients. With business acumen, you can enter the management side of the fitness industry.

**TRAINEE** You can usually join a gym or fitness center as a trainee, studying on the job for a certificate in fitness.

**GRADUATE** A bachelor's degree in sports science is not required, but it will give you detailed knowledge of physical science, anatomy, and nutrition that will help your chances of success in this career.

## ▼ RELATED CAREERS

▶ **PHYSICAL THERAPIST** *see pp. 288–289*

▶ **OCCUPATIONAL THERAPIST** *see pp. 292–293*

▶ **ATHLETIC TRAINER** Works alongside athletes to ensure they are training in a safe and smart way, allowing them to achieve their potential.

▶ **COMMUNITY HEALTH WORKER** Teaches techniques and behaviors that promote good health to groups and individuals.

▶ **NUTRITIONIST** Advises clients on eating habits for healthy living and prepares diet plans for them to achieve health-related goals. Nutritionists use scientific knowledge and research to help people on matters of nutrition to improve their health and assist with any related medical conditions.

# SKILLS GUIDE

 The knowledge to devise unique health programs based on a client's physical ability and needs.

 Good leadership skills to motivate clients to make positive lifestyle changes and to maintain them.

 Sensitivity toward clients who may suffer from a range of health difficulties.

 Good business sense and an ability to market services effectively to make a profit.

 A high level of personal fitness in order to demonstrate, guide, and supervise physical activities.

**FITNESS INSTRUCTOR** Leads classes in activities such as spinning, pilates, barre, and yoga, or provides advice and guidance on individual activities and use of weights and equipment at a gym or fitness center.

**SPORTS COACH** Teaches individuals and teams of all abilities, from beginners to pros. Coaches require a qualification recognized by the sport's governing body, and many have a background in the sport they want to coach.

**FITNESS SERVICE MANAGER** Works to ensure that members of a fitness center receive the best experience there. People in this role manage facilities and staff, with the aim of boosting customer satisfaction levels.

**PERSONAL TRAINER**
As you build your experience and reputation, you may choose to work with clients on the basis of a private arrangement or move into another area of the industry.

**OUTDOOR ACTIVITIES INSTRUCTOR** Teaches and leads groups in outdoor activities such as water sports, skiing, hiking, and rock climbing.

# COSMETOLOGIST

## JOB DESCRIPTION

Cosmetologists specialize in making people look and feel good. They provide a range of facial and body treatments—such as manicures, pedicures, hair removal, eyebrow shaping, and specialized therapies—to improve the appearance and well-being of clients. A cosmetologist may also offer advice on recommended treatments, the use of cosmetics and skin products, and makeup application techniques.

### SALARY

Newly qualified cosmetologist ★★★★★
Salon manager ★★★★★

### INDUSTRY PROFILE

Growing demand for speciality beauty treatments • Massive growth in male grooming products • Opportunities in a range of specializations and settings, from health salons to home visits

## CAREER PATHS

Cosmetologists start their careers by mastering the basics of a range of treatments, such as waxing, massage, facials, and skin care. Adding to your skills by taking courses in specialized techniques—such as piercings or advanced massage—will increase your career prospects and appeal to employers.

**COMPLEMENTARY THERAPIST** Performs a range of specialized health therapies—such as body massage, aromatherapy, reflexology, or hydrotherapy—that complement traditional forms of medical care.

**TRAINEE** You can combine work experience in a salon or spa with on-the-job beauty cosmetology training by taking a paid trainee position.

**COLLEGE GRADUATE** You can become a cosmetologist by completing a vocational college training course, which combines lectures and classes with practical experience. Full-time or part-time courses are available.

**COSMETOLOGIST** As a cosmetologist, you will continue to learn new techniques and utilize new products throughout your career. You may specialize in a type of treatment, or move into salon management or cosmetics sales.

# SKILLS GUIDE

 Good communication skills to listen to customer needs and explain treatments clearly.

 Creativity and artistic ability to keep up to date with new techniques and styles.

 Strong customer service skills for interacting with people and making them feel comfortable.

 Excellent manual dexterity to apply beauty treatments, such as skin-care products and makeup.

 Physical stamina for standing for long periods of time while giving customers their treatments.

 Precision and attention to detail for applying makeup and other treatments neatly and accurately.

**NAIL TECHNICIAN** Carries out manicures and pedicures and applies lotions, varnishes, and artificial nails. Nail technicians may also offer other treatments, such as foot massage.

**HAIR REMOVAL SPECIALIST** Uses a variety of techniques, such as electrolysis, waxing, threading, or laser treatment, to remove unwanted hair from clients.

**COSMETICS CONSULTANT** Visits salons, beauticians, and stores to demonstrate and sell new beauty products and treatments.

## ▼ RELATED CAREERS

▶ **MAKEUP ARTIST** *see pp. 32–33*

▶ **BEAUTY INFLUENCER** Creates content on social media using beauty products and makeup, generating revenue via subscribers or advertising.

▶ **BEAUTY JOURNALIST** Reviews beauty products via social media, magazines, and television.

▶ **HAIRDRESSER** Cuts, colors, shapes, and styles hair, and gives advice on suitable and attractive styles for individual clients.

▶ **IMAGE CONSULTANT** Offers advice to individual clients on their public image, including makeup styles, clothing and dress, and personal presentation. They also advise companies and corporations on a vast range of topics.

## AT A GLANCE

**YOUR INTERESTS** Beauty treatments and techniques • Health and fitness • Customer service • Art • Design • Fashion

**ENTRY QUALIFICATIONS** Cosmetologists can train on the job, but a vocational qualification is required by most employers.

**LIFESTYLE** Most cosmetologists work regular hours, but working during weekends or evenings may occasionally be required.

**LOCATION** This job can be done in a beauty salon, hotel, health spa, or on a cruise ship. Some cosmetologists visit clients in their own homes.

**THE REALITIES** Strong competition means that salaries are low. But much satisfaction is gained from helping people achieve their desired results.

# HOTEL MANAGER

## JOB DESCRIPTION

A hotel manager is ultimately responsible for the safe, comfortable, and profitable operation of a hotel. Their duties might include recruiting and managing staff, ensuring that guests receive a high level of service and enjoy their stay, and overseeing housekeeping standards and guest room amenities. Developing the business and tracking budgets are also key tasks for the manager.

### SALARY

Hotel manager ★★☆☆☆
Hotel regional manager ★★★★☆

### INDUSTRY PROFILE

Career prospects good due to high staff turnover • Growing industry • Wide range of vacancies globally, with opportunities to work internationally for large hotel chains

## ▼ RELATED CAREERS

▶ **EVENTS MANAGER** *see pp. 88–89*

▶ **TRAVEL AGENT** *see pp. 306–307*

▶ **FOOD SERVICES MANAGER** Supervises the daily operation of restaurants and other outlets serving prepared meals.

▶ **RESTAURANT MANAGER** Ensures that a restaurant operates efficiently and profitably, while maintaining the business's reputation and public profile. Restaurant managers coordinate a variety of activities—from maintenance to promotional events—and are responsible for maintaining high standards of food, service, and health and safety.

**There are more than 54,000 hotel properties in the United States.**

## AT A GLANCE

**YOUR INTERESTS** Hotel management • Travel and tourism • Business studies • Economics • Mathematics • Information Technology (IT) • Food and nutrition

**ENTRY QUALIFICATIONS** A relevant degree is helpful. Previous experience in a customer-facing role is also sought by employers.

**LIFESTYLE** Working hours are very long, and include evenings, weekends, and public holidays. Some managers live in the hotel and work shifts.

**LOCATION** Work is mostly based at the hotel, although visiting suppliers is also involved. Managers may have an office for performing administrative work.

**THE REALITIES** Dealing with hotel guests can be stressful and tiring, and living in the place of work carries its own pressures. Staff turnover is high.

## CAREER PATHS

A degree in hospitality management or a related subject is usually required to work for a larger hotel. The hotel industry also offers good prospects for nongraduates with a positive attitude, sociable nature, and an aptitude for hard work.

**TRAINEE** As a high school graduate or with some college, you can rise to a management role by taking a customer service job and working your way up.

**GRADUATE** If you have a degree in travel and tourism, business management, or hospitality, you can apply for graduate training programs run by large hotel groups.

**HOTEL MANAGER** As a hotel manager, you must balance strategic planning of business affairs with an eye for detail to maintain strong customer service. Working for a larger hotel or chain is a common form of progression.

### SKILLS GUIDE

 Good interpersonal skills and a friendly approach that makes guests feel comfortable.

 The ability to work with staff from a variety of countries and cultures, and adapt to unfamiliar locations.

 Excellent communication skills for interacting effectively with senior managers and staff.

 Leadership skills to motivate hotel staff and ensure they maintain high standards of customer care.

 The ability to come up with effective solutions to everyday problems quickly and efficiently.

 Strong commercial awareness to ensure that the hotel is run as a profitable enterprise.

**REGIONAL MANAGER** Develops and oversees the operations, marketing strategy, and finances of a hotel group in a region or country, taking responsibility for its overall profitability.

**RESORT MANAGER** Manages the daily operations of a resort complex, including overseeing the work of event organizers, hotel or restaurant managers, and grounds staff.

**CONFERENCE CENTER MANAGER** Provides a venue for business conferences, taking responsibility for staff, finances, marketing, and advertising.

**ACCOMMODATION MANAGER** Works for a large institution, such as a school, university, or hospital, ensuring that sufficient rooms of appropriate standard are available to meet customer demand.

# TRAVEL AGENT

## JOB DESCRIPTION

A travel agent organizes business or leisure travel for their customers. They may offer advice on national and international destinations, plan the trip itineraries, and take care of any ticket or passport issues that might arise. They may also make additional travel arrangements, including accommodation and restaurant or rental car bookings, and offer guidance on insurance, travel safety, vaccinations, and tours.

### SALARY

Junior travel agent ★★★★★
Experienced travel agent ★★★★★

### INDUSTRY PROFILE

Brick-and-mortar agencies facing competition from online travel sites • Demand for specialized providers servicing a particular market, such as business travelers or honeymooners

## AT A GLANCE

 **YOUR INTERESTS** Travel and tourism • Geography • History • Business studies • Languages • Economics

 **ENTRY QUALIFICATIONS** A high school education may be enough for entry-level jobs, but classes in travel and tourism or customer service are advantageous.

 **LIFESTYLE** Travel agents work normal retail hours, including weekends. They may be expected to work overtime during high season.

 **LOCATION** Travel agents usually work in an office or retail outlet. They sometimes get to travel to different destinations as part of their job.

 **THE REALITIES** Agents may have to deal with unhappy customers, which can be challenging. They often have to explain situations beyond their control.

## ▼ RELATED CAREERS

▶ **EVENTS MANAGER** *see pp. 88–89*

▶ **HOTEL MANAGER** *see pp. 304–305*

▶ **AIRLINE CABIN CREW** *see pp. 308–309*

▶ **CUSTOMER SERVICE AGENT** Answers customer queries and deals with complaints. Customer service agents also take orders and payments, arrange refunds, and maintain computer records of transactions.

▶ **LEISURE CENTER MANAGER** Runs sports and recreation centers. The job involves arranging timetables for activities, supervising a range of staff, controlling budgets, and promoting and marketing the facilities on offer.

▶ **TOURIST INFORMATION ASSISTANT** Provides information about locations, facilities, and places open to visitors. Often based in airports and major railway stations, tourist information assistants use their knowledge of transportation schedules to advise visitors.

## CAREER PATHS

There is no set career path for a travel agent. Your network of contacts in the industry will be your most useful asset in seeking higher positions. You will stand out if you specialize in a few particular destinations or sell to specific kinds of travelers, such as those with special interests.

**ASSISTANT** You may start your career as an assistant with a travel agency. This role usually combines on-the-job training with work experience.

# SKILLS GUIDE

 Good communication skills, telephone etiquette, and sensitivity to cultural differences.

 The ability to complete all necessary arrangements for customers in a careful, well-organized manner.

 The strength to stay calm and polite with clients who are difficult to please.

 Excellent attention to detail to check, order, and relay travel information accurately.

 Knowledge of other languages when talking to people of different nationalities.

**TRAVEL AGENT** Once you have become a travel agent, industry-run courses in sales or customer care will help you develop your career. With experience, you can seek professional accreditation to move to more senior positions.

**TOUR OPERATOR**
Plans and organizes group travel. The work includes organizing cruises, rail, and bus travel, or chartered flights to a selection of destinations.

**CORPORATE TRAVEL PLANNER** Arranges travel and accommodation for corporate clients, negotiating special rates on their behalf.

**CALL CENTER AGENT**
Sells travel products to customers on the telephone or the Internet, and handles product queries and complaints. May work shifts to deal with customer calls at evenings and weekends.

**RESORT REPRESENTATIVE**
Represents a travel company at a vacation resort or theme park, looking after the needs of vacationers and liaising with accommodation and travel suppliers.

# AIRLINE CABIN CREW

## JOB DESCRIPTION

Airline cabin-crew members ensure that passengers experience a safe, comfortable, and enjoyable flight. Duties include checking the aircraft's cabin, greeting and seating passengers, giving safety demonstrations, and selling and serving refreshments. Cabin crew are trained to respond to emergency and security situations, and to administer first aid. They must deal with a wide range of clients and situations.

### SALARY

Newly qualified cabin crew ★★★★★
Senior cabin crew ★★★★★

### INDUSTRY PROFILE

Strong competition for jobs • Most employees work on a temporary basis—permanent contracts are more rare • Overtime and flight allowances can increase earnings

## ▼ RELATED CAREERS

▶ **HOTEL MANAGER** *see pp. 304–305*

▶ **AIRLINE CUSTOMER SERVICE AGENT** Checks passengers onto their flight, weighs luggage, and issues boarding passes.

▶ **CUSTOMER SERVICE AGENT** Answers customer queries, handles complaints, and provides information about an organization's services. A customer service agent is often a member of the public's first point of contact with a company.

▶ **RESORT REPRESENTATIVE** Ensures that tourists have a comfortable and pleasant vacation, meeting vacationers as their flights arrive, arranging onward transportation, and offering advice once at the resort.

It is predicted that 839,000 new cabin crew members will be needed by 2036 to staff the world's commercial aviation industry.

## AT A GLANCE

 **YOUR INTERESTS** Aviation • Travel and tourism • Hospitality • Working with people • Mathematics • Languages • Geography

 **ENTRY QUALIFICATIONS** Cabin crew must have a high school education, be at least 18, and pass fitness tests. Prior customer service experience is helpful.

 **LIFESTYLE** Due to the 24-hour nature of air travel, cabin crew work irregular hours in shifts that include nights, weekends, and public holidays.

 **LOCATION** Most time is spent working in the cabin of an in-flight passenger aircraft. Significant time away from home is normal in this career.

 **THE REALITIES** Jet lag and standing for long periods make this job physically taxing. Tired or anxious passengers can be difficult to deal with.

## CAREER PATHS

Experience in customer service roles and fluency in one or more foreign languages will help gain entry to this profession. It takes between two and five years in the job before achieving promotion to more senior roles, such as managing the cabin.

### SKILLS GUIDE

 Good communication skills for understanding and attending to passengers' needs.

 The ability to work efficiently and supportively with colleagues in usually cramped cabin conditions.

 Excellent customer service to deal with passengers in a polite, professional, and sensitive manner.

 Good numerical skills for handling and exchanging foreign currency during in-flight shopping.

 Being able to think quickly to keep passengers calm during difficulties, such as emergency landings.

 Physical stamina and resilience to deal with jet lag and remain on duty for long hours in the cabin.

**HIGH SCHOOL GRADUATE** If you have a high school education, you can apply for cabin-crew training programs run by the major airlines.

**GRADUATE** You do not need a degree to work as a cabin-crew member, but undergraduate study in travel, leisure, and tourism, hospitality management, languages, social science, or business may be helpful.

**AIRLINE CABIN CREW** You take up your first job after completing training in areas including passenger care, customer relations, and security, customs, and immigration regulations. With experience, you can be promoted to a senior cabin-crew or ground-support job.

**LANGUAGES SPECIALIST** Works as part of the cabin crew on long-haul flights in which a good knowledge of specific languages is required.

**PURSER/SENIOR CABIN CREW MEMBER** Manages part of the cabin on an aircraft—such as the first-class lounge—and oversees other staff. Chief pursers are responsible for managing the whole aircraft.

**VIP CABIN CREW STAFF** Looks after very important and prestigious passengers onboard either commercial aircraft or private jets.

**CABIN CREW SUPPORT** Supports the work of cabin crew through roles including training, recruitment, and human resources. This role is generally only available to highly experienced cabin crew.

# CHEF

## JOB DESCRIPTION

A love of food and cooking is vital to succeed as a chef. The role involves planning and coordinating food production at a restaurant or other eatery, managing a kitchen, and instructing waitstaff. Chefs may cook food themselves or oversee its preparation by their staff. Many chefs are known to create unique menus and signature dishes. They also handle buying and budgeting for catering operations and restaurants.

### SALARY

Commis chef ★★★★★
Head chef ★★★★★

### INDUSTRY PROFILE

Worldwide job opportunities • Strong competition for jobs at upscale restaurants, where pay is normally highest • Industry constantly adapting to changing culinary tastes

## CAREER PATHS

Most chefs train on the job, joining a kitchen as a trainee, or *commis chef*, and studying for vocational qualifications. Ability and commitment are your keys to promotion. Working under a rated chef can give your career an extra boost.

**HEAD CHEF** Devises a restaurant menu and runs its kitchen. The role also involves making key business decisions with the aim of making the establishment a success.

**TRAINEE** Following school, trainees learn their craft by rotating through sections such as vegetables, fish, and butchery to become familiar with them all. The type and length of apprenticeship depends on the employer.

**GRADUATE** Private academies, some run by notable cooks, provide training for aspiring chefs. However, fees can be high, and there is no guarantee of employment later.

**CHEF** With experience and sufficient talent, you will climb the ladder of responsibility in the kitchen, through prep cook and line cook, to *sous chef* (the second-in-command, who may schedule staff and buy ingredients), to the position of head chef, or *chef de cuisine*.

## SKILLS GUIDE

 Excellent team-working skills to manage staff in a high-pressure kitchen environment.

 Creativity and imagination to devise unique and delicious dishes and keep the menu fresh.

 Strong interpersonal skills to maintain good relationships with staff at all levels, as well as diners.

 The ability to calculate quantities, price differences, and catering costs to run a profitable kitchen.

 Well-honed practical skills and the ability to use kitchen equipment with ease and speed.

 **CONTRACT CATERING MANAGER** Provides catering services to clients for business functions and special events.

 **INSTITUTIONAL COOK** Cooks in the kitchen of a large organization. Employers include the armed services, health providers, factories, and other workplaces.

 The average American household spends about $3,000 a year dining out.

## ▼ RELATED CAREERS

▶ **BAKER** Produces bread and confectionery products within a manufacturing operation, retail outlet, or restaurant.

▶ **BAR OWNER/PROPRIETOR** Runs premises, such as a pub or bar, that serve a variety of beverages.

▶ **FOOD SERVICES MANAGER** Supervises the daily operation of restaurants and other outlets serving prepared meals.

▶ **FOOD-PROCESSING OPERATIVE** Works on factory production lines, overseeing the mixing, cooking, and packing of food products.

▶ **KITCHEN ASSISTANT** Performs basic tasks from food preparation and checking deliveries to cleaning the kitchen and all the equipment.

## AT A GLANCE

 **YOUR INTERESTS** Food • Cooking • Business administration • Catering, hospitality, and tourism • Food production and farming

 **ENTRY QUALIFICATIONS** No set entry requirements, but qualifications in food preparation alongside relevant work experience are an advantage.

 **LIFESTYLE** Work often starts very early and finishes very late. Split shifts, evenings, and weekends are a normal part of the working cycle.

 **LOCATION** Chefs work mostly in restaurant or hotel kitchens. Catering jobs may involve traveling to locations with cooking equipment.

 **THE REALITIES** Kitchens can be busy high-pressure environments, while equipment, such as knives and hot pans, is potentially dangerous.

# MUSEUM CURATOR

## JOB DESCRIPTION

A museum or gallery curator manages a collection of historical artifacts or works of art, overseeing exhibitions and new initiatives. This role can involve acquiring, caring for, displaying, and interpreting exhibits, as well as marketing and fundraising activities. Curators also manage budgets and staff, and build relationships with donors, partner institutions, and artists and artist estates.

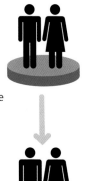

### SALARY

Curatorial assistant ★★★★★
Museum director ★★★★★

### INDUSTRY PROFILE

Funding falls during economic downturns • Employers include museums, galleries, and heritage sites • Growth in contract work, but fewer permanent positions available

## AT A GLANCE

**YOUR INTERESTS** Art • History • Languages • Archaeology • Science • Design • Education • Architecture • Information Technology (IT)

**ENTRY QUALIFICATIONS** A degree is required and postgraduate study is desirable. Relevant work experience is also useful, due to limited job vacancies.

**LIFESTYLE** Full-time curators usually have regular hours, but working on evenings and weekends is common when preparing for an exhibition.

**LOCATION** Most work is based at a museum, gallery, or heritage site. Travel may be necessary to attend conferences or deliver artifacts.

**THE REALITIES** Competition for jobs is strong, so working in a lower-paid assistant-level position is necessary to gain sufficient experience to progress.

## CAREER PATHS

Museum curators usually hold a degree or postgraduate qualification, and often contribute to research or teaching in their specialized area of interest. Reputation and expertise can lead to a role in a larger, more prestigious collection of exhibits, or a senior position in museum management.

**MUSEUM ASSISTANT** You can apply for jobs as a clerical or visitor-services assistant at a museum or gallery straight from high school. You will need good grades in history, English, or a related subject. Work experience in a museum is beneficial.

**GRADUATE** You can earn a degree in museum- or heritage-studies, but an undergraduate or graduate qualification in a subject relevant to a particular collection may qualify you to apply for junior or assistant curating posts.

## ▼ RELATED CAREERS

▶ **EVENTS MANAGER** *see pp. 88–89*

▶ **COLLEGE PROFESSOR** *see pp. 270–271*

▶ **ANTIQUES DEALER** Uses historical expertise and commercial acumen to buy and sell antique items. Antiques dealers may be employed by an auction house or work on a self-employed basis.

▶ **ARCHAEOLOGIST** Investigates past human activities by excavating and analyzing material remains, from fragments of bone or pottery to ancient ruins or buried structures.

▶ **ARCHIVIST** Stores, catalogs, and maintains a range of historically signficant documents and other materials.

## SKILLS GUIDE

 Excellent verbal and written communication skills to give talks and write articles and reports.

 Strong IT skills for creating a variety of web-based and printed materials.

 A creative flair for presenting exhibits and displays in engaging and informative ways.

 Good organizational abilities to secure a variety of new exhibits through loans and acquisitions.

 The ability to manage staff and links with stakeholders, such as governors and funding groups.

**HEAD CURATOR**
Manages the activities of a team of curators and oversees the functions of their individual departments, usually in a larger museum or gallery.

**MUSEUM DIRECTOR**
Oversees the collection held by a museum, manages personnel and operations, and ensures that the objectives set by the museum's board of governors are fulfilled.

**HEAD OF EXHIBITIONS**
Specializes in planning, organizing, and marketing permanent or temporary exhibitions at a museum.

**MUSEUM CURATOR** Most curators spend at least two years as an assistant before becoming a curator. You can choose to specialize in an area of academic research, or move into senior and management roles.

**CONSERVATOR** Preserves artifacts or works of art by controlling the environment in which objects are stored. A conservator may also restore damaged items using specialty conservation methods.

# GLOSSARY

**Accreditation**
A formal, third-party recognition of competence to perform specific tasks. Usually the reason for getting something independently evaluated is to confirm that it meets specific requirements in order to reduce risks.

**Algorithm**
A procedure, or formula, for solving a problem.

**Amateur**
A person who engages in a study, sport, or other pursuit for pleasure, rather than for financial benefit or professional reasons.

**Apprentice**
A person who works for another in order to learn a trade.

**Assessor**
A person who evaluates the merits, importance, or value of something.

**Biodiversity**
The number and variety of organisms that are found within a specified geographic region.

**Biomedical**
The branch of medical science that deals with a human's ability to tolerate environmental stresses and variations, such as in space.

**Blueprint**
A print of a drawing or other image rendered as white lines on a blue background, especially of an architectural plan or a technical drawing.

**Business acumen**
Insight into the workings of the business world.

**Commercial**
Something that is connected, or related to, business.

**Commission**
Hiring a person or group to perform a specific function or task.

**Computer hardware**
The collection of physical elements, such as the monitor, mouse, keyboard, and hard drive, that make up a computer system.

**Computer software**
The programs that are used to make a computer perform different tasks.

**Consensus**
General or widespread agreement, i.e. consensus of opinion.

**Conservation**
The act of preserving or renovating something from loss, damage, or neglect.

**Consultant**
A person who gives professional or expert advice.

**Conversion course**
A course for graduates who have a degree in a particular subject but who want to learn new skills to forge a career in a different sector.

**Curriculum vitae**
A résumé-like document used by candidates to present their skills, background, and qualifications to potential employers.

**Cyber attack**
An illegal attempt to harm someone's computer system, or the information stored on it, using the Internet.

**Cyber crime**
Crimes committed against groups or individuals using modern telecommunications networks, such as the Internet or cell phones.

**Derivative**
A special type of contract in the financial world that derives its value from the performance of an asset, such as stocks or interest rates.

**E-commerce**
A type of industry where the buying and selling of products is conducted over electronic systems, such as the Internet or other computer systems.

**Eco-friendly**
A term that is used to describe a product that has been designed to do the least possible damage to the environment.

**Ecosystem**
A community of plants, animals, and smaller organisms that live, feed, reproduce, and interact in the same area or environment.

**Ethnographic**
Relates to ethnography, the systematic study of world people and cultures.

**Executive**
A senior manager in an organization, company, or corporation.

**Fellow**
The title of a senior teaching position at a university or similar institution. Someone who is a fellow has been awarded a "fellowship."

**Freelance**
A person who is self-employed and who is not committed to a particular employer on a long-term basis.

**Hacker**
Someone who breaks into other people's computer systems, for the most part illegally.

**Haute couture**
A type of clothing for women, usually made from expensive, high-quality fabric, that is made to order for a specific customer.

**Hedge fund**
An investment fund, typically formed by a number of different investors,

that uses a wide range of techniques to try and generate the highest possible financial return.

## Hybrid working
A flexible working arrangement that allows a person to work in more than one location, such as home and the office.

## Information technology
The study or use of systems (especially computers and telecommunications) for storing, retrieving, and sending information.

## Infrastructure
The basic physical or organizational structure needed to operate a business, society, or enterprise.

## Interpersonal skills
A term often used in business to describe a person's ability to relate to, and communicate with, another person.

## Legislation
The act or process of making laws.

## Module
A standardized part or independent unit that can be used in conjunction with other parts or units to form a more complex structure, such as in a computer program or building.

## Networking skills
The ability to build and maintain contacts and relationships with people in the business world. Possibly one of the most important skills for aspiring entrepreneurs.

## Overtime
The amount of time someone works beyond normal working hours.

## Patent
The official legal right to make or sell a unique invention for a particular number of years.

## Periodical
A publication, such as a magazine or scholarly journal, that is produced on a regular basis; it might appear every week, every two weeks, once a month, once a quarter, or once a year.

## Personnel
The people who work for a particular company or organization.

## Portfolio
A collection of work intended to demonstrate a person's ability to a potential employer.

## Portfolio career
Using skills, experiences, and networks to generate income from different sources of work and/or multiple employers.

## Postgraduate
A student who already has one degree who is studying at a college or university for a more advanced qualification.

## Private sector
Businesses or industries that are owned by individuals or groups, usually for profit.

## Procedure
A set of established methods for conducting the affairs of an organized body, such as a government, club, or business.

## Protocol
A code of correct conduct, often referring to affairs of state or diplomatic conduct.

## Prototype
The first example of something, such as a machine or other industrial product, from which all later forms are developed.

## Public sector
The portion of the economy consisting of the government and enterprises which are owned by the government.

## Revenue
The income a government or business receives from a particular source, such as taxes or the profit made on a property or investment.

## Sabbatical
A period of leave from one's customary work. Usually applies to college staff or teachers, who are often granted a period of leave (usually paid) every seven years.

## Self-employed
An individual who earns his or her livelihood directly from their own trade or business, rather than as an employee of another.

## Simulator
A machine, used for training purposes, designed to provide a realistic imitation of the controls and operation of a vehicle, aircraft, or other complex system.

## Stakeholder
A person or a group of people who own a share in a business.

## Third sector
The part of an economy or society comprising nongovernmental and nonprofit organizations or associations, including charities, voluntary and community groups, and cooperatives.

## Trainee
A person undergoing training for a particular job or profession.

## User interface
The visual part of a computer application or operating system through which the user interacts with a computer, often by choosing a command from a list displayed on the screen.

## Vocation
An occupation, especially one for which a person is particularly suited or qualified.

## Welfare
Financial or other aid provided to people in need, especially by the government.

# INDEX

# ABOUT THE AUTHORS

**Consultant and Principal Author: Sarah Pawlewski**
Sarah is a careers guidance professional with more than 25 years' experience. She runs her own consultancy and works with clients of all ages across schools, colleges, and industry. She holds degrees in psychology and career guidance, and is a member of the Career Development Institute.

**Contributors:** Professional Careers Advisers Linda Bozzo, Christine Rowley, Imogen Gray, Heather Towers, and Claire Sutcliffe; Bianca Hezekiah, authenticity reader; Nicholas Schaefer.

# ACKNOWLEDGMENTS

**The publisher would like to thank the following people for their assistance with this book:**

Kavita Sharma for consulting; Priyanka Sharma-Saddi and Saloni Singh for the jacket; Priyaneet Singh, Hina Jain, Jennifer Chung, and Sarah Edwards for editorial assistance; Ankita Mukherjee, Heena Sharma, Priyanka Singh, Vidit Vashisht, Vikas Chauhan, and Jessica Lee for design assistance; Vishal Bhatia and Pawan Kumar for DTP assistance; Ann Baggaley for proofreading; Elizabeth Wise for indexing.

Thank you for your expertise: Erin Aiello, Niki Alexiou, Scott Arouh, Stacey Barrack, Matthew Barry, Christopher J. Beatty, M.D., FACS, Steven Benenati, Lisa Berry, Bob A. Bloom, Alex Bronshteyn, James Carrig, Jack Chapman, Kathleen Cirioli, Emily Cohen, Stephanie Davies, Ben Deutsch, Shane Dinneen, Anne Dodgen–Averitt, Kathleen A. Dunne, Samantha Ecker, Libby Ellwood, Michael Fasulo, Mariana Fazakas, Miriam Garber Finkelstein, Paulette Galbraith, Melissa Gangi, Warren Geist, Christina Giovinazzo, Heather Givner, Brian Goldblatt, Ben Gorban, Jeff Halliday, Art Hance, Sarah Hayes, Jacob Hess, Megan Hodges, Jason Huwe, Michelle Huwe, Sean James, Duane Joseph, Ryan Judge, Jason Kahner, Jonathan Keefer, Donny Kempster, Rachel Kempster, Dana Kurilew, Annmarie Larocca, Jessica Lee, Mike Lux, Fotini Marcopulos, Edward Marks, Cathy Marshall, Max Marshall, Christopher Marton, Michelle Masilon, Amy Maya, Melissa Maya, Frank Mee, Jen Molter, Michael Monteverdi, Rachel Nault, John Norris, Roland O'Leary, Nate Ogdahl, Amanda Oldenburg, Renee Orlando, Tom Orlando, Anthony Paci, Christina Pease, Brandon Pecoraro, Mike Pecoraro, Jenna Perfette, Sara Elands Peterman, Kristen Renda, Danielle Ricciardi, Robert Roglev, Alex Rosa, Mark Salerno, Elizabeth Sargent, Alex Schloop, Jason Schwankert, Adam Siegel, Dan Siegelstein, Hartley Singer, Lauren Singer, Andrew Scott Taylor, Jeffrey Taylor, Amanda Thyne, Andrew Thyne, Becky Thyne, Lars Tibbling, Matt Tomczuk, James M. Toolan, Ben Trubits, Karole Vail, Vince Venditti, Bobby Wayne, Jennifer Wenger, Peter West, Hilary Westgate, Mandala Wojnar, Audrey Wojtkowski, Stacia Woodcock, Liz Yang, Meghan Yatsko, and Jon Zweigbaum.